easter gospels

The Resurrection of Jesus
According to the Four Evangelists

ROBERT H. SMITH

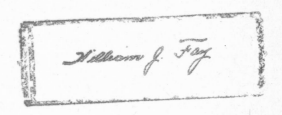
AUGSBURG Publishing House • Minneapolis

EASTER GOSPELS

Copyright© 1983 Augsburg Publishing House

Library of Congress Catalog Card No. 83-70518
International Standard Book No. 0-8066-2024-2

Scripture quotations unless otherwise noted are from the Revised
Standard Version of the Bible, copyright 1946, 1952, and 1971 by the Division of Christian Education of the National Council of Churches.

Manufactured in the United States of America

contents

ACKNOWLEDGMENTS

Looking back over the whole process leading to the conclusion of this manuscript, I realize that it would be impossible even to list the names of all the people in whose debt I stand—countless generous teachers and helpers, including family and students. (Perhaps some would not even want to be named, lest they be associated with the shortcomings of this work!)

Nevertheless, I must at the very least make explicit my gratitude to the good people at the Ecumenical Institute for Theological Studies in Jerusalem (Tantur), where Meta, Maria, and I were so graciously received in the fall of 1978, to Robert Fortna of Vassar College for gentle advice and encouragement in the early stages of research and writing at Tantur, to Everett Kalin, colleague at Christ Seminary-Seminex for his painstaking and detailed critique of the manuscript in its final stages, to Ralph Petering of St. Louis for his interest and support, and to the Aid Association for Lutherans for a grant supporting a study leave.

At more than one level it seems appropriate to dedicate this work to a woman witness: my mother Gertrude, my first teacher in the many meanings of Easter.

St. Louis
1983

ROBERT SMITH

ABBREVIATIONS

ASTI	Annual of the Swedish Theological Institute.
BAGD	W. Bauer, W. F. Arndt, F. W. Gingrich, and F. Danker, eds., A Greek-English Lexicon of the New Testament and Other Early Christian Literature.
BDF	F. Blass, A. Debrunner, and R. W. Funk, eds., A Greek Grammar of the New Testament and Other Early Christian Literature.
BZ	Biblische Zeitschrift.
CBQ	Catholic Biblical Quarterly.
CTM	Concordia Theological Monthly.
Currents	Currents in Theology and Mission.
EphThLov	Ephemerides Theologicae Lovaniensis.
EvTh	Evangelische Theologie.
ExpT	Expository Times.
IDB	Interpreter's Dictionary of the Bible.
IEJ	Israel Exploration Journal.
Int	Interpretation.
JAAR	Journal of the American Academy of Religion.
JBL	Journal of Biblical Literature.
JR	Journal of Religion.
JTC	Journal of Theology and the Church.
JTS	Journal of Theological Studies.
NovT	Novum Testamentum.
NTS	New Testament Studies.
RB	Revue Biblique.
SJT	Scottish Journal of Theology.
ThS	Theologische Studien.
ThZ	Theologische Zeitschrift.
TLZ	Theologische Literaturzeitung.
USQR	Union Seminary Quarterly Review.
ZKG	Zeitschrift für Kirchengeschichte.
ZNW	Zeitschrift für die neutestamentliche Wissenschaft.
ZThK	Zeitschrift für Theologie und Kirche.

Introduction

Perhaps another book on Easter and the resurrection could be issued without apology, covered simply by passing reference to the intrinsic importance of the subject matter. After all, Easter ranks with Good Friday and Christmas in importance among the holy days of Christendom. These days, and those events in heaven and on earth which they celebrate, have always been the heart of the living body of Christian imagination and devotion. Indeed, it would not be far from the truth to declare that while these three abide, the greatest of them is Easter. Paul Althaus has said that "there has never been a message about the Christ that was not an Easter message."[1]

Of course, Althaus' statement is an extravagant hyperbole. It is literally true only as long as one defines "message about the Christ" so as to exclude as unorthodox, heretical, or un-Christian all those documents, sermons, and platforms that have purported to be Christian but which make no reference to Easter or even actually deny the historical truth of Jesus' resurrection.

For example, the source document known as Q circulated in the earliest days of the church before Matthew and Luke wrote their gospels, and it contains no resurrection account. Furthermore, 2 Thessalonians, Philemon, Titus, 3 John, 2 Peter, James, and Jude are New Testament writings entirely lacking in any overt reference to Jesus' resurrection. However, they do presuppose it. The writers of these letters emphatically confess Jesus as the Lord in whom we live and as the Savior whose glorious epiphany we await.

7

Modern post-Enlightenment christologies represent a different kind of challenge to the statement of Althaus. Serious moderns, holding membership in almost every Christian denomination, have pictured Jesus as rabbi or mystic, pacifistic advocate of lost causes or violent revolutionary, tragic hero or wandering charismatic, or as the embodiment of the ideals of a Victorian gentleman, the Boy Scout movement, or big business. These modern christologies also do not have Easter at the center of their messages. Nevertheless, Althaus is correct when he effectively fixes attention on the fact that Jesus' resurrection or exaltation climaxes the very earliest songs and creeds of the church (e.g., 1 Cor. 15:3-5; Rom. 1:3-4; 4:25; 8:34; Phil. 2:6-11; Col. 1:15-20; 1 Tim. 3:16; 1 Peter 3:18-20), that it is the climax in each of our canonical gospels, and that it is the presupposition of the very existence of the early church and of the writings of the early church.

Friends and foes alike acknowledge the centrality of the resurrection in the New Testament and the church, and the present book, without quibble about the relative brilliance of the resurrection in the constellation of Christian convictions, appears under the assumption that Easter is important enough and sufficiently strong to withstand the assault of one more attempt at interpretation.

Defining the Present Work

While another study of the resurrection does not need justifying, the scope, the aim, and the method of this study do. A beginning can be made by declaring what this book does not intend to be or to do.

It is not another attack upon, nor another apology for, the historical reality of Jesus' resurrection or the reliability of the traditions of his empty tomb and post-crucifixion appearances to his disciples. From the beginning the resurrection has been doubted, denied, mocked, and explained away by insiders as well as by outsiders. The Easter narratives have suffered as outrageously as the heroes in the roll call of Hebrews 11: tortured, banished, scourged, chained, stoned, sawn in two.

Ancient and modern Christians, as well as old and new pagans, have regarded the resurrection of Jesus as a willful deception, a misunderstanding based on a swoon and later spontaneous recovery, a mistaken interpretation consequent upon the women's visit to the wrong tomb or their visit to the right tomb emptied by a gardener anxious to preserve his flowers and vegetables from the feet of the curious, a projection of the myth-making and myth-needing heart of the human animal. Learned literary analyses, focusing on discrepancy in the texts and working under the spell of the causal nexus of all things with all things in the universe, have concluded that there really never was a resurrection nor an empty tomb nor angels nor a gardener; there were only visions of Jesus by Peter, or perhaps not a vision but only a growing conviction of his continuing life, or a fresh perspective on the majesty of his cross.

This book is not another attack, nor on the other hand is it one more defense of the historical truth of Easter. There are many such apologetic works, including works of dazzling and original scholarship. The reality or historicity of the resurrection has been defended in many ways: as according neatly with modern anthropology and the structure of human hope; as a real event but transcendent and therefore visible only to the eye of faith; as a unique event without analogy except in the future; as an event requiring a finer net of assumptions than usual for its apprehension; as a dated experience affecting a historical figure of recent memory and so different from the return to life of Attis, Adonis, and Osiris, whatever the formal resemblances may be. The truth of the resurrection has been argued by pointing to the rhythms of nature and to lesser transformations and victories of life over decay, to parallels in the history of religions, and to the trustworthy character of the earliest witnesses. Reference has also been made to the effects in early Christian history such as the observance of Sunday by a band of religious Jews, the production of those vibrant writings constituting the New Testament, the crossing of hard boundaries and the inclusion of Gentiles into a new community, the celebration of Baptism and Eucharist not merely as memorials, but as acts of incorporation into the Christ. Additionally, the resurrection has been defended as a reality by reference to the transformation in ancients like Peter and Paul and in moderns like Malcolm Muggeridge and Charles Colson. It has, of course, also been defended by shouters venomously deriding doubters and unbelievers or simply thundering with conviction or anxiety, "It is written!"

Naturally not all books on Easter fall into the category of defense or assault. Many good or bad books attempt to state the meaning of the resurrection for the New Testament as a whole or for contemporary Christian faith as a whole. Other books investigate the way to investigate Easter or the ways Easter has been regarded in the past in order to begin to make sense of the host of approaches and the many tools, methods and assumptions with which investigators sift the data and construct their hypotheses.

Now it is both instructive and disturbing that, in spite of sharp differences, many (not all) of the attackers and defenders apparently agree on the definition of Easter faith. They both seem to assume that "having Easter faith" or "believing in the resurrection" means assenting to the proposition that he was really raised from the dead, that his death was reversed and his body with all its limbs and organs was revitalized in some marvel of transformation, that his tomb was emptied of its catch, that a divine, transfiguring event occurred a few days after the crucifixion.

However, that does not seem to be the central concern of the witness of the New Testament. The earliest Christian writers seem to have assumed such an event. They presupposed its having happened, but they spent surprisingly little time defending it or arguing for it. They were concerned less with arguing the truth or reality of the resurrection than with defining the significance of the resurrected one, whom they all agreed was really and marvelously alive in their midst.

Luke comes closer than the other evangelists to asserting and defending the reality of Jesus' resurrection (Luke 24:36-43), and yet even he has other and more basic concerns. John is terribly misunderstood when Thomas (20:24-29) is viewed as a modern skeptic, questioning miracles and demanding empirical evidence. Too much of the wrong sort of thing has been made of Matthew's remark about the rumor of the theft of Jesus' body (28:15).

Neither Paul in 1 Corinthians nor the evangelists in their resurrection narratives argue that Christian faith can be expressed adequately in some such phrase as "God really performed a miracle of transformation and resurrection on the third day." Jesus' resurrection is not the end and goal of their argumentation, but the beginning.

Accepting and presupposing the reality of the resurrection, apostles and evangelists used that tradition in a variety of ways. The present work focuses on how each one of the canonical gospels uses the shared Christian tradition of the resurrection of Jesus. How does the resurrection function in their writings? What tasks does the Easter material perform? How do they put the resurrected Christ to work? The focus is not so much on history as on the texts, on writings, on traditions. The book does not attempt to penetrate through the texts back into history, at least not back into the last days of the life of Jesus, not back into the shoes of Joseph of Arimathea and the guards and Mary Magdalene and Peter on April 7-16 of the year of our Lord 30.

On the other hand, the book does attempt a task both historical and literary, that of standing in the shoes of the evangelists in Syria or Asia Minor or Greece or Rome in the years between 65 and 95, in the second and third generation after Good Friday and Easter, and of interpreting the documents in the light of what can be known about the communities in which they arose.

So this book is neither attack nor apology. It is an attempt to listen to the evangelists carefully and sympathetically in their social and historical contexts, in order to see what they held dear about the resurrection of Jesus.

Strategy

The strategy of the book is simple. A single chapter is devoted to each one of the evangelists. Each chapter has three sections, featuring in turn the situation of the evangelist, commentary on his resurrection narrative, and a summary of the evangelist's view of Easter.

It would help to know with precision the historical situation of each writer. While the gospels as writings do have an integrity and life of their own, and it is proper to use upon them all the literary critical talent and imagination an interpreter possesses, still it would be useful to know who the original readers were, where they lived, and under what circumstances. Having at our disposal the biographies of the authors would also be more help than hindrance.

The effort to locate each evangelist not only geographically and chronologically but in terms of the varied currents of values and ideas, of experiences and deeds, inside the church and the world involves a good amount of guesswork. Ernst Käsemann remarked in his Shaffer Lectures that "introductions to the New Testament," the class of modern books devoted to these subjects, could to a large extent be placed into the literary genre of fairy tales.[2] It may as well be admitted from the start that this book indulges necessarily in some guesswork, but the guesses are moderate, modest, and centrist, even when they represent a choice among possibilities or a guess that might have some small claim on originality.

The paragraphs on background not only contain some guesses but are deliberately narrow. For example, Luke exhibits throughout his gospel and in the early chapters of Acts a very strong sympathy for the poor and a sense of the dangers of wealth. He advocates radical sharing and encourages Christians to accept poverty without regret. Obviously, Luke also exhibits a keen interest in missionary outreach and in the inner life of prayer. Some readers may be surprised to find

these and many other matters treated hardly at all in the introductory section on Luke. Instead, the focus is on Luke's attitude toward Roman power, his careful recommendation of the majesty of Jesus and
the glory of the kingdom of God, and questions of continuity in the
church through the passage of time.

It is not the case that poverty and riches, missions, or prayer are
unimportant. Rather, it seems that Luke 24 and Acts 1-2, read in the
light of the rest of Luke-Acts (and Luke-Acts read in their light), reveal that the author is absorbed in connecting Jesus' resurrection
with issues of Roman power and the passing of generations. Therefore
those issues are featured in the introduction to the section on Luke's
gospel, to the exclusion of other issues with which Luke and his community also wrestled.

So the brief introductory sections below involve some
guesswork—as little as possible—and also a narrow concentration
upon one of two issues confronting the community, and this concentration entails some simplification and constriction of vision. But the
guesses and the focusing are offered in the twin convictions that the
Gospels as a whole justify them and they in turn help to illumine the
Easter narratives.

The second section of each chapter consists of verse by verse commentary on the resurrection narrative of the evangelist. The commentary was written with the usual assumptions about the canonical gospels. It supposes that Mark is the first of the four to have been
written, that Matthew and Luke had Mark's gospel (up through 16:8)
in written form on the table in front of them as they composed their
own gospels, that they had access also to other written and unwritten
materials, and that Matthew and Luke wrote independently of one another. It also assumes that John's gospel was not written in total isolation from the synoptic tradition, although the exact nature of John's
relationship to the synoptics cannot be ascertained and we must simply be content with great and frustrating ignorance. Moreover, it is
assumed that each of the evangelists was a bright and enterprising
author and theologian, not merely a blue pencil artist or scissors and
paste expert. At the same time, it is acknowledged that the originality
of the evangelists was held in check by the availability of traditions,
by reverence for them, and by the critical powers of their own
communities of readers.

While the sections of commentary operate with the usual widely
held assumptions about sources, no effort is made to travel backwards
in time from the present state of the text through underlying written

traditions and oral sources to the actual historical events of Easter Sunday. Such an itinerary treats the present text too glibly and permits it simply to recede from view. The words of the evangelists are treated as though they were windows into the history of Jesus of Nazareth.

Of course, source and tradition criticism have often been used in this fashion to construct a story which we do not have, and then that invented account is permitted to overshadow the story we do have—or rather the stories, since we have four related but distinctively different accounts of the Easter events in our canonical gospels. These should occupy the foreground of our attention.

The effort is made in the sections of commentary to enter into the world which each evangelist has constructed in his gospel, to listen to each evangelist on his own terms, and to stand in his shoes or eavesdrop as he addresses his first audience, in order to understand, if at all possible, the use each makes of the Easter traditions in his particular situation.

The third and final section of each chapter recapitulates some of the material in the first two sections, summarizing briefly the way the evangelist has shaped and used the tradition of Jesus' resurrection in his particular situation.

In addition, these final sections scan the entire gospel under consideration with an eye for Easter motifs. What does each author say about Easter outside his resurrection narrative? How has he anticipated Easter? Does the way the evangelist presents the resurrection in his Easter narrative relate to patterns discernible earlier in his gospel? Has the evangelist consciously employed literary devices preparing his readers for the narrative of Jesus' resurrection? Did Easter so overwhelm and transform the evangelist that he has unconsciously reshaped memories, individual traditions, and his entire composition, so that in its entirety or in unexpected parts it enunciates the message of the resurrected Lord?

This final section of each chapter offers only a rapid reading of the gospel and is more suggestive than exhaustive. But Easter faith is so closely associated with faith in God and reliance upon his presence, effectiveness, and goodness that every sentence in the gospel can, from a certain angle, be regarded as an expression of Easter faith. Good Friday and Easter were realities of such enormous power that it would be odd indeed if they had not stamped their mark on the testimony of the evangelists from the beginning and not only at the end. These final sections in each chapter could be almost endlessly enlarged. They tend, however, to be brief, concentrating ordinarily on material with readily apparent reference to the resurrection.

Omissions

Much is omitted from this work. It contains nothing on Q, nothing except for passing reference on Paul, Hebrews, the Apocalypse, or any of the other writings of the New Testament beyond the Gospels. Furthermore, the study concentrates on the canonical gospels and does not look beyond them at the gospels of Thomas, Peter, or any of the other apocryphal documents which once circulated as Scripture in parts of the early church.

Because of their special status, the various endings of Mark have been included for treatment, even though Mark 16:8 is the original ending of the gospel.

Easter Faith

It is surprising, in view of modern preaching and teaching on the resurrection, to note how little the evangelists use the resurrection of Jesus for purposes of soothing the anxieties of Christians regarding their future. They do not seem interested primarily in comforting their contemporaries by making Jesus' resurrection into evidence for a resurrection in general. The evangelists do not use Jesus' resurrection as proof that there really is life beyond the grave. They do not focus chiefly on proclaiming his rising from death as a sign that believers will one day also shuck off their grave cloths and vacate their tombs.

Nor do the evangelists use the Easter materials to teach what many churches have claimed they teach. The several branches of the Christian church have used individual verses out of the Easter narratives as proof texts for a variety of dogmatic positions, including such matters as the primacy of Peter, ordination to a hierarchically organized priesthood, the dominical institution of Baptism, the presence of Christ in the Eucharist and in scriptural meditation, the deity of Christ, the doctrine of the Trinity, the unique dignity of Mary as a second Eve, the priesthood of all believers, the necessity of orthodox faith, the inspiration and inerrancy of the Scriptures, the truth of prophecy, and the promise of charismatic endowments.

Then what connections do the evangelists make? What use do they make of the traditions of Easter? It is perhaps foolhardy to attempt to summarize any of the conclusions of the body of this work in a few dangerously brief sentences. However, the following may at least hint at the direction in which the discussions below proceed.

The Easter texts testify to a powerful change in Jesus, but they do it in order to empower the readers for new life and renewed ministry. The focus in all the Easter texts on ministry and service is remarkably strong.

To people buffeted and confused by unjust suffering and malice, Mark proclaims the resurrection as the vindication of the crucified, and through his Easter narrative he summons Christians to minister and serve joyfully in spite of all the hostility they encounter.

Especially to teachers in the church, full of their own importance and proud of their spiritual gifts, Matthew proclaims the resurrection as the exaltation of the Teacher of the Sermon on the Mount. He is not merely the once and future Lord, but the present one in the midst of the congregation.

To readers overawed by Caesar's mighty power and tossed about by conflicting winds of doctrine, Luke interprets the resurrection and ascension as the enthronement of Jesus as Lord and Christ of a universal kingdom of peace, wherein life is ordered by the word of his chosen witnesses.

John's gospel achieved its unique form by meditation on the rejection of Jesus in his homeland, the excommunication of the believers from the synagogue, and the wrenching experience of the death of the Beloved Disciple. To people who felt adrift and alone in a world of death and darkness, the evangelist had learned to speak eloquently of the glorified Jesus as the way to oneness with the Father and to eternal life as a present possession.

mark

The Setting: Persecution

The puzzle of Mark's gospel[1] is not how Jesus can be both human and divine, son of Mary and Son of God. The mystery has to do rather with the cloud brooding over this Jesus as he proceeds to a lonely and forsaken death. Over all his days and all his words and works, over his power and his weakness, over his speech and his silence, there falls the shadow of the cross.[2]

The darkness of that shadow hardly seems relieved by the curiously brief and enigmatic resurrection paragraph at the close of the gospel. How can such a portrait be "the good news of Jesus Christ" (1:1)? How can this somber and sobering document be called a "gospel"? The answer is to be found in the situation addressed. But what exactly was that situation?[3]

One opinion is that Mark wrote in order to combat an incipient docetism that was devoted to the kerygma of the triumphant Christ but indifferent to the tradition of the words and deeds of the historical Jesus. Another is that Mark was moved to write his gospel in order to defeat a divine-man Christology, one in which Jesus was pictured as a charismatic wonder worker in his earthly life and was then portrayed in his heavenly life since the resurrection as an exalted Lord whose powers the Christian can now share mystically or sacramentally. In opposing such heresies, which make light of the cross as a momentary interruption in an otherwise glorious career, Mark is supposed to have

17

gone to the opposite extreme, outdoing Paul in his emphasis on the
cross. Proponents of this view say that in Mark the darkness of the
cross is not brightened by any resurrection appearances or promises
of appearances. The final pericope of the gospel (Mark 16:1-8) speaks
not of appearances and reunion but only of the failure of the disciples
and the absence of Jesus, according to this way of thinking.[4]

A far different interpretation of Mark's ending is offered below.
Here it may be said that Mark by no means eliminates references to
power and the Spirit in the career of Jesus or in the life of the early
church. His strategy is not simply to substitute the story of the cross
and weakness for another, opposing story of resurrection power. As
Paul had done before him, so Mark stressed the paradoxical power of
the suffering and death of Jesus in weakness, subordinating but not
eliminating the tradition of the miracles and words of Jesus. Indeed,
the fresh combination of the Pauline proclamation of the cross with
the narrative tradition of Jesus' words and deeds ranks as the great
contribution of Mark's originality and genius.

Furthermore, the assumption that Mark represented one school
of theological thought against another defines his situation too narrowly and too coolly as one of heady intellectual debate.

Another suggestion recently offered about the background of this
gospel is that Mark is "a foundation document for an apocalyptic community" of people located sociologically in a situation of deprivation
and geographically in backwater Syria.[5] The theory, as displayed in all
its fullness by its proponents, has much to commend it. Nevertheless,
if Mark really were an apocalyptic writing composed for an apocalyptic community, there would surely be in it far more symbolic interpretation of the Old Testament, far more use of such stock apocalyptic
figures as monsters and dragons, far more speculation on days and
times and puzzling numbers, as there is in the Book of Revelation.
Mark does contain apocalyptic elements, but they are bits and pieces
of traditional thought and piety, part of the mental furniture of the
age. They occupy the fringes of the author's imagination and do not
hold the center. Mark does not announce the imminent cataclysmic
end of the world and summon his readers to withdraw from their
worldly occupations and entanglements. He does not call them to re-
tire to a pure and safe existence of quiet waiting. His attitude is more
robust.

Mark commends a life focused not on spectacular events to occur
in the immediate future but on patient ministry in the company of the
crucified but resurrected Jesus. He calls his readers to joyful service

in the world of this present time in spite of whatever awful, numbing horrors of persecution may be visited upon them. The disciples are beloved children of God no matter what appearances may seem to be saying to the contrary. Such a positive attitude towards life is not at all characteristic of apocalyptic.

The gospel itself gives every indication that it was written for Christians battered by the experience of persecution and suffering (8:34-38; 10:28-30; 13:8-13). That much seems indisputably clear. What is not so clear is which precise persecution is in view.

Two separate catastrophes are known to have broken upon Christian communities in the middle sixties of the first century: 1) Nero turned his cruel attentions upon the Christians in the city of Rome (A.D. 64-65), and 2) a short time later the Christians of Judea were caught in the maelstrom set churning by the Jewish rebellion against their Roman overlords in the holy land (A.D. 66-73).

The convulsions of the Jewish-Roman war in Judea have been suggested as the key to Mark's writing. While the war ravaged the land, all the Jewish inhabitants suffered, whether they were adherents of the synagogue or members of the church. According to ancient tradition, the Christian community of Jerusalem, refusing to join their Jewish compatriots in the national uprising, abandoned the Holy City and made their way across the Jordan River to Pella, some 60 miles north and east.[6]

The Christians found themselves in a tragic situation, caught in a terrible pincer: zealous Jews regarded them as traitors and the Romans were not able to distinguish them from other Jews, so they had enemies to the right of them and enemies to the left.

It has been suggested that Mark was one of the Christians who fled Jerusalem for the north just before the outbreak of the war. He interpreted the gathering storm as the eschatological tribulation, the final shaking of the universe immediately preceding the parousia (Chap. 13), and then sometime between A.D. 67 and 69 wrote his gospel in an effort to persuade Christians to gather in Galilee to meet the returning Lord.[7]

But there are too many difficulties in the way of accepting the notion that the war in Judea is the setting for the gospel of Mark. Among many other things, it must be said that if Mark were writing in Palestine, he would not have had to explain Jewish customs and notions (7:3-4; 12:18; 14:12; 15:42), or the climate (11:13) and currency (12:42) of Palestine, nor would he have had to translate Aramaic words and phrases (3:17; 5:41; 7:11, 34; 15:22, 34). The glosses, translations, and explanations point to a non-Palestinian and generally non-Jewish readership.[8]

Once it was thought that the many Latin loanwords in the gospel pointed to authorship in Rome, but then it was argued that most of them are commercial or military terms that would be found wherever Roman legions were stationed. Nevertheless, the explanation (12:42) of the two copper coins *(leptēs)* as equivalent of a *quadrans*, a coin not in circulation in the East, tells in favor of a western rather than an eastern provenance.[9]

Internal evidence points to Gentile-Christian rather than to Jewish-Christian readers. The Gentile mission and therefore the existence of Mark's community is grounded firmly in Jesus' own ministry (3:13ff.; 6:7ff., 30; 13:10). Jesus felt responsible for the crowds that gathered about him in the pagan Decapolis (6:37), and the gospel pointedly asserts that Gentiles benefit from the ministry and dying of Jesus (10:45; 11:17; 14:8-9, 24; 15:38-39; cf. 12:1-11).[10]

Many will venture to go no farther than to say that the gospel was produced somewhere in the Roman empire for a Gentile-Christian audience in the mid-60s of the first century. And yet, the proposal that Mark composed his gospel at Rome in the late 60s or early 70s for a Christian community whose memory was scarred by the persecution under Nero needs to be taken seriously. No other background meshes so well with so much of the available evidence or explains so well why Mark has pictured Jesus as he has.[11]

Tacitus (born in A.D. 57-58), writing around the end of the first century or beginning of the second, says that a great fire broke out in Rome on July 19 in the year 64 and raged for six days, completely destroying three districts, reducing seven more to a few scorched ruins, and leaving unscathed only four of the total of fourteen. Homes, palaces, and temples were ruined. Many citizens perished in the flames, and others lost all their worldly goods. Looters prowled the streets and even fanned fires. Nero devised emergency shelter and brought in food from Ostia, but the populace was bewildered and mean. They heard that during the fire Nero had stood on his private stage and had in song compared the fate of Rome with the destruction of ancient Troy.

Nero undertook to rebuild the city, improving its architecture and water supply. The Sibylline books were consulted and the gods propitiated. Still the suspicion persisted that Nero had deliberately set fire to the city to clear the way for a greater Rome. At that point, says Tacitus:

To suppress this rumor, Nero fabricated scapegoats—and punished with every refinement the notoriously depraved Christians (as they were popularly called). ... First, Nero had self-acknowledged Christians arrested. Then, on their information, large numbers of others were condemned—not so much for incendiarism as for their antisocial tendencies. Their deaths were made farcical. Dressed in wild animals' skins, they were torn to pieces by dogs, or crucified, or made into torches to be ignited after dark as substitutes for daylight.[12]

Thus, Tacitus says, the Romans pounced on known Christians and on those who freely acknowledged their faith and then extracted from them—by what exquisite tortures we are not told—the names of fellow Christians. Persecutors are notoriously interested in the leaders of offending movements and are willing to offer concessions to the small fry in exchange for testimony against the leaders. It always happens in religious and political persecutions that some refuse to give the evidence sought, while others, anxious to save their own skins or their own families, betray erstwhile friends. Still others, if they think it will help them, deny any connection with the persecuted faith or renounce their connection and change their creed. Those who can manage it simply go underground or get out of town. Treachery, betrayal, defection, fear, flight, the agony of decision—these are some of the central realities pertaining to the situation addressed by Mark.[13]

Persecution tests more than physical courage. It inflicts spiritual wounds, especially when the persecuted are innocent by any ordinary standards of morality and justice. The Roman Christians regarded themselves not only as guiltless but as the elect, the privileged people of God, and persecution plunged them into dismay. How could God permit his own children to be maligned, abused, tortured, put to death?

In their Baptism the Christians had heard the voice of the Father covenanting with them as his beloved children: "You are my son, my daughter." Afterwards they could no doubt point to experiences assuring them of God's fatherly concern in their daily lives. Charismatic endowments were plentiful in early Christian communities, and perhaps some members of Mark's community were able to perform signs and wonders, even though there is no evidence that the majority were blessed with healing powers, or that they enjoyed the more spectacular gifts of the Spirit or revelled in such gifts as the Corinthian enthusiasts had.[14]

The hopes and expectations of Mark's original audience were not so different from those of most Christians in subsequent ages. They found suffering dismaying, especially suffering inflicted by a cruel and sadistic opponent completely lacking in sympathy and bereft of the most elementary understanding of the nature of their faith. Misrepresented as dangerous to the state and as haters of humankind, they were hounded and killed without mercy. They cried out, as Christians have regularly cried out, "Why has God let this happen to us? Why has God forsaken us?"

Furthermore, once persecution had ceased, state and populace turned to other affairs, and a different set of problems inevitably arose. What should the survivors do about those who had turned state's evidence and those who had lapsed, if such persons now sought readmission to the Christian community? How should the community handle the resentment and suspicion between those who had borne the brunt of suffering and those who had fled the city but kept the faith? How could the whole community make sense out of the experience of suffering and assimilate it as something positive, working not to the erosion of faith but to its deepening?

The times were tumultuous. Nero, deposed by the senate in favor of Galba on June 8, A.D. 68, committed suicide the next day. Immediately insurrection and political unrest erupted everywhere. In the next year and a half Galba, Otho, and Vitellius succeeded one another rapidly. Finally, an eastern coalition under Vespasian defeated Vitellius and the western forces in December of 69, restored peace and order, and reunited the empire.[15]

The exact time and place of the writing of Mark's gospel remains at best an educated guess, a conclusion based on hints both inside and outside the gospel itself. But what should be clear is the fact that Mark is addressing innocent sufferers, persecuted people. They believed they were children of God, and yet their sufferings made them feel forsaken by God.

Mark heard the cry, felt the anguish, and saw the spiritual danger. The members of the community were tempted by persecution to discouragement, alarm, anxiety, unbelief, or false belief.

Mark responded by offering to his readers a fresh and profound interpretation of the Christian tradition, emphasizing the parallels between their own experience and that of Jesus.[16] In his portrait of Jesus, Mark emphasizes both Jesus' sonship and his forsakenness.

Mark pictures Jesus as teaching and healing in Galilee (Part One, 1:1—8:26), journeying through Galilee to Perea (Part Two, 8:27—

10:52), and arriving at the Holy City of Jerusalem (Part Three, 11:1— 16:8).[17] The chief audience of Jesus in the first part of the gospel is the crowds. It is true that he turns aside from the crowds to speak to his disciples (1:35; 3:13-19; 4:10, 34; 6:30, 45-54; 8:14-21), but the overwhelming impression Mark gives is of Jesus' interaction with the general populace in villages, in synagogues, on hillsides, and at the sea. People press about Jesus to hear him, to see and touch him, to bring their sick to him.

The crowds do not entirely disappear from the second section of the gospel. They are there in the background (8:34; 9:14ff.; 10:1, 46), but the foreground is occupied by the disciples, pictured as being in direct, prolonged, and intimate conversation with Jesus (9:30-31).

Then in Part Three, the relationship of Jesus with the Jerusalem authorities is the new and dominant feature, even though the disciples and crowds continue to be present significantly almost to the end. Local authorities were present in the first section, but it is really in the third section of the gospel that the powerful in the land mount the stage as major actors in direct contact with Jesus. There at the end, the action occurs not just in Judea but in Jerusalem, and not just in Jerusalem but in the temple precincts, in the courtyard of the high priest, and in the Roman praetorium of Pontius Pilate.

The subject matter of Jesus' teaching changes as his geography changes. Jesus' ministry in Mark's gospel opens with the declaration that "the kingdom of God is at hand" (1:15), and the authority of Jesus, the kingship of God, the contest with demonic powers, and the struggle for faith are major themes of the opening chapters.

A shift in theme occurs with Peter's conferral of the royal title of "Christ" upon Jesus (8:29). Jesus then begins in the central section of the gospel to speak pointedly and repeatedly of his rejection, suffering, death, and vindication, especially in the three great passion predictions (8:31; 9:31; 10:33-34) and in the climactic ransom saying (10:45).

In the final section of the gospel, Mark seems to shift once again to new themes, the temple and the Messiah. Of course, the "Messiah" or "Christ" is by itself no new topic (1:1; 8:29; 9:41; see also the variant reading at 1:34), but throughout the entire final section of the gospel these two topics continually emerge, usually somehow paired.

Jesus receives muted messianic acclaim (11:10) as he approaches the city and the temple. The following day he returns to cleanse the temple (11:15-19), and then day by day he is in the temple, teaching (cf. 14:49) and disputing, particularly about his authority (esp.

11:27-33) and the nature of messiahship (esp. 12:1-11, 35-37). Talk of temple (13:1-3) and Messiah (13:6, 21, 2, 26, 32) continues in the Little Apocalypse (Chap. 13).

At his trial the charges revolve around the twin topics of his relationship to the temple (14:58) and his identity as "Christ, the Son of the Blessed" (14:61; 15:2, 9, 12, 21). The same two topics form the subject matter of the taunts hurled at him as he hangs on the cross (temple in 15:29-30; Christ, King of Israel in 15:31-32). Then, as he dies, temple and messiahship (kingship or sonship) are featured once again: the curtain of the temple is torn in two (15:38) and the centurion confesses Jesus as God's Son (15:39).

Each of the three main sections of Mark's gospel is characterized also by different forms of activity on the part of Jesus. The earlier chapters are studded with miracles, as Jesus casts out demons, heals the sick, raises the dead, feeds the hungry, stills the storm. In 1:1—8:26 there are at least fifteen miracles, but in the next section (8:27—10:52) there are only two, and journeying to Jerusalem rather than any healing is the characteristic action of this section.

In the final section of the gospel (11:1—16:8) Jesus performs only one act usually classified as a miracle, the cursing of the fig tree (11:12-14, 20-21). It differs from the healings and feedings of Part One and seems negative rather than positive in its effects. It serves a primarily didactic or symbolic purpose. It must be read in conjunction with the cleansing of the temple, with which it is structurally intertwined. Splendid in appearance, the temple will be judged because it does not bear the desired fruit, and there is a hint that a new time or season of fruitfulness lies in the future with a new community.

From the point of view of the action of Jesus, it is clear that miracles belong to Part One and that weakness and dying belong to Part Three, while Part Two is transitional, as Jesus wends his way from Galilee and ministry to Jerusalem and suffering.

So from many points of view Jesus seems to "progress" in Mark's gospel from teaching to silence, from deeds of power to weakness, from freedom to captivity, from popularity to forsakenness.

The bottom line might appear to be that Mark's Jesus is a progressively forsaken figure, gradually losing his power and his following, until at the last he utters from the cross that terrible cry, "My God, my God, why have you forsaken me?" (15:34). And yet, that is only one side, the dark side, of Mark's portrait. Mark's eye of faith perceives light and strength in, with, and under the darkness and the forsakenness. There is light also after the darkness, but not only after it or beyond it. Light is there wrapped in the darkness. So Mark writes with irony, and his words seem full of paradox.

Thus Mark's gospel is punctuated by a series of great declarations that Jesus is the Son of God. Mark varies and alters the confession of Jesus, so that sometimes it is "Son of God" and other times it is "God's Son" or "My beloved Son" or "Son of the Blessed."

The title is there in Mark's opening phrase (1:1, omitted by some ancient manuscripts but probably part of the original),[18] and it is found in the mouth of demons (3:11; 5:7; cf. 1:24). That the title is uttered by unclean spirits might seem to debase it or diminish its value, but Mark features the sonship of Jesus at three critical moments: his baptism, transfiguration, and crucifixion. "My beloved Son" is the Father's confession and declaration concerning Jesus (1:11; 9:7). Jesus himself finally asserts his sonship both in the prayer in Gethsemane (14:36) and in the trial before the Sanhedrin (14:62), and he is acclaimed as God's Son by the Roman centurion (15:39) beyond the cry of forsakenness (15:34), as though to contradict that cry, or to offer a counterbalance to it, or to compel readers to view it and review it for fresh possibilities.

The entire gospel has been read by some as a narrative shaped by an ancient enthronement ritual. In this reading, Jesus' baptism corresponds to the adoption of the new king, his transfiguration to the ceremonial presentation, his crucifixion to the actual enthronement, and the centurion's confession to the people's acclamation.[19]

It almost seems that Mark has offered two divergent readings of Jesus in his gospel: Jesus is acclaimed God's Son in the beginning, in the middle, and at the end; but crowds fail to understand, disciples misunderstand, and authorities reject him utterly, while all abandon him.

And yet, Mark perceives intimate links and connections between the two sets of facts about Jesus. The suffering is only apparently a defeat or a contradiction of sonship, for in Mark's perspective suffering has intrinsic value and is eventually triumphant. The forsakenness and suffering are predicted by Jesus and so are presented as somehow under his control. They are, furthermore, freely accepted by him as divinely willed. Jesus shared with his disciples not only his certainty of victory beyond death in his resurrection (8:31; 9:31; 10:33-34), but also his vision of triumph and of benefits accruing to many precisely in his dying (10:45; 14:22-24).

Jesus is revealed as the Son of God and King of God's people at the end, not in spite of his suffering, but exactly in and through his suffering service. Mark was reminding his contemporaries, children of God and disciples of Jesus, that their experience of deprivation and persecution by no means contradicted their status as children of God. Sonship, far from being incompatible with service and suffering, is intimately meshed with them, both in the case of Jesus and in the case of his disciples, whom he called to "take up your cross and follow" (8:34). That word in Mark means moving even toward martyrdom in full confidence of the Father's care. So Mark is writing about the sonship and suffering of Jesus not merely to insist that Jesus really is the Son, but to interpret the sonship of Jesus as well as the sonship of his disciples.

Mark's community was shaken by persecution, and the pictures of Jesus current in the community were not adequate to console and strengthen the sufferers for patient endurance, for joy in service, for mutual forgiveness.

Mark's achievement was a fresh rendering of the traditions of the words and deeds of Jesus. He brought them all to the foot of the cross. All the traditions about Jesus—as teacher, exorcist, and healer—were brought by Mark under the control of the cross, so that there is no Jesus without the cross or without faith, and no faith without the cross of Jesus.[20]

Quite obviously there is no Christian faith or Christian confession or Christian discipleship without the cross. All this holds true of Mark's appropriation and transmission of the resurrection traditions. It is precisely the crucified Jesus and no other who is the risen Lord of the church. It is most important to note how the resurrected one both is and is not described. He is not described as seated in glory at God's right hand, as remote and resplendent in heaven, as bearing scepter and crowned with gold, as robed in majesty and clothed with might, as seated at a banquet table in a celestial mansion, as mounted on a white horse and wielding a sharp two-edged sword, or as coming upon the clouds of heaven to judge the nations. He is portrayed in the angel's message as leader of the church in its universal mission and ministry. He summons his scattered disciples and leads them forth.

The Original Ending of Mark

Mark 16:1-8   And when the sabbath was past, Mary Mag'dalene, and Mary the mother of James, and Sa-lo'me, bought spices, so that they might go and anoint him.[2] And very early on the first day of the week they went to the tomb when the sun had risen.[3] And they were saying to one another, "Who will roll away the stone for us from the door of the tomb?"[4] And looking up, they saw that the stone was rolled back; for it was very large.[5] And entering the tomb, they saw a young man sitting on the right side, dressed in a white robe; and they were amazed.[6] And he said to them, "Do not be amazed; you seek Jesus of Nazareth, who was crucified. He has risen, he is not here; see the place where they laid him.[7] But go, tell his disciples and Peter that he is going before you to Galilee; there you will see him, as he told you."[8] And they went out and fled from the tomb; for trembling and astonishment had come upon them; and they said nothing to any one, for they were afraid.

The final paragraph of Mark in Codex Sinaiticus and Codex Vaticanus, the oldest and best of the great ancient Greek manuscripts of the New Testament, consists of 16:1-8. The first copies of Mark to reach Africa, Alexandria, Caesarea, and Antioch of Syria end with verse 8, and since the African text derived from Rome, the earliest Roman copies also probably ended with verse 8.[21]

Nevertheless, today many—certainly not all—deny that Mark could have planned to end his gospel at verse 8 and suggest a variety of reasons for the abrupt conclusion.

Some think that Mark actually wrote a longer gospel, but that some pages have been accidentally lost. Stephen Neill,[22] for example, thinks not only that the original ending has been lost, but also that the original opening is gone. He imagines that two pages of the original gospel (he assumes it was a codex and not a scroll) are missing—the first and the last. The present opening verse (1:1, "The beginning of the gospel of Jesus Christ the Son of God") is in his opinion a scribal note meaning that "this is where a new gospel begins."[23] Neill thinks the lost opening contained a very brief nativity story and some kind of transitional material preparing for the appearance of John the Baptist, while the lost ending narrated a resurrection appearance to the women (cf. Matt. 28:9-10) and their sharing of the news with the disciples.[24]

Others imagine that Mark never reached the ending he had planned and that he was cut off in mid-flight by illness, imprisonment, or death.

Modern scholars have theorized variously about what this hypothetical lost ending of Mark might have contained. In addition to a meeting with the women along the road, a favorite is an appearance of Jesus to Peter and the other disciples. B. H. Streeter guessed that Mark originally closed with an appearance to Mary Magdalene, followed by an appearance to Peter and the others while they were fishing on the Sea of Galilee, and that John derived his version of these incidents (John 20-21) from the now lost conclusion of Mark.[25]

The feeling that Mark 16:8 is too abrupt is very old. Matthew and Luke followed Mark and incorporated his gospel almost wholesale into their own, so that theirs are revised and expanded versions of Mark. Both of them felt the need for a fuller conclusion and supplied it, each in his own way.

Every attempt by ancient scribes to augment the present final paragraph with the so-called Short Ending, Long Ending, and Freer Logion (see below) is a declaration from some element in the ancient church that it found that concluding paragraph to be no conclusion at all.

Modern scholars, for their part, have called the eight verses of Chapter 16 abrupt, inartistic, impossible, inappropriate, and even unbearable as an ending to a Christian gospel.

Why all the dissatisfaction, ancient and modern, with 16:8 as the conclusion to the gospel? A few basic reasons for the negative evaluations are mentioned repeatedly:

1. The last word in verse 8 is the Greek conjunction *gar*, translated by the English conjunction "for." That a book written in the Greek language could end with *gar* has been long and vigorously denied. No other example of a Greek book ending thus has ever been found.

Gar is a weak, unaccented word in the Greek sentence, and the feeling of the final clause might be conveyed by a paraphrase: "they were afraid, you see." The voice drops and the whole ends on a muted note.

Nevertheless, examples have been collected of clauses, sentences, paragraphs, chapters, and long sections of books all ending with *gar*, and the majority view today is that it would not at all be impossible for an entire book to end this way.[27]

2. By the time Mark reaches 16:8 he has not yet, it is asserted, succeeded in counterbalancing the enormous weight of injustice and iniquity chronicled in the preceding chapters. The gospel as it stands, we are told, is not sufficiently good news to enable Mark's first or last readers to live with joy in the face of suffering and with the confidence that God's good and gracious will shall overcome. Bruce Metzger calls the final clause "a melancholy statement."[28] The commentary below will argue to the contrary.

3. It has been said that Mark has himself led the reader to expect at least the fulfillment of the promises of 14:28 and 16:7, that is, an ap-

pearance of the resurrected Jesus to the disciples. In particular, some look for an appearance of Jesus to Peter as the one scene which could most satisfactorily close the action of the gospel.

Mark 16:1-8 is certainly difficult, but is it really impossible as the original conclusion to the gospel? It is muted or reserved, but its reserve is a dramatic and kerygmatic asset.

If Mark had offered an account of the appearance of Jesus to the women or to Peter or to any of the others, he might have encouraged the impression that the members of the first generation enjoyed privileges denied to later Christians.[29] By so closing his gospel, he might also have fostered the notion that Christian faith is fundamentally backward-looking and focuses primarily on the past acts of God in the history of Jesus.

Mark's curiously muted conclusion puts the brakes on curiosity and prevents the readers' imaginations from completing the gospel in terms of a traditional happy ending.[30] Mark has concluded his gospel hopefully and mysteriously. His ending has the effect of throwing the readers back upon themselves, placing them in the position of having to make a decision for or against "Jesus and Galilee," and that means for or against discipleship and ministry, for or against different kinds of futures for themselves.

The unfinished character of the gospel directs readers to the time beyond that recorded in Chapter 16 and so to their own relationship with God and his Christ. That the gospel does not come to rest within the framework of the narrative, that it does not offer a neat resolution of all the tensions inherent in the plot, means that the gospel can not and dare not be viewed as completed in the past. Mark did not want his story to be read, perhaps even believed, and then easily set aside.

Mark has refused to write a story over which the reader can exercise such control. The narrative is not at the reader's disposal but is open-ended. It is tantalizing, and it challenges readers to supply an ending in their own lives. The one end the author desired above all others was that the readers become disciples, take up the cross, and follow Jesus on his way.

The gospel of Mark, as it was known by both Matthew and Luke, ended at 16:8,[31] and therefore the short form of the gospel, however abrupt it may seem, was in circulation in the 70s and 80s of the first century and was supplying the church's needs, at least in some segments of the church. Today there are still those who regard it, short and muted as it is, as a masterpiece of awesome force, full of suspense, mystery, indirection, and challenge. They find it fully as satisfying in

its own way as the longer endings and further episodes of the other canonical gospels, and as more satisfying than the fantasies of the
various endings supplied to Mark by well-intentioned church people
and scribes of the second century.

The following commentary works with the assumption that Mark
intended to close his gospel at 16:8.

Mark 16:1-8:   He Goes Before You

16:1   The events of Jesus' condemnation, execution, and burial
rolled on in solemn cadence as the author recorded the sun's journey
across the sky and announced the passage of time in three-hour segments on that Friday (Chap. 15). But then it was evening. Jesus died
and was buried, and the Sabbath came. Mark has not a single word
about that Sabbath. The rush and flow of time is momentarily
stemmed, as narrative and narrator break off. The break in the narrative appears to mirror another and deeper discontinuity.

What is the end of the one who taught with authority in synagogues on the Sabbath (1:21-27), who called himself lord even of the
Sabbath (2:23-28), who aroused the fatal antagonism of defenders of
the peace of the Sabbath (3:1-6)? That sabbath and its defenders seem
finally to have mastered him. But then "the sabbath was past," and
Mark plunged in to narrate the events of a new day, the first day of the
week.

The women had not fled but remained steady. They are
latecomers to Mark's narrative, appearing for the first time in the account of the passion, even though Mark ties them to earlier times by
declaring that they, like the men around Jesus, hailed from Galilee.
They had followed Jesus and ministered to him in the north, and were
part of a larger company of women who had accompanied Jesus south
to Jerusalem (15:41).

In short order Mark offers three lists of names of women (15:40,
47; 16:1). The lists are not consistent, and fully satisfying explanations
of the differences are hard to come by. Perhaps Mark knew two different lists (15:47 and 16:1) preserved by two different communities and
has combined them in 15:40.[32]

It does not take us very far to note that Mary Magdalene is the
only woman named in the resurrection accounts of all four Gospels
and that John especially develops her portrait and role; or to see that
Matthew identified Salome as "the mother of the sons of Zebedee"
(Matt. 27:56; cf. 20:20); or to remark that Jesus' mother is absent (but

present in John 19:25-27), and that strangely enough Jesus had brothers named James and Joses (Mark 6:3), the same names given to the sons of a Mary at the tomb; or even to say that women in Judaism were disqualified from bearing witness in court.[33]

In spite of difficulties in figuring out who these women were and why the three lists differ, Mark manages to make at least three positive points with his lists: 1) He reminds the reader of other nameless women in his narrative who served Jesus (1:31), clung to him in faith (5:25-34; 7:24-30), and in spite of opposition and even ridicule displayed their devotion (14:3-9). 2) Mark once again in these notes establishes Galilee as the place of ministry and discipleship (1:9, 18), while he simultaneously deepens the impression of Jerusalem as the center of opposition (3:8). 3) The presence of these women is a sign of promise at a moment when Jesus' following appeared to have collapsed and all hope for the future seemed to have vanished utterly.

Mark intends the final paragraph of the gospel to be a word of hope, and it is nonsense to imagine that Mark composed it as a last attack upon the disciples or as an advertisement of the failure of the women.[34]

It was customary for relatives to visit the grave of a loved one for three days after burial, since the soul was thought to hover near the tomb thinking it might return to the body, and mourning reached its height on the third day when death was judged irreversible.[35] And yet the motive Mark here assigns to the women regularly provokes doubts in the minds of commentators. In the climate of Judea how could friends or relatives possibly think of entering a tomb and laying hands on a body that had been lifeless for 36 hours?

However, Mark says very simply that the anointing of Jesus' corpse was the motive for the women's visit. Luke follows Mark in ascribing that same purpose to the women (even though both have recorded earlier anointings, Mark 14:3-9; Luke 7:36-50), while John has Joseph of Arimathea and Nicodemus as anointers immediately before burial, and Matthew, for reasons of his own, says only that the women went "to see the tomb."

However, the real point of Mark's description, whatever its difficulties, is that the women, for all their loyalty and courage, walked to the tomb without expecting Jesus' resurrection. They reckoned only with death and were fully convinced by what they had already witnessed that they were near the end of their relationship with Jesus. They went out only to pay their final respects and to offer the parting gesture of a ritual washing and anointing of his corpse.

16:2   Clearly Mark is talking about Sunday morning, and therefore what he will next report occurred "on the third day" according to Jewish as well as Roman reckoning. What is at first sight unclear is how "very early," the early part of the last watch of the night (3-6 A.M.), can be equated with "after the sun had risen." This is not the first time that Mark has offered in tandem two notes of time apparently conflicting. He has done it previously at 1:32, 35; 4:35; 13:24; 14:1-2, 12, 30; 15:42. In all these cases the second note seems to be intended as a more precise rendering of the first.[36]

But Mark has more in mind than the time of day. Tension exists not only between his notes of time, but more importantly between the dark mood of the women and the fact that Jesus had already risen. The present passage is connected with the notes of time in Chapter 15 and especially with the description of the awesome darkness that fell over the whole earth at Jesus' crucifixion (15:33). The risen sun is a signal that he has triumphed and lives.[37]

16:3-4   Between verses 3 and 4 one Old Latin manuscript offers a direct answer to the women's question about who would move the stone for them. It is a striking addition more in keeping with the tone and imagery of the apocryphal Gospel of Peter or the longer ending of Mark (16:9-20) than the sobriety and reserve of the authentic body of Mark:

> However, suddenly at the third hour of the day darkness came over all the earth. Angels descended from heaven, and then, rising up in the glory of the living God, they ascended with him (Jesus), and immediately it became light. Then the women approached the tomb.[38]

The addition is interesting but hardly original, and it tells far more of the religious imagination of the scribe than of the mind of Mark.

Mark pictures the large stone before the tomb as the one all-absorbing topic of their conversation on the way. They are not counting on any other reality than the obviously invincible power of death. Since Christian readers knew the outcome ahead of time, Mark's narrative would serve to provoke those readers to criticize the obtuseness of the women and so to distance themselves from the same or parallel moods or musings. Thus, for all the negative tone and content of the opening verses of the paragraph, they are effective both as preparation and foil for news to come and as a device geared to the strengthening of basic Christian posture and convictions.

Mark's remark about the great size of the stone (4b) comes late, but delayed explanations are not unusual in his gospel.[39] By severing the remark from its more natural place at the end of verse 3, Mark has thrust it into the foreground, so that the stone's removal, completely unexpected and outside the competence of the women, is understood to be a marvel, inexplicable on any ordinary grounds.[40]

Of the canonical evangelists, Matthew lavishes most attention on the stone and the power that rolled it aside. He insists that the tomb was opened not by any earthly agency, but by an angel of God (Matt. 28:2). The Western text (D) of Luke 23:53 describes the stone as so large that 20 men could scarcely roll it. According to the Gospel of Peter (37), the stone moved aside of its own power.

16:5 In Mark, Luke, and John the first visitors to the tomb on Easter went right in. In Matthew's narrative, with its focus on the power behind the rending of the tomb, the angel of the Lord sits upon the stone outside the tomb, and the women therefore converse with him in the open air.

According to Mark, the women upon entering the tomb saw "a young man"—an angel—dressed in a white garment.[41] The encounter between heavenly messenger and earthbound women brings the reader to the heart of the paragraph and the climactic statement of the entire book. From the beginning of the gospel the reader has been led to ask when and how the kingdom of God promised by Jesus (1:15) would invade the earthly sphere. The crucifixion appeared to be a total victory for all the tired old authorities of religion and state, and to brand trust in Jesus as vain and simpleminded. The presence of the angel in the final paragraph of the gospel means that God has the final word in the story of Jesus and in the history of his people.

Recognition of the centrality of the angelic word can help to sharpen the usual analysis of the form of the paragraph. It has become customary to say that, from the point of view of form, there are in the Gospels two kinds of resurrection narratives. The New Testament offers no narrative of the resurrection itself, no description of the moment of Jesus' awakening, the casting aside of the stone, or the triumphal emergence of Jesus. That kind of narrative can be found for the first time in the apocryphal Gospel of Peter from the middle of the second century. The New Testament is reserved and offers only 1) empty tomb narratives (Mark 16:1-8 and parallels) and 2) resurrection appearance narratives (Matt. 28:16-20; Luke 24:13-53; John 20:19-29; John 21).

However, Mark 16:1-8 is more than "an empty tomb narrative." That label focuses on the content more than on the form, and then even from the point of view of content the label is less than fully adequate.

The empty tomb, together with the women and their spices, belongs to the setting. The gem of incomparable worth in this paragraph is the angelic declaration. Formally speaking, the paragraph has much in common with pronouncement stories, trim narratives which serve as settings for a significant pronouncement or saying. The real center of this story is the message carried by the young man.

Only once previously in his gospel has Mark reported any angelic activity (1:13) and the expectations roused by the angel's presence here at the end are therefore all the greater.

That is, only one other angelic visitor or comment is recorded, unless the "young man" who fled away naked from Gethsemane (14:51-52) is also to be understood as an angel. He is the only other figure in Mark to be referred to by the word "young man." Furthermore, attention is drawn in both passages to the manner in which the young man is clothed and to his posture. Mark portrays them in parallel fashion and so invites comparison:

14:51-52	16:5-6
young man *(neaniskos)*	young man *(neaniskos)*
dressed *(peribeblēmenos)*	dressed *(peribeblēmenos)*
in a linen cloth	in a white robe
fled away naked	sitting on the right side
(complete silence)	(good news)

Mark encourages readers not simply to make a literary or stylistic comparison but to interpret the two passages together. In the earlier passage the young man left his sheet or garment (it is not clear whether it is the one or the other) behind and fled away naked, that is, in horror and dread, as Amos 2:16 said the strong man would flee on the terrible day of the Lord.[42] In the later passage the young man or angel is "sitting," the traditional posture of the teacher (Mark 4:1-2; 13:3; Matt. 5:1-2; Luke 4:20), and he is "on the right side," the side of favor or good fortune (cf. John 21:6) or of special dignity and success (Mark 10:37; 12:36; 14:62; Matt. 25:33-34). Thus his bearing already indicates that he has come to teach and his teaching is good news from God.

The two references to a young man are a pair of bookends bracketing the passion and resurrection of Jesus. A young man fled in hor-

ror and dismay when Jesus was arrested. Can he be an angelic interpreter or reflector of the terror shaking heaven and earth? ("No angel
can fully bear that sight.") But then, after Good Friday and after that
Sabbath, a young man sits calmly and fully clothed (cf. 5:15), ready to
proclaim good news.[43] Indeed, he bears the Easter kerygma, compressed into briefest compass, and that good word of the resurrection
of the crucified is the climax not only of the paragraph but of the entire gospel.

The women reacted to the appearance of the angel with
amazement, fear, and shock. Throughout his gospel Mark has depicted human reactions to encounters with the awesome power of Jesus in similar language. The language is designed not only to describe
Mark's understanding of the feelings human beings experienced in
contact with Jesus, but even much more to communicate Mark's evaluation of the encounters themselves—God really is breaking into human life and seizing power through the person and career of Jesus.

16:6 The young man's first word is a needed reassurance.
When the hard line dividing heaven and earth is erased and the holy
God confronts his erring creatures, then according to the ordinary
human calculus of right and wrong the result might well be
explosive—a confrontation fatal to the sinful and full of blessing only
for the righteous. Even though the women had ranged themselves
alongside Jesus, who ate and drank with tax collectors and sinners
(2:15-17) and criticized the righteousness of the religious authorities
(7:1-23), they approached his tomb with as much faith in Jesus as a
stone, mesmerized by the seeming invincibility of death and by the apparent triumph of the enemies of Jesus and of God. The women reacted as frail and errant humans always react to a theophany or angelophany in biblical narrative—with fear and trembling (Gen. 28:17;
Exod. 3:6; Judg. 22-23; Isa. 6:5; Ezek. 1:27); but the angel greeted them
with words preparing for joy.

Mark then offers a formulaic summary of the good news of
Easter, addressed even more to his readers than to the women. After
all, the women did not need to be told what they were looking for, but,
for the sake of proclaiming good news to the readers, Mark has the
young man open his announcement by rehearsing a highly compressed biography of Jesus.

The Easter kerygma proclaims God's resurrection of Jesus, and
Jesus is briefly described as "of Nazareth" and "who was crucified."
"Of Nazareth" may not be the best translation of the Greek adjective
"*Nazarenos*" (Mark 1:24; 10:47; 14:67; 16:6; cf. Luke 24:19). He is "the

Nazarene," and that word does more than locate Jesus geographically.[44]

To his Jerusalem opponents, "Nazarene" meant that Jesus was
untutored in the law and reckless of its demands, a self-taught, un-
authorized preacher hailing from the rural backwaters of Galilee up
north. In John's gospel Nathanael voiced the southerner's disdain,
"Can anything good come out of Nazareth?" (John 1:46) Nazareth was
an insignificant village of a few hundred peasants. But to his friends,
"the Nazarene" was a title full of the memories of Jesus' extraordinary
mission of teaching, healing, and exorcism in Galilee conducted with
the very highest authority.

Furthermore, the Nazarene was "the crucified" (cf. 1 Cor. 1:23;
2:2; Gal. 1:1). Opposition had run the full course. Roman and Jewish
officials had condemned and executed Jesus as one whose activities
and claims dangerously undermined the foundations of the basic religious and political institutions. He had been made to suffer a cruel
punishment of the most terrible humiliation and shame. Jews and
Christians knew that a person hanged on a tree was regarded by
Scripture as one cursed (Deut. 21:23; Gal. 3:13). Never in the ancient
world outside of Christianity is the cross ever a symbol of anything
good or positive. It is always disgusting, repulsive, obscene.[45]

Nevertheless, the divine messenger proclaimed that this one, this
crucified Nazarene, had been raised. By translating *egerthe* in the active voice, "Has risen," the RSV makes the resurrection sound like Jesus' own doing, but Mark accepts on the one side the total destruction
of Jesus at the hands of inimical powers, and on the other side the miracle of the intervention of the Father. That Jesus had been raised
means that God has in his own time and fashion heard the cry of Jesus
(14:32-43; 15:34). God did not let Jesus drop.

Mark's Roman readers, battered by persecution, needed to hear
that death too has a lord and is not so almighty as it appears. When
Jesus was crucified, it seemed that all the seed had been trampled
underfoot, eaten by birds, choked by weeds, and scorched by sun.
Death left no remainder, but only a dry and barren place. But God
raised him from the dead, and the dry ground began to fulfill the
promise of an abundant harvest.

Mark focuses in the case of Jesus and of his readers on suffering
unto death, but Mark has in view more than simple expiration, the cessation of biological functioning, the heart's final beating and then the
silence and the cold. Death is an enemy all right, but the story of Jesus
and the situation of Mark's readers defined other enemies, allies of

that death, that made death the more miserable and hateful. All through his gospel Mark has had in view such cohorts and consorts of death as the lust for power and privilege rather than a hunger and thirst for the kingship of God, the judgment that Jesus' way with sinners was dangerous, the charge of blasphemy, the malady of unseeing eyes and calloused hearts.

Death is an enemy, but death is not alone. The death of Jesus was the seal of all the works of all his opponents, both human and satanic, and it was the frustration of all the good performed and all the hopes engendered by Jesus in his ministering.

When God raised Jesus, he not only trumped the suffering and the death, but he also overturned all the verdicts, judged all the judges, confounded all the critics, and vindicated Jesus and his cause once and for all. Resurrection means eschatological action, a deed of God expected for the end of history. God has reached into the midst of ongoing history to raise up Jesus of Nazareth who was crucified and to render the ultimate verdict upon him; in him the time is fulfilled and the kingdom of God really has drawn near (1:15).

So resurrection means vindication and it means also exaltation. Jesus was not simply brought back to life. He was transformed so that people could not point to him and say, "Look, here is the Christ!" or "Look, there he is!"(Mark 13:21). The word he spoke to his judges has been fulfilled: he is enthroned at God's right hand (14:62); therefore, the angel said more than that the tomb is empty when he declared, "He has been raised; he is not here. Look! Here is the place where they laid him."[46]

"They," his enemies, killed him and brought him down to the grave, but God has raised him up. The sentence contrasts human and divine action. The empty tomb is silent witness to the utter futility of all human opposition to God and an eloquent sign of the eventual victory of filial trust and obedience.

16:7   Even vindication and exaltation together do not exhaust the angel's declaration. The resurrection means that the activity of Jesus continues. His ministry of teaching, healing, and calling to discipleship had been brought to a halt by his death. But the resurrection sets all that activity of the Nazarene into motion once again.

Call it rehabilitation. The angel has words of rehabilitation for Peter and the disciples. Far from expressing any vendetta against the disciples, the words recorded here are pure grace.[47] They are a lordly absolution pronounced upon "his disciples and especially Peter" or "his disciples and even Peter." In spite of having sworn undying devotion with an oath (14:31), they had all forsaken him and fled (14:50) like sheep scattered at the death of the shepherd (14:27). Nevertheless, the resurrected one did not write them off and summon others in their place, but began all over again with these failures. The one foundation of the church, the Markan community included, is divine mercy.

The phrase "going before you" has been read in two different ways. It has been taken temporally and interpreted to mean that Jesus is heading north to Galilee and will arrive there some days before the disciples. But with a direct object, the verb "go before" *(proago)* more naturally means to lead, to go at the head of, as a shepherd leads the sheep (14:28), as Jesus walked as leader at the head of the band of disciples and drew them along in his wake going up to Jerusalem (10:32), as the crowds "went before" *(proagontes)* and "followed after" Jesus when he entered Jerusalem (11:9).

The angel declared that Jesus, raised from the dead, was now gathering the scattered disciples, once again taking his place at the head of the flock, and calling his sheep to follow after him.

He was leading them "to Galilee." Galilee is for Mark (and Matthew) more than a geographical locale. Some interpreters are convinced that Galilee functioned for Mark as a land of salvation or of revelation, as a *terra sancta* or *terra christiana,* as the place of eschatological expectation, or as the locale of acceptance and belief.

Objections have been raised against all such nonliteral, nongeographical interpretations of "Galilee," but they must be taken seriously and be given greater precision, if possible. It is a fact that Galilee had a bad reputation among Judean Jews as a district inhabited by people who neither knew nor observed the law (cf. John 1:46). Not only did Jesus hail from Galilee, but he also chose to work in Galilee precisely among those ignorant and sinful masses despised by the more conservative southern brethren. Jerusalem was the place where the tradition located the eschatological fulfillment (Test. Zebulon 9:8), but after his resurrection Jesus called his disciples again to Galilee. That call may well entail a verdict on Jerusalem, but for Mark the accent lies on Galilee as a place and symbol of lowly service, of patient ministry, of passionate mission. As Jerusalem was for Mark the place of rejection and death, the city of opposition, so Galilee was the place of Jesus' ministry of teaching and healing, and it was the land where that mission was to be resumed.[48]

The disciples had been privileged failures the first time around. At the end the angel told them in effect, "The past is forgiven, and you are now receiving a second chance to be disciples." Furthermore, that ending takes the reader back to the first pages of the book, back to a fresh consideration of the entire way of Jesus. The reader is taken back to the beginning, back to Galilee where Jesus first announced the nearness of the kingdom and called people to repentance and faith (1:15), where Jesus gathered disciples and went before them (1:16-20), from which the report of Jesus' activity spread abroad to many people in other districts (3:7-8).

When Mark records the word that the resurrected Jesus leads disciples to Galilee, he means that "Jesus the Nazarene" was not laid forever to rest at the crucifixion but that now, in a new manner, he takes up his mission as leader of the disciples. Back to Galilee means back to the beginning, back to a ministry of proclaiming with authority the new teaching that the kingdom of God has drawn near. There in Galilee disciples participating faithfully in mission will "see" Jesus.

The traditional interpretation of the words "there you will see him" (16:7b) is that the angel promised resurrection appearances of Jesus like those recorded in Matthew 28, Luke 24, and John 20 and 21.

Noting that the form of the verb "you will see" *(opsesthe)* is exactly the same one which occurs in 14:62, where Jesus spoke to the high priest about the coming of the Son of Man with power, some interpreters have suggested that the angel is promising not resurrection appearances but the final advent of Jesus, the end of the age, and the judgment of the quick and the dead. They argue that a different form of the verb (namely *ophthe*, "he was seen" or "he appeared") is regularly used to indicate resurrection appearances (Luke 24:34; 1 Cor. 15:5, 6, 7, 8) and that "you will see" *(opsesthe)* is a fixed expression for the parousia (Mark 13:26 par.; John 16:16; 1 John 3:2; Rev. 1:7).[49]

Resurrection appearances or parousia? Focusing on the form of the verb "to see" *(horao)* is not enough. The verb is very common. It appears frequently and is used with a variety of meanings. It is simply not true that *ophthe* is a technical term for resurrection appearances, nor is it true that *opsesthe* is a technical term for the paraousia. These words and forms are used with other meanings, and those events are described with completely different words as well as with other forms of the verb "to see."

A third possibility looms beyond resurrection appearances or parousia. It is helpful to focus on the use of seeing in the structure of Mark's gospel. Mark makes a significant reference to seeing at the end of each of the three great sections of his work. The public ministry of Jesus among the throngs (Part One) closes with 8:22-26, the healing of a blind man. The central section of the gospel (8:27—10:52), in which Jesus teaches his disciples privately and attempts to unpack for them the mystery of his passion, also closes with the healing of a blind man in 10:46-52. Mark thereby signals to his readers that it takes a miracle to open eyes to see the truth in Jesus, and the truth is that the time is fulfilled and that God is bringing in his kingdom through the Nazarene, the crucified, that is, through one who served and suffered.[50]

At the end of the third great section of the gospel (11:1—16:8) the disciples, unseeing and offended up to that point in the narrative, are promised sight for their blind eyes. The expectation with which the gospel closes is that the disciples, as they receive the Easter message and follow Jesus in his renewed mission, will at long last really see.[51]

16:8   If Mark presented the angel's word as the Good News of the resurrection of Jesus, and if verse 7 points to the absolving, gathering, and enlightening of the disciples, what is the meaning or function of verse 8, in which the women appear on the face of it to disobey the messenger of God? Is there a contradiction between verses 7 and 8, as many interpreters declare? Were the women really disobedient to the heavenly vision?

The first part of verse 8 is no problem. Confronted by a heavenly visitor, the women react with that trembling which always overtakes sinful mortals faced with the holy and divine. "Trembling and astonishment" seized the women, just as people were amazed when Jesus cast out a demon (Mark 1:27), healed the paralytic and forgave his sins (2:12), raised Jairus' daughter from the dead (5:42), stilled the storm (4:41), walked on the water (6:49-51), or cured the deaf man with the impediment in his speech (7:37). In the central section of the gospel, where miracles nearly cease, his disciples are amazed at his words about suffering (9:32) and at his determination to go to Jerusalem (10:32). In the passion narrative Pilate marveled at Jesus' silence (15:5) and at his rapid death (15:44). But above all, from beginning to end, it is the word or teaching of Jesus which amazes his hearers (1:22; 6:2; 10:24, 26; 11:18; 12:17). Thus the first half of verse 8 declares that the women were awestruck in the presence of a fresh deed and word from God.

The second half of the verse is more difficult: "They said nothing to anyone, for they were afraid." Some scholars have attempted to demonstrate that 16:8a ("trembling and astonishment") refers to a positive, numinous awe, while the "afraid" of 16:8b *(ephobounto)* expresses a negative, cowardly fear, leading to a disobedient silence. But the "fear" (same word-stem as in 16:8b) in 4:41 and 9:5-6 refers to awe at the divine and has nothing to do with cowardice. And in all three of these cases the awe or shock is accompanied by a loss of words or momentary silence. Perhaps 11:18 is a case of a lack of sheer physical courage, but the one other occurrence of "fear" in Mark's gospel (10:32) is ambiguous and could mean either "afraid" or "awestruck."

Trembling, astonishment, and fear are frequent responses to divine revelation in Mark. In fact, Mark's vocabulary for describing human reactions to divine activity or teaching is richer than that of the other evangelists. Five of the 12 words (six different roots) which Mark uses in his gospel in order to describe human responses to divine intervention are not found in the other gospels at all.[52]

Mark's recording of reactions is a kind of editorial comment. By speaking of human awe, Mark signals his conviction that an event or announcement passes human inventing or human grasping. Terrible depths underlie it and an aura of mystery surrounds it. It is God's doing and it is marvelous.

But does it make sense to characterize the "fear" of the women at the end of verse 8 as numinous awe? And how does that relate to their silence?

Answers begin to emerge from a scrutiny of the structure. The two halves of verse 8 are parallel to one another:[53]

    A And they went out and fled from the tomb
    B for trembling and astonishment had come upon them
    A' And they said nothing to anyone
    B' for they were afraid.

Discovery of the parallelism leads to a twofold gain. In the first place, the reaction of B is parallel to that of B'. The fear of B' is not different in kind from the astonishment of B. This is no case of cowardice but one more example of awe in the face of a divine intervention in human response to moments of revelation (Exod. 15:16; 1 Cor. 2:3; 2 Cor. 7:15; Eph. 6:5; Phil. 2:12; cf. Heb. 12:21). In verse 8 "trembling" in B is paralleled by "fear" in B', and the two belong indissolubly together as elements in a single response.

Furthermore, doubling is a Markan habit, and it reaches a crescendo in the closing paragraph of the gospel. Among other repetitions or doublings, the paragraph includes a double note of time (very early, after sunrise, 16:2), two references to the removal of the stone (16:3, 4), a pair of participles (seated and dressed, 16:5), repetition of the same verb in narrative and direct discourse (they were afraid, be not afraid, 16:5-6), a twofold description of Jesus (the Nazarene, the crucified, 16:6), double imperatives (go and say, 16:7), doubling of response (trembling and astonishment, 16:8), repetition of a conjunction ("for" is used twice in 16:8), and a double negative (in Greek: "nothing to no one," 16:8; cf. 1:44; 5:3). The impression that 16:8b is a repetition of 16:8a or a doubling is strengthened by the observation that doubling is part of Mark's style.[54]

Just as the responses in verse 16 (B and B') are parallel to one another, so also the events of A and A' are parallel. Both A and A' describe the behavior of the women during the same limited, circumscribed period of time. For a short time they can be said to have run from the tomb. For the same brief period of time, while they ran from the tomb, they said nothing to anyone.

The difficult passage (v.8) might almost be paraphrased with the words: "Awestruck and dumbfounded, they ran straight from the tomb to the disciples, without stopping to greet anyone on the way."

Corroboration for the interpretation that the silence of the women was confined to the limited time of the flight is to be found in the clause, "They said nothing to anyone" (16:8b). A similar statement occurs in 1:44 where Jesus directed the man he had cleansed of leprosy, "See that you say nothing to anyone; but go, show yourself to the priest, and offer for your cleansing what Moses commanded" (1:44). The command to silence in that incident was in effect for a limited duration, namely, until the former leper got to the priest. Then he was to indicate that he had been cleansed. Could he do that without speaking and identifying himself and declaring why he had come? Obviously not.

The language of the command to the leper is readily explainable. Jesus was commissioning the man to perform a task which took precedence over the natural impulse to shout aloud his good news to all and sundry whom he might chance to meet along the way. There is a similar injunction to silence in the Old Testament. Elisha once sent his servant Gehazi on an urgent errand to the house of the Shunammite woman, whose son had fallen ill. Elisha directed Gehazi as follows: "Gird up your loins, and take my staff in your hand and go. If you meet any one, do not salute him; and if any one salutes you, do not reply; and lay my staff upon the face of the child" (2 Kings 4:29). Furthermore, when Jesus sent out the 70 two by two, he gave those bearers of the word strange instructions: "Salute no one on the road.

Whatever house you enter, first say, 'Peace be to this house' " (Luke 10:45).

Thus the silence of the women, closely combined as it is with a command to deliver a message and with their rushing from the one who had given the commission, has a special and peculiar meaning. In the total context of Mark 16:1-8 "saying nothing to any one" is an idiomatic expression for singleminded devotion to a duty which overrode all other obligations, including the sacred obligation to greet people they might have met along the way. The women were not diverted from their duty by the knots of women gathered at the wells of the city or bustling with jars through the streets. They hurried directly to the disciples to deliver the news to them first of all.[55]

The pericope opens on a dark and negative note. The women moved slowly toward the cemetery to perform their sad duty of completing the last rites for their erstwhile Master. Their lives had arrived at a dead end, and it was impossible for them even to move aside the great stone, let alone remove the barrier of death that stood between them and Jesus. But at the end of the pericope they ran quickly from the tomb back to the disciples, astonished by the miracle and grace of the resurrection of Jesus. The wonder of the resurrection is mirrored in the movement of the women. Their initial realistic facing up to the impressive power of death is in sharpest contrast to their final awe at the good news God's messenger had conveyed to them. Their speech and demeanor in the first half of the paragraph are a sombre contrast to the energy they display at the end.

Additional Note: Silence and the Women

Julius Wellhausen is apparently the first in a long line of modern commentators to speak of a contradiction between verses 7 and 8, between the angel's command to take a message (v. 7) and the women's silence (v. 8). Wellhausen further noted that Paul, writing in 1 Cor. 15:3-8, knew nothing of the women's experience and report. Wellhausen's remarks are exceedingly brief, but the idea of a contradiction between the last two verses of Mark is found in developed form in Wilhelm Bousset, on whose work Rudolf Bultmann built his own exegesis of the passage. According to these interpreters, the reference to fear and silence in verse 8 answered the question why the story of the empty tomb had remained unknown in the Christian community for so long. The church is supposed to have spoken at first only of visions or appearances of the spiritual, resurrected Christ (1 Cor. 15:3-8). Originally, according to this theory, it had no empty tomb story. Mark is supposed to have provided verse 8 as a cover story to aid in introducing the relatively late account of the empty tomb.[56]

Julius Schniewind, Ulrich Wilckens, and Albert Descamp are among many who see some kind of connection between the silence of the women and the theme of the messianic secret in Mark.[57] Silence and secrecy, according to this view, are preoccupations of the author who does not believe that the truth of God is easily, publicly, or directly observable like some piece of natural data. Revelation is always indirect and the epiphany is hidden behind a veil, capable of being discerned only by the eye of faith.

Beginning with the observation that women were not eligible to bear witness in the courts of ancient Israel, many have asserted that the silence of the women and their lack of relationship with the apostle constitute a form of apology. Von Campenhausen suggested that Mark's ending was designed as an argument against people who were saying that the disciples had tampered with the grave and had stolen the body of Jesus.[58]

To that charge the passage is thought to respond that the disciples, far from having staged the empty tomb in deceit, did not even know anything about the empty tomb until later. There was no link between the disciples and the empty tomb, because there was none between the disciples and the women, thanks to the fear and silence of the latter. On the other hand, Grass thinks that people may have been calling the disciples secondhand witnesses, dependent on the testimony of women, and declaring that their Easter testimony was therefore unreliable. Read in that light, the passage defends the primacy and originality of the disciples' testimony. It rests not on the word of the women (cf. Luke 24:11) but is grounded instead on other events and experiences of those first Easter days, especially on the appearances of Jesus to them, alluded to in Mark 16:7.[59]

Martin Hengel denies any apologetic element in Mark's story. Rather he thinks Mark relates how the women were scandalized even as the men had been earlier in Gethsemane. The flight *(ephygon)* of 16:8 corresponds to that of 14:50, and both mean the collapse of faith. For these women the empty tomb was the sign, not of victory, but of defeat—now the corpse of the Lord had been robbed and his tomb desecrated. They were witnesses of the resurrection without knowing it. The later evangelists found Mark's picture unbearably bleak and attempted to connect the empty tomb with the later appearance, but Hengel thinks the appearances were originally independent.[60]

Still others have proposed the theory that Mark 16:1-8 is not an apology for the Twelve but a polemic against them. Only the women and not the male disciples were witnesses of the death, burial, and resurrection of Jesus. According to this line of thought, the passage originally exhibited a contrast between privileged, faithful women and frightened, disloyal men. 16:8b was added in order to explain that the women, hitherto portrayed positively, were incapacitated by fear and therefore never delivered the angel's message, with the result that the disciples never met the resurrected Jesus, never were commissioned as apostles, and never were forgiven their apostasy. Representative of a form of this interpretation, Theodore Weeden thinks Mark was involved in a vendetta against the disciples. Following Weeden, John Crossan says that verses 6 and 7 express Mark's faith and that of his Galilean community, while verse 8 declares Jerusalem's failure.[62]

The silence of the women is difficult. The passage is by no means crystal clear. It has been argued in the commentary preceding this note that the women's fear is numinous awe and that their silence is a sign of the closemouthed commitment of messengers to a sacred task. If that is correct, then the various interpretations summarized in the preceding half dozen paragraphs are not only wrong, but unnecessary.

Summary: Vindicated Leader of Disciples

Mark proclaims the resurrection of Jesus as good news for Christians perplexed and chafing under the rough hand of persecution and suffering. He uses the traditions of Easter to stiffen their resistance, to sustain their faith, and to direct their energies to ministry.

The tragedy of the death of Jesus was not simply that a man's heart stopped beating, but that Jesus' ministry had been stopped, and that the deed had been perpetrated by a coalition of relatively good people, dedicated to holiness and serious about their religious traditions, renowned for their justice and proud of their laws. The combined opposition of respected religious and legal institutions was dismaying, and resisting such forces and contradicting them seemed unreasonable and even hateful. The danger was that the Christians of Mark's community, under the pressure of persecution, would duplicate in their own lives in the late 60s or early 70s the capitulation of the first disciples a generation earlier, that they would abandon discipleship and ministry for the sake of their lives and sanity.

To his contemporaries Mark proclaimed that the itinerary of Jesus' ministry, including collision with the great social, religious and

political powers and resulting in rejection and death, was the path
mysteriously ordained not only for Jesus but for all the children of
God. The resurrection of Jesus was the ultimate end of that way of
service. Indeed the resurrection was God's majestic yes to the lowly
way of Jesus.

Mark's account of the first Easter is passing brief and his testimony to the resurrection is reserved. Mark offers no description of
Jesus' body and no great final words of the resurrected one.
Nevertheless, his account of the transfiguration (9:2-8) shows how
Mark would have portrayed the resurrected Jesus if he had wanted to:
his whole appearance underwent a glorious metamorphosis, as his
body glowed with divine light and his clothing shone with unearthly
brilliance (cf. 1 Cor. 15:51; 2 Cor. 3:18; Phil. 3:21; Rev. 1:13-15), while
the cloud of God's presence enveloped him (Exod. 16:10; Num. 14:10;
Ezek. 1:4; 2 Macc. 2:18; Mark 13:26; 14:62) and the voice of God confirmed his status.[63]

Mark preferred a more reserved conclusion, and for its part the
transfiguration has a more important function than to show how
Mark might have pictured the resurrected Jesus. At the moment when
the death of Jesus and the martyrdom of his disciples first came into
clear view (8:31-37), Mark signalled by means of the transfiguration
narrative that the way they travel is the way of life and light rather
than darkness and death. The transfiguration is a proleptic vision of
future glory given ahead of time as encouragement to disciples dis-
mayed by the prospect of the cross and therefore reluctant to be in
discipleship.

Furthermore, Mark's Jesus had spoken earlier in the gospel about
his resurrection quite openly and explicitly in the passion predictions
(8:31; 9:31; 10:33-34) and rather indirectly elsewhere. For example, in
the parable of the sower (4:1-9) and in the parable or allegory of the
tenant farmers (12:1-12) Jesus proclaimed his future triumph and the
victory of the kingdom.

These two parables belong together and complement one another.
One is Jesus' initial teaching in parables, and the other is his last (4:2;
12:1), so they bracket most of Jesus' public proclamation.

These parables clearly resemble one another in choice of imagery
and in inner dynamics. Both feature the cultivation of the land, a field
of grain in the one case and a vineyard in the other, and in both instances the desired goal is the yield of fruit or a harvest. Again in both
parables antagonistic powers work actively to frustrate the fulfillment of the expectation of a yield.

In the first parable natural forces (birds, sun, and thorns) threaten the crop, and in the second human adversaries conspire together. In that second parable the drama seems heightened as the tenant farmers first beat and kill the owner's servants and then finally kill the owner's son as they plot to seize the vineyard as their own and wrest it from the owner and the rightful heir.

Both parables are embedded in literary contexts heavy with opposition to Jesus, and these parables interpret those contexts and that opposition. In spite of all resistance and rejection, Jesus foresaw the ultimate triumph and victory of the kingdom, as clearly as a farmer forsees a harvest beyond every hostile force (Chap. 4). In the later parable Jesus described the opposition of the tenants as arising out of deep rebellion against the owner and a dark design to seize the inheritance. Then Mark pictures Jesus as asking his audience what the outcome of that rebellion will be (12:9), linking the parable to the context. The question is answered by the sudden introduction of Psalm 118: "The stone which the builders rejected has become the head of the corner" (12:10). The new imagery of construction and building blocks seems awkward, since the fundamental images of the parables are agricultural. Nevertheless, the link with the wider story of Jesus is secured. It is clear that the parables proclaim the eventual exaltation of Jesus and frustration of his opponents.

Furthermore, the parables speak not only of Jesus, but also of the fortunes of the church. It has often been observed that "the word" in the interpretation of the parable of the sower (4:14-20) is not only Jesus' word or Jesus' ministry of proclamation, but also, at another level, it is the church's word or the church's ministry of testimony, something extremely important to Mark (13:10; 14:9).

The central role played by the word in the first parable is paralleled by the role of the son in the second. The fortunes of the word and of the son run parallel to one another. Mark sees the church in its ministry of the word as continuing the work of Jesus and as paralleling Jesus in mission, in suffering opposition, and in divine vindication.[64]

Unexpected triumph is the subject of the small seed that produces the great shrub (4:30-32). And in his last days in Jerusalem Jesus declared that the Sadducees, by denying the resurrection of the dead, betrayed their ignorance of the essence of Scripture and their failure to reckon on the power of God (12:18-27). Later, at the Last Supper, he vowed to drink no wine until he might drink it new in the kingdom of God (14:25); afterwards he promised that he would gather the scattered sheep and go before his disciples again (14:28; cf. 16:7), and he proclaimed his coming glory (14:62).

So, for all his reserve and brevity, Mark does prepare for the account of the resurrection. Furthermore, because it is the climax of the way of Jesus and the fulfillment of his words, the resurrection undergrids the reliability and trustworthiness of all the promises recorded in the gospel: the promise of the imminent arrival of God's own reign (1:14-15; 4:22-23), the promise of Satan's final overthrow inherent in the temptation narrative and in the exorcisms (1:13, 23-27; 3:22-27; 5:1-20), the promise of the ultimate outpouring of the Holy Spirit, the great counterforce to all the unholy spirits (1:8; 13:11), the promise of wholeness and salvation given with the healings and raisings from the dead and declarations of forgiveness (e.g. 2:1-12), the promise of fellowship with God bound up with all the meals and especially Jesus' last meal (2:15-17; 6:32-44; 14:22-25), the promise of entrance through the narrow gate into life and the kingdom (10:23-27), and the promise of eternal life beyond all separation, loss, and persecution (10:29-30).

The resurrection is thus the climax of the life of Jesus and the crowning element in a literary pattern of promise and fulfillment woven into the fabric of Mark's narrative.[65] That pattern promotes a sense, not of optimism to be sure—Mark is starkly realistic about earthly and cosmic powers of opposition—but of expectation and of hope.[66] Clinging to faith and hope in face of persecution is vindicated by his resurrection as something greater and finer than naivete, stubbornness, or madness. The resurrection confirms the truth of Jesus' assertion, given in the context of dispute with the Sadducees, that all people, disciples or not, always have to do with the living God (12:24-27).

Especially at the end of the gospel, when Jesus appears totally friendless and powerless, Mark narrates a number of fulfilled predictions: Jesus told his disciples that they would mysteriously find a colt ready (11:2-6) and a room prepared (14:12-16), and ahead of time he correctly declared that one would betray him (14:18-21, 43-45), another would deny him (14:30, 66-72), and that all would forsake him (14:27, 50). The fulfillment of those smaller predictions prepares the reader for the fullfillment of the larger promise of the resurrection.

Even if there had been no preparation previously in the narrative, the announcement of the resurrection of Jesus by the angel in Chapter 16 would be climactic. Resurrection is by definition not just another miracle along the way, but is an eschatological event.[67] It is the beginning of the end of the world, and it cannot be separated from the last judgment, the dissolution of the present world order, and the dawning of the new world of God. Mark's composition compels readers to move through the little Apocalypse (Chap. 13) as a kind of preface to the narrative of Jesus' passion and resurrection (Chap. 14–16). Mark thereby indicates that Jesus' suffering and vindication are not merely personal events in Jesus' biography but are cosmic and eschatological events, signaling the end of the old age and the beginning of the new.

At the beginning of the gospel, the temptation report hints broadly that Jesus is inaugurating the new world in which God's power triumphs over all his enemies, wild beasts are pacified, and angels minister to God's people (1:12-13; Isa. 11:6-9; Ps. 91:11-13; Test. Naphtali 8:4).

Jesus' own first words in the gospel are a declaration that history is rushing to its appointed glorious climax (1:14-15), and the clear implication is that that climax is bound up with his appearance. Nevertheless, he was from start to finish opposed, misunderstood, and rejected; even if initially he seemed successful, Mark's gospel portrays him on one level as progressively forsaken until the awful cry of dereliction was uttered on the cross (15:34).

But all the struggles and the cross itself were followed by the resurrection, and, what is more, they were cast in a new light by the resurrection. Easter spells out God's own verdict on Jesus and his way. That Jesus has been resurrected signals that he really is the stronger one (1:7; 3:27) and the kingdom of God (1:15; 11:10) and God's whole new world (2:19-22) is indeed drawing near in him.

Jesus is revealed by the resurrection as having acted, not by the power of Satan (3:22), but by the authority of the heavenly Father. He is not a destroyer, but a builder of a new temple and new community (14:58, 62). He is not ineffectual and despised in the eyes of God, but the triumphant Son of the Father (9:7; 15:34-39). He is not a blasphemer (2:7; 3:22, 28; 14:64), but is rather God's agent and Messiah upon the earth (14:62). The resurrection is God's judgment against all the false judgments passed upon Jesus and it is God's judgment in favor of Jesus.

Vindication of Jesus' Way

But Mark's account of the resurrection and his gospel as a whole is more than a defense of Jesus' person, more than a vindication of his unique sonship, something other and more than an essay on his divinity. Mark has composed a vindication of Jesus' way and a defense of

Jesus' call to discipleship. His gospel is an apology for steadfastness and filial trust in the hardest of times.

On the way between baptism and crucifixion Jesus silenced easy confession and sought faith. Faith is not mere mental perception or recognition of his person and status, not a matter of adding together miscellaneous clues and arriving at the correct sum, not agile penetration of the tantalizing veil nor even sudden intuition of the truth behind the incognito.

The truth about Jesus is hidden, concealed, paradoxical. His claims are neither blatant nor easy of apprehension. The hearers cannot gain control of the revelation. Rather it is in control, lively, challenging, urgent, running across the grain of ordinary human expectation and desiring. Jesus, with his ministry and his cross, is the action of the Father calling to faith, to risk, to venture, to service, to the joy of discipleship in spite of the cost.

Mark moves through discussion, disputation and debate, through admiration, argument and contemplation, through them and not merely around them, and beyond them to the call to discipleship. Jesus is a wise teacher, but more. Jesus is a compassionate healer, but more. He is a powerful exorcist, but more. And faith is more than knowledge of his history and more than admiration for his wisdom, compassion or power. Faith and discipleship are indissolubly joined, and discipleship means traveling the way of the cross behind Jesus. There is neither faith, nor discipleship, nor even any real Jesus without the cross.

Mark continually focuses on the relationship between Jesus and the Twelve. That relationship is the stuff of which his gospel is made, to a far greater extent than is true of the other three gospels. Mark's gospel is the story of Jesus' quest for disciples; and as the story of Jesus and his first disciples, it is simultaneously the story of the faith and discipleship of Mark's readers.

In composing his gospel, Mark counted on his readers to identify with the disciples. It is natural for Christian readers of the gospel in the 60s or 70s of the first century to see themselves in those very earliest Christian disciples.

Jesus' opening call to the disciples to follow him (1:16-20) is full of the grace extended likewise to the readers, and that call to follow him on his way also expresses a norm for judging the subsequent behavior of the disciples. Faithful following in discipleship is the standard.

At first the disciples are portrayed sympathetically and positively, and Mark's readers are encouraged in their tendency to identify with them, but then, gradually and steadily, Mark exposes the flaws and inadequacies of the Twelve.

In Part One (1:1—8:26) they are closer to Jesus than the crowds as they accompany Jesus through villages and towns and enjoy private explanations. In spite of everything, the reader has high hopes for them. But in Part Two (8:27—10:52) those hopes are dashed. Peter thinks that he has penetrated Jesus' secret, and he confesses him in ways that the crowds fail to do, but in so doing he exposes his false understanding and opens himself to sharp criticism from Jesus (8:27-33). The nine out of the 12 disciples who were not on the mount of transfiguration with Jesus are unable to cure the deaf and dumb boy, brought by his father in hopes of healing. Jesus does heal the lad and implies that the nine were incapable of the act because of a deficiency (9:29). James and John want to share the glory of Jesus' rule, sitting on his right and on his left (10:37). Mark's record of their request is full of irony: they obviously do not know what they are asking; two men will indeed be at Jesus' right and left as he is proclaimed King (15:27), but James and John do not want the cross.

In Part Three (11:1—16:8) one disciple betrays, another denies, and all of them forsake Jesus (14:50). By fleeing, they express their utter failure in relation to his call to believe the gospel (1:15), to follow him (1:16-20; 2:14), to remain with him (3:14), and to listen to him (4:3, 9, 20). Their discipleship simply dissolves.

The reason for their collapse is described in various ways. They are full of fear and anxiety about themselves and lack trust toward God (4:38-40; 6:49-50; 9:28-29). They cling to their lives and fear losing them (8:34-38). They desire honor and power (10:37), or at least some crumbs of reward for their sacrifices (10:28).

Jesus says that their minds are intent not on the things of God but on the things of humans, even of Satan (8:33), and their thoughts are worthy of pagan or Gentile unbelievers (10:42). But especially prominent is the language of sight and blindness.

The truth about the crowds and about the disciples, demonstrated repeatedly, is that they have eyes that see not and ears that hear not (4:11-12; Isa. 6:9-10). That is an old biblical way of describing spiritual obtuseness and unbelief.

The disciples have been given the secret of the kingdom and should have been able to see and hear (4:11), but Part One comes to a close, and Jesus raises questions about the hardness of their hearts, the sight of their eyes, and the hearing of their ears (8:14-21). Part One

then concludes with the story of the healing of the blind man of
Bethsaida (8:22-26).

The healing of the blind man occurred gradually or in stages.
That may be meant to indicate the difficult and nearly intractable nature of the illness and so be designed to magnify Jesus' final overcom-
ing of the malady. More probably, it signifies that people, in the first
place the 12 disciples, come to faith in Jesus not easily or quickly, and
not necessarily once and for all in the twinkling of an eye, but by
grades through repeated and perhaps painful encounters with the divine Word.

In fact, the healing immediately precedes the pericope in which
Peter offers a confession that is only half correct: "You are the
Christ." It is also half wrong and Peter requires more enlightening,
since at this stage he rejects the association of suffering with messiahship and therefore also with discipleship.

Once again, as at the end of Part One so also at the close of Part
Two, Mark narrates the healing of another blind man, a beggar named
Bartimaeus (10:46-52). The account of his cure is full of symbols of
faith and discipleship. In spite of his blindness and the scolding of the
crowd, Bartimaeus persisted in confessing Jesus as "Son of David"
and calling on him for mercy. When he was told that Jesus had summoned him, he immediately threw aside his beggar's mantle, knowing
he would need it no longer, and springing up he approached Jesus and
made his request for healing. Once he was well, he began as model disciple to follow Jesus on his way from Jericho up to Jerusalem and the
cross.[68]

The two healings, rounding off Parts One and Two of the gospel,
indicate that it will take nothing less than a miracle of divine intervention to heal the blindness of crowds and disciples, enlightening
them with regard to Jesus and the cross. Discipleship, taking up the
cross, entering the kingdom of God, and salvation are not within human possibilities. They are given by God, with whom all things are
possible (10:27).

The call to faith and discipleship, echoing and resounding
through the entire gospel, is met time and again with misunderstanding, inadequate confession, and dismal rejection, with the result that
Jesus in his passion is totally alone, forsaken, without disciples, without any human possibilities.

And yet, God still gave him disciples and confessors and possibilities even at the end. Bartimaeus followed him, an anonymous woman
anointed him ahead of time for burial (14:3-9), an unnamed landlord

made provision for the last supper (14:12-17), a pagan centurion confessed him (15:39), a member of the Jewish council buried him (15:42-46), and several women paid their respects to the corpse (15:40-41, 47; 16:1). The darkness of the end was penetrated repeatedly by shafts of light.

Mark offers a portrait of the Twelve that is far from flattering, but the disciples do serve very well as examples for a community which had undergone the trial and testing of persecution. Mark recalls their failures in order to remind his own community what kind of people they themselves do not really want to be or even need to be.

There are redeeming features, if not in the disciples, then in the Jesus whose call to them was not stilled even by death. Jesus predicted his own postcrucifixion return to leadership (14:27-29), and the "young man" at the tomb echoes Jesus' words, full of hope for all failures and traitors, promising a new beginning (16:7).

The final paragraph of the gospel is not a third account of curing blindness (in addition to 8:22-26 and 10:46-52), but it does contain, as one of its most puzzling elements, the promise that the disciples will "see" Jesus in Galilee. Commentators generally perceive two possibilities only: either Mark is referring to the parousia (the final coming of Jesus) or he has in mind appearances of the resurrected Jesus like those narrated in Matthew 28:16-20, Luke 24:13-52 and John 20:19-29. But in continuity with the healings recited at the end of Parts One and Two, Mark actually has in view the miraculous gift of spiritual sight. In spite of everything, the disciples were not repudiated. Jesus' own family is not rejected. The story is open ended,[69] and as the call to discipleship sounds forth, as the resurrected Jesus begins his work afresh and issues his proclamation (1:14-15) again and again, the stronger one is at work, his family comes into being (3:31-35; 10:28-31), and he himself begins to build the new temple not made with hands.

16:8

Mark has few direct comments on the time of the church after the resurrection. But scraps of evidence indicate that Mark knew that the angel's message was heeded so that some members of the Christian community were fishers of men (1:16-17), preached with authority (3:14-15; 6:7-13), confessed his name and gospel to Jews and Gentiles in all nations (9:9-10; 13:9-13; 14:9), and renounced the security of family and wealth (10:28-30). Some faltered under pressure and were ashamed of Jesus and his words (8:38), but others remained steady even to the point of martyrdom (8:27-33; 13:11), convinced that heaven and earth can pass away sooner than his word and promise (13:31).

To a community shaken by persecution, Mark wrote of the victorious crucified one. He shared his confidence that innocent suffering, in the case of Jesus and in their own cases, is not evidence of God's disfavor, absence, or impotence. The cross, terrible as it certainly is, speaks the truth about the blindness of the best of institutions and people and about the intrigues and plots hatched in ambitious hearts. It is eloquent also of obedience, trust in the mysterious will of the Father (8:31; 9:31; 10:33-34; 14:32-42), and the redemptive power of innocent suffering borne in love (10:45; 14:22-25). God, by the resurrection, does more than reverse the terror. He affirms the sufferers together with their service and their steadfastness. The resurrection in Mark is vindication of the way of Jesus and of his call to discipleship.

matthew

The Setting: Struggle for the Higher Righteousness

Matthew was involved in a struggle over the right understanding of the Scriptures (Torah), Jesus, and the Spirit. On the one hand, he was deeply disturbed by a permissive or antinomian trend apparent among some charismatics who regarded certain dramatic spiritual endowments as the essential marks of membership among God's people. On the other hand, he recognized the danger of a legalistic insistence upon the rigorous observance of the letter of the Torah, whether the written law of Moses or the orally transmitted legal tradition of the elders, as prerequisite for membership in the people of God. As he attempted to deal with the challenge of the charismatics or enthusiasts parading under the banner of freedom and the spirit without falling into the trap of legalism, he focused on Jesus as the teacher of the church and on the higher righteousness taught by Jesus.

Not a Jewish-Christian Gospel

Studies of Matthew and his background or community have traditionally stressed the evangelist's concern for the correct interpretation of the Torah, the rabbinic character of his argumentation, his insistence on the literal fulfillment of Old Testament prophecy in Jesus, and the fiery confrontations between Jesus and Jewish authorities. Notorious are the extremely harsh remarks Matthew reports

55

concerning scribes and Pharisees, the scriptural scholars and the lay people devoted to the keeping of the whole law. Not to merely anonymous "crowds" (Luke 3:7), but to "scribes and Pharisees" John the Baptist thundered, "God can from these stones raise up children to Abraham" (Matt. 3:7). In Matthew's gospel that word of the Baptist serves as a prophecy illuminating the way tax collectors, harlots—and Gentiles—enter the kingdom before the leading representatives of Judaism (21:31-32).

Matthew castigates scribes and Pharisees as hypocrites practicing ostentatious alms, prayer, and fasting because they are in love with human praise (6:2, 5, 16; 23:5-6). They are deaf to the prophets (3:7; 12:24), desire a sign (12:28), and try to entrap Jesus (22:34). The Pharisees are blind guides (15:14; 23:17, 19), preaching Moses but not practicing him (23:3), binding burdens on people without aiding them (23:4), converting people not into children of God (5:9) but into children of hell (23:15), tithing over and above the literal demand of the law but neglecting justice, mercy and faith (23:23), straining out gnats and swallowing camels (23:24), cleansing the outside and keeping up appearances but remaining inwardly as dirty and unclean as a tomb full of bones (23:25-28), praising the prophets but acting like their murderers (23:29-34). The seven woes on the Pharisees in Chapter 23 darkly mirror the Beatitudes of Chapter 5.[1]

Matthew's gospel alone records the strange word of Jesus about accepting the authority of the rabbis at least in principle (23:2-3), and worries about people having to flee from the final catastrophe not only in winter but on the Sabbath (24:20; cf. Mark 13:19). The latter is often taken as a sure sign that the gospel arose in a Christian community so closely bound to its synagogue origins that it was still observing the letter of the Torah.

Working with these bits and pieces of data like a detective with his clues, scholars have for a long time concluded that the arguments and claims of Matthew's gospel can best be understood in the light of deteriorating relations between Christian church and Jewish synagogue in the last few decades of the first century. In the next few pages that conclusion is examined and finally rejected.

In A.D. 70 the rebellion of the Jews in their Palestinian homeland against the vastly superior power of Rome had ended disastrously. Judaism was shaken to its foundations. Institutions basic to the life of the people were ripped apart and destroyed.

The triumph celebrated jointly by Vespasian and his son Titus in Rome in A.D. 71 displayed, among other spoils of victory, items of plunder from Jerusalem's temple: the seven branched candelabrum, the table of shewbread, the trumpets, and a copy of the law.

The holy city and holy temple of the Jews were reduced to rubble (compare Matt. 22:7 with Luke 14:16-24; cf. 21:43). Judaism itself nearly expired.

Before the war Judaism in Palestine had been polyglot and pluralistic. Various factions and accounts had lived side by side, jostling one another, sometimes acting in concert and frequently attacking one another's positions, competing for influence among the wider populace. Judaism was anything but monolithic or monochrome, simple or homogeneous. Sadducees and Pharisees, Essenes and Zealots, priests and lay people, pacifists and revolutionaries, observers and nonobservers filled the land.

Everything was different in the aftermath of the fighting. The war destroyed the Essene communities like that of Qumran, scattered the members of that ascetic fraternity, and dashed their apocalyptic hopes. Defeat discredited the Zealots and other advocates of a holy war of revolution against Rome. The aristocratic Sadducees and high priestly families had previously exercised an influence out of all proportion to their numbers because of the signal importance of Jerusalem and the temple, but after the war survivors had no real power. Their denial of the resurrection as a modernist doctrine found only in more recent Jewish writings (cf. Matt. 22:23-33) was anathematized by the ascendant Pharisees.[2] With the destruction of the temple, the priests very nearly lost their reason for being, although the notion of rebuilding the temple kept alive hope for their own further personal service.

The future of Judaism rested with the Pharisees. Already before the war they were identified with institutions (synagogue and school) which could and did survive the disaster of 70, and which could serve as a basis for the renaissance of a severely threatened Judaism.

Under a Pharisaic sage named Johanan ben Zakkai and the council he gathered around himself at the town of Jamnia, the synagogue assumed new and greater importance. Practices which had formerly been the exclusive prerogative of the temple and the priests were shifted to the synagogue. Authority formerly reserved for the Sanhedrin in Jerusalem began to be exercised by the Bet Din, the high court or council of rabbis at Jamnia. The president (Nasi = prince or patri-

arch) of the council located at Jamnia (and at succeeding sites) re-
placed the Jerusalem High Priest as spokesman for all Jews.

It was ruled legitimate to blow the ram's horn or shofar in the
synagogue to announce the onset of the Sabbath and other feasts.
Prayer was interpreted as the equivalent of sacrifice, and the doing of
deeds of piety took the place of the performance of ancient ritual. The
council assumed liturgical authority, determining the religious calen-
dar of feasts and fasts, and people looked to it also for ethical and legal
decisions.

Judaism did not die in the fires that consumed Jerusalem and
temple, but was reborn and reformed around the Pharisaic program
and the sages centered at Jamnia.

So it was that, with the virtual disappearance of Sadducees,
priests, Zealots, and Essenes, the Pharisaic synagogue and the Christian church were the two Jewish religious communities (mixed with
Gentiles on the Christian side) to survive the war with vitality and
with programs for the hard tasks at hand, with comprehensive interpretations of Scripture and history, with deep convictions regarding
the doing of the will of God and the identity of the people of God, and
with vigorous and gifted teachers and leaders.

Christians emphasized reading the Bible, or Old Testament, as
story and promise in such a way that Jesus was interpreted as an act
of God like the deeds of God in creation, exodus, and return from exile,
except that Jesus was the full and stunning climax of all those previous deeds. The Jews still held that Torah was both law and lore, both
command and story, but more and more emphasized its legal character in opposition to the Christian reading. Jesus as Christ and Son of
God was the rallying cry of the daughter community, while torah as
law became fundamental for the other.

Gamaliel II, grandson of the Gamaliel of Acts 5, succeeded
Johanan ben Zakkai as president of the council at Jamnia and
assumed, as one of his most urgent duties, the task of defining Judaism over against heretical elements, including Christians. Decisions
were reached about which books were holy and utterly authoritative
and which, though useful, were to be relegated to a lesser niche or removed from the community altogether. He called for a revision of the
synagogue prayer, now known as the Eighteen Benedictions, which
would serve to stiffen the backbone of orthodoxy and both anathema-
tize and effectively expel heretics. The twelfth benediction was composed or revised to include the phrase,

Let Christians and heretics perish in a moment,
let them be blotted out of the book of the living,
and let them not be written with the righteous.

It would have been impossible for a Jewish-Christian to utter
aloud this phrase or say "amen" to it. The ruler of a synagogue could
ask a suspected Christian member of the synagogue to serve as the
representative of the congregation and lead the praying of the Eighteen Benedictions. If he refused or stumbled in the recitation, he would
be exposed as a Christian and expelled (Mark 13:9; Matt. 10:17; John
9:22; 12:42; 16:2).[3]

Many scholars insist that Matthew's gospel must be interpreted
as a product of this dialogue or polemical exchange between synagogue and church in the 80s or 90s of the first century. Church and
synagogue competed for the hearts and loyalties of the Jews. Each religious community regarded itself as the genuine people of God, heirs
of the history stretching back to Abraham and forward to the day of
judgment.   *A*

Some modern interpreters have even gone so far as to depict the
author of the gospel as a converted scribe or rabbi, arguing his case for
a Christianized Judaism with former colleagues who still bowed to the
spiritual authority of Johanan or to his successor Gamaliel in the rabbinic assembly at Jamnia. Matthew is viewed as a Jewish Christian
teacher struggling against Pharisaic Judaism, attempting to prove
that Jesus is the Messiah, showing by his words and deeds that scripture is perfectly fulfilled in him; or Jesus is a new Moses, giving a new
Pentateuch (the five great Matthaean sermons in Chap. 5-7, 10, 13, 18,
24–25), liberator and founder of a new people consisting of all who
confess him (16:13-19), while those who deny him, even if Abraham is
their father, cease to be God's people (3:9; 27:25). In this
interpretation, Matthew's views of the identity of Jesus and the
church are featured.

However, sometimes Matthew's Jewishness and his relation to
the synagogue are pictured rather differently. In a time when pagans
were flocking into the church and threatening to dilute the Jewish element inside the church, Matthew as Jewish-Christian scribe is
thought to have had as much difficulty with the Gentile mission as Peter and James a generation or so earlier (Gal. 1–2). In this view, Matthew is thought to be almost pro-Jamnia and anti-Gentile. He is
viewed as a very conservative Christian, anxious to uphold Jewish tradition against the slogans of the Gentile converts who prized freedom

more than the discipline of the law. He is viewed as a Christian and a confessor of Jesus as the Christ, but as one who does not believe that it is possible to have the true Christ without the Jewish traditions. He is a conservative reformer of deep ethical seriousness. This interpretation is right in fixing upon the law and a life of righteousness as of central importance for Matthew, but it seems nevertheless to be mistaken about Matthew's environment and the manner in which Matthew expounds law and righteousness.

Matthew's gospel presents numerous impressive indications that the author was not even a Jew, let alone a former rabbi actively participating in the debates between church and synagogue described above. Such debates may have belonged to the past history of his community. Perhaps they had made a strong and lasting impression, but they were no part of the community's present. Matthew is conscious of a considerable distance between the churches of Christians and the synagogues of Jews. That is shown by the fact that he speaks of "their" scribes (7:29), "their" cities (11:1), and "their" or "your" synagogues (4:23; 10:17; 12:9; 13:54; 23:34).

Distance between the communities is implied in other passages. Surely at one level the author sees his Jewish contemporaries mirrored in the one son who uttered a quick "yes" to his father's command, that is, to the law offered at Sinai, but then went off and neglected to carry it out, while the other son (= Gentiles) at first spoke an equally quick "no," but then later repented and did his father's bidding (Matt. 21:28-32). Matthew, like Mark, retells Jesus' parable or allegory about the people who abused and killed the owner's servants and finally his son, with the result that the owner put those wretches to death and leased the vineyard to others (21:33-43). Matthew alone records the comment of Jesus, "The kingdom of God will be taken away from you (chief priests and Pharisees, 21:45; 22:15) and given to a nation (*ethnos*, cf. 28:19) producing the fruits of it" (21:43; 27:25). Furthermore, Matthew's version of the parable of the great supper differs significantly from Luke's telling. In Matthew, the guests rejected the invitation to the wedding banquet and killed the king's servants so that their city was laid waste and destroyed, and others were invited to take their place at the wedding banquet of the king's son (Matt. 22:1-10; cf. Luke 14:16-24).

All this seems to be a transparent reflection on the crucifixion of Jesus, the destruction of Jerusalem, the influx of Gentiles into the church, and the rhetoric of a church whose split from the synagogue belongs to the past. It is taken for granted that the two communities now go their separate ways.

Was Matthew a Gentile-Christian?

Many recent investigators have begun to question the traditional picture of close relations between church and synagogue in Matthew's time and place and to theorize that the author may have been a Gentile, knowing Judaism only at second hand, or at least that he may have been a member of a predominantly Gentile-Christian community, which has definitively broken off from Judaism and exhibits the universal outlook of the Gentile mission.[5]

Matthew exudes the confidence that Christians are emancipated from the Jewish laws and traditions governing foods and washing of hands (15:1-20; Mark 7:1-23). In the entire gospel there is not a single word for or against circumcision. That Jewish rite, fundamental to every other ordinance, is never once mentioned (contrast Luke 1:59; 2:21; Acts 15:1; 16:3; Gal. 2:3; 5:1-12).

Matthew views the church as a mixed body consisting of good and evil (22:10; cf. Luke 14:13), sheep and goats (25:32), wheat and tares (13:25), Jew and Gentile, the law-observant and those ignorant of the details of Mosaic legislation. He was also obviously an advocate of assertive openness to the Gentiles (28:18-20).

Matthew was no Jewish-Christian legalist, even though he is often misunderstood as one. Most emphatically he denied the propriety of separating good and evil in the church. That belongs to God and is reserved for the last day (13:40-41, 49-50). The church is called and ordained to forgiveness, mutual encouragement, and the winning of the erring brother or sister (Chap. 18).

Not only was Matthew probably a Gentile-Christian, but more and more it seems he was battling, not against the Pharisaism of Jamnia, but against some form of Christian enthusiasm, characterized by the sort of antinomianism and libertinism which confronted Paul at Corinth. Another way of putting it is to say that Matthew opposed some brand of early Christian radicalism.[6]

This view is quite different from the one which understands Matthew's gospel as a Christian defense of the church and as a blast against the synagogue and its leaders.

It is beginning to appear that Matthew's gospel is better understood as a polemic against movements and leaders inside the church. Matthew's gospel is only superficially anti-Pharisaic or anti-synagogue. It has in view Christian aberrations.[7] Matthew had serious concerns about certain Christian prophets. He wrote his gospel in order to counteract and instruct spirit-enthusiasts or charismatics of an antinomian sort who were disrupting Christian communities. The evidence for such a reconstruction follows.

A Spirit of Boasting and of Freedom

Matthew recalls the attacks of Jesus upon certain charismatics. Towards the end of the Sermon on the Mount, Matthew records Jesus' warning to the community about "false prophets in sheep's clothing" (7:15-20).[8] These enemies of the community are Christians (sheep), not Jewish or pagan outsiders. They confess Jesus in language sufficiently orthodox: "Lord, Lord" (7:21-22). That is the cry of both sheep and goats in the parable of the last judgment (25:37, 44), and throughout the gospel it is the specifically Christian way of addressing Jesus.

It is a perfectly correct formula to use in hailing Jesus. More than that, it is probably not just liturgical convention or brief creed but inspired or ecstatic utterance (see 1 Cor. 12:3). Nevertheless, in spite of their inspired and orthodox confession, those Christian prophets are exposed as false by the fact that they are not bearing good fruit (7:15-20). They are "evildoers" or, more literally, "workers of lawlessness" (7:23).

Lawlessness *(anomia)* is a Matthean word and a Matthean worry. It is used to define the posture of scribes and Pharisees once (23:28), but is used of Christians three times (7:23; 13:41; 24:12). Looking ahead to the days of the church and the end of history, Jesus says that many people under the pressure of suffering and hatred will give up their faith and begin to betray and hate one another (24:10), acting exactly as their unbelieving enemies do. Then false prophets will arise in the community and fan the flames of betrayal and hate with their deceptive teachings (24:11). The last and worst estate of the Christian community (not the world or the synagogue) is then described as the multiplication of lawlessness and the chilling of love (24:12). Elsewhere, in a parable addressed to the church, Matthew pictures Jesus as warning that at "the end of the age" (13:40; 28:20) the angels will gather up all the doers of lawlessness and cast them into the fire (13:36-43).

Their exclusion from the kingdom comes as a surprise to the lawless (7:22-23; 25:1-13, 14-30, 41-46; 22:11-14). But why are they startled? How could they possibly have expected to get in? On what basis? Apparently on the basis of their charismatic endowment. That is, they esteemed their spiritual gifts and powers as infallible evidence of

God's indwelling and therefore of God's favor and acceptance, and so of their status as the children or people of God.

They had no doubt that they were spiritual people, God's people, because the gifts of the Spirit were clearly displayed among them: exorcisms, prophecy, the power to do miracles, and perhaps also tongues and spiritual utterance. The possession of the Spirit and the manifestation of the gifts of the Spirit had become their boast and the ground of their confidence (7:15-23). All this could easily be misunderstood. It must be emphasized that Matthew, like Paul, is basically positive about the Spirit and about spiritual endowments. The very fact that Matthew speaks not simply of prophets and charismatics but of "false" prophets shows that he assumed that there are "true" prophets and so "true" charismatics. Christian discipleship is described in terms of charismatic deeds and charismatic speech in Jesus' mission discourse (10:5-20). Jesus was himself conceived by the Spirit (1:18, 20) and endowed with the Spirit at his baptism (3:16; 4:1), and in the power of the Spirit he performed charismatic deeds of healing, exorcism, and raisings of the dead (11:2-6; 12:28). Jesus also strenuously denounced blasphemy against the Holy Spirit (12:31-32).

Furthermore, Matthew appears to use "prophet" alongside "little ones," "righteous person," and "disciple" as synonymns. All of them are the equivalent of "Christian" (10:41-42). If "prophet" is a synonym for "Christian," then Matthew has a very high view indeed of the charismatic endowments in the congregations. Even if "prophets" designates only some especially gifted Christians, it is still a fact that Matthew thought of all Christians as possessing the Spirit or as being alive in the Spirit (see Rom. 8:9). Of course, Matthew's estimate of the Old Testament prophets is incomparably high.

Nevertheless, as positive as Matthew may be about the Spirit, he time and again betrays his uneasiness with certain charismatics. For example, his formulation of the Beatitudes, which may be designed especially for church leaders, appears to include anticharismatic cautions.[9]

"Blessed are the poor *in spirit*" (5:3, underlined words not in the parallel in Luke 6:20) may be aimed at those who boast of their spiritual riches, just as "Blessed are the meek" (completely absent from Luke's list) may have in view those who are puffed up and arrogant because of their endowments (cf. Matt. 11:29; 21:5; 1 Cor. 4:6, 18, 19; 5:2; 8:1; 13:4).

"Blessed are those who mourn" (5:4) may have in mind mourning over sin rather than boasting of freedom from the law, as Paul says some Corinthians were doing as they exhibited their spiritual liberty (1 Cor. 5:2; cf. Matt. 9:14-15 where penitential fasting and mourning are parallels).

Elsewhere in the Sermon on the Mount, and in other passages also, Matthew records sayings of an anticharismatic cast. Jesus' recommendation of prayer uttered secretly behind closed doors, spoken simply, without babbling or prating (Matt. 6:5-7), resembles Paul's distinction between myriads of words spoken in a tongue and five words spoken with the mind (1 Cor. 14:19).

Jesus in Matthew 7:11 declares that the Father knows how to give "good things" (not "the Holy Spirit" as in Luke 11:13) to those who ask him.

Matthew omits the generous saying at Mark 9:38-41 (cf. Luke 9:49-50) concerning exorcisms performed by a charismatic leader who does not follow Jesus. It is simply unthinkable to Matthew that a true prophet and true charismatic is not simultaneously a disciple of Jesus.

According to Matthew 25:31-46, it is not notorious public sinners who are excluded from the kingdom, nor is it the charismatically endowed who enter. It is doers of deeds of loving kindness, people who have exhibited love towards the deprived and disinherited, who are called sheep and righteous, and they enter the kingdom.

Finally, Matthew is silent about Pentecost. He neither has Jesus promise a Pentecostal experience or a future advent of the Paraclete (but see Matt. 10:20; cf. 3:11), nor does he describe the outpouring of the Spirit upon the community of the disciples in the days following Easter. And yet, there is nothing incomplete about the portrait Matthew has drawn, nor is it necessary to fill in any gaps with paragraphs or scenes taken from the other gospels or from the Acts of the Apostles.

Instead of promising the gift of the Spirit, Jesus declared, "Where two or three are gathered in my name, there am I in the midst of them" (18:20), and he said, "Lo, I will be with you always" (28:20). Of great significance in this context is the fact that the very name he bears is Emmanuel, which means "God with us" (1:23). It is central to Matthew's whole presentation of Jesus that he describes the enduring presence of God not in terms of the Spirit's being outpoured and filling Christians, but in terms of the majesty of the crucified and resurrected Jesus enthroned with his word in the midst of the congregation.

Once again, it must be emphasized that Matthew was not wrestling with charismatics in general. He is very far from uttering a blanket condemnation of the gifts of the Spirit or of inspired people.

In Matthew's view all Christians are endowed with the Spirit (3:11; 10:20). But some charismatics—some prophets, some visionaries, some healers, some inspired leaders—boasted of their gifts. Furthermore, and this is extremely important for understanding Matthew's situation and gospel, on the basis of their particular inspiration these prophets and leaders offered new teaching not in harmony with the words of Jesus. Matthew was prompted to say loudly and clearly that Jesus is himself still present as the one Lord and Teacher of the church.

Matthew's gospel is a teaching gospel. It bears the marks of having been produced by a master teacher, may well have been designed as a handbook for teachers, and is certainly full of the teaching of Jesus. It is not merely what Jesus taught once upon a time in the days of his flesh. Matthew rather holds before the congregation the present teaching of the exalted Jesus.

The teaching of the troublesome enthusiasts or radicals can be reconstructed to some extent by paying attention to the positive teaching in Matthew's gospel.

Matthew does not represent Jesus as a literalist or strict constructionist with regard to the law, nor is he on the other hand a reductionist who carelessly sweeps aside all commandments save that of love alone. Matthew shows that what he looked for is the higher righteousness, one which surpasses that of scribe and Pharisee and not one which merely imitates them (5:20; 3:15; 6:1; 21:32; 23:23). Indeed, he reacted against a legalism or ethical rigorism which demanded an observance of the entire law as the essential mark of the people of God. He presses through and beyond mere fasting, praying, almsgiving, handwashing, abstinence from foods, sabbath observance, and tithing. He takes these traditional disciplines for granted as practices of his community and sees problems in both mere external observance and also in easy abandonment of these disciplines.

Righteousness, love, and mercy are at the heart of Jesus' teaching in Matthew. The entirety of the ethical content of the Sermon on the Mount is bracketed by the saying on the higher righteousness (5:20) and the Golden Rule (7:12; cf. Acts 15:29D; Tobit 4:15; Hillel in b. Shab. 31a; Didache 1:2). Asked regarding the first and great commandment, Jesus replied that love for God and love for one's neighbor are first and second, not in rank or order of importance, but as two sides of a single coin or as mother and daughter—bone of its bone and flesh of its flesh—a single love comprehending heaven and earth.

Mercy takes precedence over sacrifice (9:13; 12:7; cf. Hosea 6:6; 1 Sam. 15:22). Mercy *(eleos)* means gracious acts, deeds of kindness or love (cf. Matt. 25:31-46). Matthew portrays Jesus as weighing religious and ethical practices and declaring that the heaviest matters in the law are justice and mercy and faith (23:23). All these taken together add up to perfection or genuine religious and ethical maturity *(teleios,* 5:48; 19:21). Confronted with people who located the heart of their religion in pyrotechnic displays of spiritual virtuosity and who regarded all references to the law of God as threats to their spiritual liberty, Matthew recalled the teaching of Jesus with its profound and firm insistence upon love, discipleship, the higher righteousness, and service in the world of human need.

Far from being a Christian legalist, insisting on the continuing validity of every detail in the Mosaic law, Matthew criticizes hypocritical, rigoristic adherence to the law and defends openness to the Gentiles. Far from brushing aside the law in the name of Christian freedom, Matthew struggles for the higher righteousness.

The rigorists whom Matthew opposes are not the rabbis of Jamnia, and the advocates of total freedom are surely not the pupils of Paul. Who are they, then?

The last decades of the first century witnessed numerous disturbances caused by inspired teachers and prophets inside various Christian congregations. The epistles of John testify to the disruptive activities of false prophets in the Johannine communities. The false prophets do not confess that Jesus is the Christ, the Son of God in the flesh. They boast that they are above sin and that they know God, and yet they do not keep the commandments of God. Keeping the new commandment of love and confessing Jesus are the criteria for judging between true and false prophets (1 John 4:1; cf. 2 Peter 2:1; Rev. 2-3). Criteria are also established by the Didache, a Christian book sharing many features with Matthew's gospel. It was probably produced at about the same time or a little later than Matthew (ca. A.D. 90-110) and in roughly the same area, namely Syria. The Didache warns about false prophets. These itinerant teachers and missionaries are revealed as false if they seek hospitality for more than two days, if they ask for a banquet, for money or for gifts, if they go into an ecstatic trance, or if, in general, they do not exhibit knowledge of the Lord accompanied by righteousness. The behavior both taught and practiced by the Lord is the standard of judgment in the Didache (Chap. 11-13).

The church in Syria and Asia Minor, and perhaps elsewhere, was both nourished and disturbed by prophets, prophetesses, and other inspired, wandering teachers at the end of the first century. The attitude of Matthew has much in common with that of the authors of the gospel and epistles of John, the book of Revelation and the Didache.

The polemical edge in Matthew's gospel is opposed primarily to inspired teachers and prophets, and those antagonists of Matthew were inside the church. But why then does Matthew assign so much space to Jesus' confrontations with Jewish authorities—scribes and Pharisees and priests?

Matthew uses the memory of Jesus' conflicts with scribes and Pharisees, with kings and governors, not to polemicize the men of Jamnia or any other outsiders, but to issue a stern warning to teachers inside the church—teachers and leaders who are, in a sense, the heirs or the counterparts of the scribes and Pharisees, as the church has been constituted as the people of God in the last times, enjoying privileges once belonging exclusively to Israel. Matthew is speaking to fellow Christians and especially to fellow teachers, warning them that, although they are children of God and sons of the kingdom, they nevertheless can and inevitably will lose their status if they neglect the will of God and his righteousness.

Matthew recalled Jesus' harsh words on scribes and Pharisees not to refute contemporary rabbis, but to combat what he regarded as parallel movements inside his own community.[10] Merely possessing the law, or being attached to the law in a loose external fashion, without deep inner devotion to the underlying intention of God's will, means that the church will lose its status as God's people and be cut off and excluded from the kingdom as they thought the scribes and Pharisees had been (Matt. 23). Matthew summed up Jesus' words on false prophets in the same context (24:4-12) as proof that there is no substitute for doing the will of the Father. Admiring the law or verbally affirming the grandeur of the will of God is not sufficient.

Matthew applied the past warnings of Jesus to the present condition of the church; or it would be more accurate to say that the words of Jesus recorded by Matthew continue to be the authoritative teaching of the resurrected one. The view that Matthew is aiming not at outsiders but at insiders is confirmed by the resurrection narrative. It is only against the background of Matthew's struggle for the church's identity and integrity that his resurrection narrative yields its full meaning.

Matthew 27:62-66: Seal the Tomb

Matthew 27:62-66 [62]Next day, that is, after the day of Preparation, the chief priests and the Pharisees gathered before Pilate [63]and said, "Sir, we remember how that imposter said, while he was still alive, 'After three days I will rise again.' [64]Therefore order the sepulchre to be made secure until the third day, lest his disciples go and steal him away, and tell the people, 'He has risen from the dead,' and the last fraud will be worse than the first." [65]Pilate said to them, "You have a guard of soldiers; go, make it as secure as you can." [66]So they went and made the sepulchre secure by sealing the stone and setting a guard.

What exactly is the point of this account, found in Matthew's gospel alone? At first the answer seems clear enough: this paragraph belongs together with material in 28:4 and 28:11-15 which concludes with the note, "This story (namely, that Jesus' disciples came by night and stole his body) has been spread abroad among the Jews to this day."[11]

It is customary to say that Matthew, to counter that slander, includes material to show how ridiculous and impossible the charge of deception really is. Such may possibly have been his motive. But the wording of the slander seems weak, and for its part, Matthew's rebuttal seems half-hearted. Can this really be the voice of the church locked in serious debate with the synagogue across the street? Instead of offering arguments with some chance of convincing unbelievers, Matthew merely heaps ridicule on an opposing position. His words would hardly impress any but the least thinking unbeliever.

It seems far more likely that Matthew's real aim is shoring up his readers—his Christian readers—by sharply reminding them not only that the resurrection of Jesus serves as the dividing line between believer and unbeliever, as the watershed between the old age and the new, but also and especially that belief in Jesus' resurrection entails allegiance to the teaching and example of the earthly Jesus. This paragraph is a summons, therefore, to Christian readers to ponder his resurrection deeply and to appropriate it rightly.

This material exhibits parallels to the material on the slaughter of the innocents at the beginning of the gospel (2:16-18). That earlier account is not anti-Herodian or anti-institutional, except possibly in a very extended sense. It serves to show the vanity of any opposition and is designed to encourage adherents in their allegiance. No matter what steps the enemies may take, God has them in derision and his plans will not be thwarted by human nay-sayers. The narrow escape in the beginning (flight to Egypt, 2:13-15) foreshadows the resurrection at the end, and both are narrated so as to appeal to the reader's imagination and heart.

27:62   Matthew pictures the chief priests (26:3, 14, 47, 57, 59; 27:1) and the Pharisees (Chap. 23), guardians of the sanctity of the Sabbath (12:1-14), as profaning the Sabbath by meeting with Pilate to conduct business on the day of rest (contrast John 18:28).

27:63   The Pharisees address Pilate respectfully (see below) and recall that Jesus had said, "After three days I will rise again" (16:21; 17:23; 20:19). They avoid referring to Jesus by name (see 1:21) and instead speak only of "that deceiver" or "that liar" (*planos;* cf. Test. Levi 16:3).

27:64   They plead their case that the governor secure the tomb and so prevent the disciples from stealing the body and spreading a false report of resurrection among the people. As they voice their fears, they predict the post-crucifixion Christian message precisely, "He has risen from the dead" (28:6-7). And from their point of view that "last fraud" or "last lie" (*eschatē planē*) will be worse than the first.

27:65-66   Whether Pilate himself set a Roman guard, or merely told the Jewish authorities to do whatever they wanted, is perhaps beside the point. Matthew alone among the canonical evangelists pictures the tomb as not merely closed with a stone, but also sealed and guarded. The Gospel of Peter later (ca. A.D. 150) embellished this tradition by describing how the Pharisees, together with elders and scribes, assisted the soldiers in rolling into place a great stone across the mouth of the tomb and in sealing the stone with seven seals. Then the Pharisees pitched a tent before the tomb and settled down to keep a personal vigil and prevent any tampering or deception (Gos. Pet. 8:28-33).

So on the day when Israel was commanded to rest, the enemies of Jesus are portrayed as hard at work in a vain effort to secure and seal their verdict upon him and upon the church's proclamation.

Throughout Matthew's material the Pharisees are pictured as operating on an assumption very dear to Matthew: there can be no separation between the earthly Jesus and the exalted Jesus. Or, to put it another way, there is no separating the earthly Jesus with all his deeds and teachings from the message of his resurrection. What the old enemies of Jesus object to is not just the report of the empty tomb and resurrection. For them, resurrection is not an impossible thing.

What they find impossible is the idea that Jesus, of all people, has been raised from the dead. They deny that their old opponent, with all his attacks on their positions and with all his own interpretations of the Father's will (5:21-48), could have experienced the divine vindication of resurrection. They reject not resurrection, but the resurrection of Jesus. They reject not God's ability to work wonders, but the possibility of God's having chosen Jesus as his agent in the past or present or future.

In a few words this paragraph brings to mind all the controversies of Jesus that have filled the book to this point, and it reminds the reader that the Pharisees had once come to Jesus seeking from him a sign proving that he acted and spoke on the Father's authority. Jesus had answered that they would receive only the sign of Jonah (12:38-42; 16:1-4). That means that they would receive as a sign the tomb emptied after three days, which would serve as a sign alongside the prophecies of scripture and the promises of Jesus.[12] Or it could be that his burial, his entombment in the earth, is itself the sign of Jonah.[13] In his death and burial his enemies would find the sign they really wanted, and they would believe that sign and interpret the word about his resurrection in the light of the sign of his tomb as a fraud and deceit. Either way, Matthew is warning the reader to make better decisions than those seekers after signs who, when they received the sign, tried to cover it up.

There is irony in the narrative in the way chief priests and Pharisees are pictured as correctly vocalizing both Jesus' promise (27:63) and the Christian kerygma (27:64) and in the way those religious leaders acknowledge the pagan governor's authority, addressing him as "sir" or "lord" (*kyrie;* 8:2, cf. John 19:15).

There is also humor, as Jesus' opponents take what they regard as realistic precautions: a squad of soldiers to stand guard at the tomb, a stone against the door, a seal on the stone. They act the way Darius had when he cast Daniel into the lions' den, ordered a stone laid upon the mouth of the den, and then sealed the stone with his own signet (Dan. 6:17).

That is humorous, because the earth has already been shaken once, splitting the rock, popping the stone covers off the tombs, rousing the dead (27:51-53), and marking the death and resurrection of Jesus as the end of the old world and the beginning of the new. And Matthew and his readers know it will happen again, revealing all the precautions of the Jewish and Roman leaders as hopeless and puny.

Matthew uses this paragraph not so much to refute Pharisees as to remind Christian readers, and especially Christian teachers, of two things:

(1) The Christian message of the resurrection of Jesus is not "the final deception" (*hē eschatē planē*) but is the ultimate and deepest truth.

(2) And therefore Jesus is not "the deceiver" (*ho planos*) leading God's people astray but is—not was, but is—the one great Teacher and Master of the people of God (cf. 23:8-9).

Matthew 28:1-10:   He Has Been Raised

Matthew 28:1-10   Now after the sabbath, toward the dawn of the first day of the week, Mary Magda-lene and the other Mary went to see the tomb. ²And behold, there was a great earthquake; for an angel of the Lord descended from heaven and came and rolled back the stone, and sat upon it. ³His appearance was like lightning, and his raiment white as snow. ⁴And for fear of him the guards trembled and became like dead men. ⁵But the angel said to the women, "Do not be afraid; for I know that you seek Jesus who was crucified. ⁶He is not here; for he has risen, as he said. Come, see the place where he lay. ⁷Then go quickly and tell his disciples that he has risen from the dead, and behold, he is going before you to Galilee; there you will see him. Lo, I have told you." ⁸So they departed quickly from the tomb with fear and great joy, and ran to tell his disciples. ⁹And behold, Jesus met them and said, "Hail!" And they came up and took hold of his feet and worshiped him. ¹⁰Then Jesus said to them, "Do not be afraid; go and tell my brethren to go to Galilee, and there they will see me."

Matthew's narrative of the events of Easter morning presupposes Mark's. It is a revised version of Mark's report.

28:1   Where Mark says that women arrived at the tomb early on Sunday morning "to anoint the body" (Luke follows Mark in that), Matthew says that "Mary Magdalene and the other Mary (who had witnessed the burial, 27:61) went out *to see* the sepulchre."

Matthew omits any mention of anointing because he does not want so much as to hint that any of Jesus' friends could have entered the tomb or touched the body. They could go and pay their respects from a distance, but, because of the guard, they would not have been able to approach too closely. Access to the tomb was denied them, and the emptiness of the tomb could not possibly have been their doing.

28:2   Matthew turns from negative defense to positive assertion. Opening the tomb was the work of God alone: "a great earthquake" (27:51, 54; 8:24) means that Easter is God's doing, acting as he had at Exodus and Sinai (Exodus 19:18; Psalm 68:8; 114:7; cf. Hebrews 12:26) and as he had promised to do at the end of the old age and the beginning of the new (Isaiah 13:13; 24:18-20; Ezekiel 37:7; 38:19-20; Joel 3:16; Haggai 2:6). He gives a sign in the earth beneath as he had granted a sign in the stars above at Jesus' birth (2:1-12). What is solid, enduring, and dependable if not the great eternal rocks, so unlike shifting sand (7:24-27)? The earth is stable (5:18; 24:35), and when it begins to split open the end is at hand (24:7; Rev. 6:12; 8:5; 11:13, 19; 16:18).[14]

Not Mark's "young man" (16:5) nor any human agency, but an "angel of the Lord" or "the angel of the Lord" (Exodus 3:2-6; Acts 7:30) was responsible for opening the tomb. Angels do not simply hymn or herald his birth and resurrection, but act as his agents and servants (1:20, 24; 2:13, 19). When he let himself be arrested, Jesus had declared that he could call on the Father to put twelve legions of angels at his disposal (26:53). There is here an unexploited parallel to the other early resurrection materials in which the resurrection is understood as enthronement over spiritual powers (Phil. 2:10-11; 1 Peter 3:22; 1 Tim. 3:16; Eph. 1:21). They are servants; he is the Son (Hebrews 1:5—2:9).

28:3   The angel himself shone like a bolt of lightning, and he was clothed in a garment like glistening snow. With a few strokes of the pen, Matthew recalls the splendor of the transfigured Jesus (17:2) and the Lord's promise that the righteous will one day shine like the sun in the kingdom of their Father (13:43; Dan. 12:2-3). The angel has descended from the world of light where the Father's will is always obeyed (6:10) and is clothed in the burning purity, awesome splendor, and undying glory of the heavens (Isa. 1:18; Ezek. 1:4; Dan. 7:9-10; 10:6; Rev. 1:14). In Mark the "young man" is primarily a messenger, but Matthew portrays the angel as an apocalyptic figure, throwing the stone aside and opening a whole new age in cosmic history.[15]

28:4   The guards faint dead away and are thus removed from the stage, enabling the angel and the women to conduct their conversation privately. Their quaking with the earth and then their fainting also help to answer the question of how the guards could possibly have remained unbelievers in the presence of the angel of the Lord. They never heard his message. Matthew may intend some irony here as well: On Easter the dead one comes to life (see 27:51-53) and those regarded as living and powerful fall into a deathlike faint.

28:5-7   The wording of the message of the angel in Matthew is almost exactly the same as in Mark. The slight differences can be accounted for in various ways:

(1) The verses containing the angel's message have been arranged artfully so that beginning and end are parallel:

5a The angel said to the women	8b and ran to tell his disciples.
5b Do not be afraid;	8a so they departed quickly from the tomb with fear and great joy
5c for I know that	7e Lo, I have told you.
5d you seek Jesus who was crucified.	7d There you will see him.
6a He is not here;	7c and behold, he is going before you to Galilee;
6b for he has risen, as he said	7b that he has risen from the dead,
6c Come, see the place where he lay.	7a Then quickly go and tell his disciples

(2) Mark's references to "Nazareth" and "Peter" have been dropped, because Matthew will close his gospel on a universal note with the great scene on the mountain in Galilee, and he does not want to have Nazareth, a definite and known Galilean site, clouding the picture. Also, the final appearance with its command and encouragement is for the whole church in all the days ahead, and the naming of Peter could easily have obscured that.[16]

Jesus is no longer called "the Nazarene" by Matthew (as he is designated by Mark), but he still retains his identity as "the crucified." He had ended on a cross because he had taught and acted with authority in opposition to the received opinion and current orthodoxies. He had earned for himself powerful enemies by claiming that he heard the Father's voice calling him to identify himself in meekness with the outcast and to share the burdens of the oppressed (3:13-17; 8:14-17; 11:25-30; 21:5; 26:36-46). Full of obedience and trust as the Son of God, he gave himself (26:63-64; 27:40, 43, 54), sealing with his blood a covenant of forgiveness for all (20:28; 26:26-29).

(3) The heart of the Easter message in Matthew as in Mark is that "Jesus the crucified ... has been raised from the dead." That event occurred, says the angel in Matthew's gospel, "just as he said." Note how his enemies had used the same phrasing in the preceding paragraph (27:63-64). Matthew once again connects earthly Jesus and resurrection as closely as possible.

28:8   Mark's ending (16:8) was too enigmatic or too reserved for Matthew. His own gospel will conclude with the great epiphany of

Jesus in the presence of his disciples, assembled in Galilee on the basis of the message carried to them by the women. Hence, Matthew alters the final words of Mark (16:8) to make it unmistakably clear that the women certainly did deliver the news entrusted to them.

28:9-10   As the women left the tomb and were on the way, Jesus himself met them. At first it seems that the incident offers little that is new. It seems to be a kind of duplicate of the scene with the angel, except that Jesus himself is now involved. The women fell before him and kissed his feet, acknowledging not only that he is alive but that he lives as exalted Lord (contrast the behavior of the priests at 26:65-68 and of the soldiers at 27:27-31). This meeting is like the climax of the narrative of the stilling of the storm (14:22-33) and it resembles the actions of the Magi who were led by a star to Jesus' feet (2:2, 8, 11).

Jesus offered the women no proof of his corporeity (cf. Luke 24:37-43) and they made no attempt to hang onto him (as in John 20:17). The brief recital of the encounter is designed to serve at least three purposes:

(1) To set the stage for the great scene in Galilee where his disciples fall down before him and worship him (28:17) in contrast to those who continue to oppose him (28:11-15).

(2) To soften the colors and modulate the severe tones of that final scene (28:16-20), lest Christian devotion to the exalted Jesus be misinterpreted as slavish obeisance to an oriental despot. It is properly interpreted as the awestruck response of friends and "brothers" (12:46-50; 25:40; John 20:28; Ps. 22:22) to whom Jesus has revealed the Father's demanding and gracious will. He is the firstborn among many brethren (Rom. 8:29; Heb. 2:11-18).

(3) To make it clear that what leads to discipleship and lays the foundation of the church is not visions of angels, some ambiguous sign like the empty tomb, some spectacular sign like the Magi's star, ecstatic seizure, or prophetic inspiration of Christian leaders. It is rather the word of Jesus, for Jesus himself is Lord of his church, and he here announces that he is once more gathering his disciples in Galilee (4:18-22).

Matthew 28:11-15:   Spread This Story

Matthew 28:11-15   [11]While they were going, behold, some of the guard went into the city and told the chief priests all that had taken place. [12]And when they had assembled with the elders and taken counsel, they gave a sum of money to the soldiers [13]and said, "Tell people, 'His disciples came by night and stole him away while we were asleep.' [14] And if this comes to the governor's ears, we will satisfy him and keep you out of trouble." [15] So they took the money and did as they were directed; and this story has been spread among the Jews to this day.

Sandwiched between the worship of the women in Jerusalem and the worship of the eleven in Galilee is the scene of the bribers and the bribed who deny Jesus' resurrection. Choices are being set before the reader.

The brief scene is reminiscent of the gathering of the Magi before Herod the Great inside his palace at the beginning of the gospel (2:1-12), and it is a stark contrast with the scene on the mountain in Galilee (28:16-20). In all three scenes there are authorities wielding impressive power and holding high office. Before them stand people who have seen signs or heard reports and who arrive as suppliants and seekers. The authorities dispose of matters, issuing instructions and offering assurances.

28:11 Not one but two reports of the events at the tomb arrived back inside Jerusalem. While the women carried one message, some of the guards bore another.

28:12 The chief priests met with the elders of the people just as they had done previously when they first plotted against Jesus (26:3), paid out money (26:14-15), arrested (26:47), and tried him (26:57; 27:1). The same body of persons is meant by "chief priests and Pharisees" in 27:62. As they had "sought false testimony against Jesus" (26:59-60), so once more they arranged to have their version heard. They distributed bribes, suppressed the news of resurrection, and spread a false report.

From that time on, the message of the angel (28:5-6) has been only one of the reports making the rounds about the first Easter morning. It has never circulated without some such counterclaim as the one proposed the same day by the most responsible religious leaders in the land.[17]

28:13 The soldiers were told to include as part of their account the tale that they had fallen asleep. They thus destroy their own credibility as witnesses by admitting that they had had their eyes closed while there transpired those events which they purport to interpret.

28:14 Furthermore, the council reassured the guards that they would handle Pilate and keep the guards out of trouble.

28:15 In the final analysis, the soldiers are pictured as disciples of the priests and elders. Just as the eleven were told by Jesus to teach people *(didaskontes autous)* all he had commanded (28:20), so the soldiers spoke not just as they had been "directed" but as they had been "taught" or "instructed" *(edidachthēsan)*. Again, the reader is being asked, "Whose disciple do you want to be? And who is your teacher *(didaskalos)*?" (cf. 23:8).

The scene is described with the same irony and humor that fill 27:62-66. This paragraph is again a sharp call to the readers to make a right decision.

Luke's narratives of beginning and end exhibit none of the crisis atmosphere of Matthew's. Luke's infancy narrative is homey and pastoral, focusing on events in the family and among relatives and on their expanding knowledge of the wonderful child born in the days of the Augustan peace. Priests and prophets step onto the stage to acclaim him. Sages marvel at his wisdom. Angels announce his advent. And Luke's resurrection narratives are dominated by a steadily growing comprehension of Jesus' lordship.

However, if the sun shines on the Lukan Jesus, darkness glowers in Matthew. In the beginning his legitimacy is in doubt, and, when suspicion has been swept aside, highly placed enemies seek to take the young child's life. Soldiers fill Bethlehem with weeping when they murder the innocents, and the infant Jesus has to flee for his life and only narrowly escapes. So also at the end, plots are hatched and money changes hands, so that when the seal on the tomb fails to do its job, rumors are spread branding his disciples as graverobbers and his resurrection a hoax.

The whole Matthean atmosphere, all the way from infancy to death and resurrection, is one of conflict. Of that there can be no doubt. Matthew believes that fateful decisions must be made by the readers, and his work is full of sharp debate and argument as he does his best to press his readers for the right choice.

Matthew 28:16-20: I Am with You

Matthew 28:16-20   Now the eleven disciples went to Galilee, to the mountain to which Jesus had directed them. [17]And when they saw him they worshiped him; but some doubted. [18]And Jesus came and said to them, "All authority in heaven and on earth has been given to me. [19]Go therefore and make disciples of all nations, baptizing them in the name of the Father and of the Son and of the Holy Spirit, [20]teaching them to observe all that I have commanded you; and lo, I am with you always, to the close of the age."

Of all the alterations of Mark's Easter narrative introduced by Matthew, none is more significant than the fact that Matthew does not regard Mark 16:1-8 as the climax and conclusion of the record about Jesus but caps his story instead with the great final scene in Galilee. The word of Jesus fittingly concludes Matthew's gospel.

Matthew could have offered a much different kind of ending. He might have pictured the enthronement of Jesus along the lines of Daniel 7:13-14, with the presentation of the resurrected Son of Man before the Ancient of Days, his solemn investiture with power and dominion over all peoples, and the declaration that his kingdom would never be destroyed. Or Matthew might have portrayed Jesus as an awesome figure with face like the sun shining in full strength, with eyes like flames of fire, wearing robes decorated with emblems at once royal, priestly, and military (Rev. 1:12-20). Or again, the gospel might have closed with a Christian hymn celebrating the movement of Jesus through obedient death to glorious triumph over things in heaven, things on earth, and things under the earth (such as Paul has preserved in Philippians 2:6-11) or one on the all-embracing reach of his epiphany and sway (1 Tim. 3:16).

Matthew has chosen to close his gospel not with a visual or pictorial representation of Jesus' assumption of power, but with the words of Jesus, the church's one teacher and master (23:8-10), addressing the issue of legalism and antinomian enthusiasm.

For a time it was popular to think of Matthew 28:16-20 (or 18-20) as reflecting the ritual of the enthronement of a king: (1) Elevation or Conferral of Authority, (2) Presentation and Proclamation of the Elevated, and (3) Assumption of Power and Acclamation by Subjects. Similar patterns were discerned in 1 Timothy 3:16, Philippians 2:9-11, and Hebrews 1:5-14. For much of its special imagery Matthew was thought to be indebted to Psalm 2, or more often to Daniel 7 and the presentation of the Son of Man before the Ancient of Days.[18]

Lately, interpretations have begun to shift away from enthronement and back to message, since Matthew 28:16-20 does not picture an enthronement but rather records the words which the enthroned or exalted one utters to his people. Many terms have been used to define either the present or the reconstructed, underlying form of the material: elements of a church order (Holtzmann), cult legend and I-saying (Bultmann), mythical revelation speech like 11:25-27 (Dibelius), farewell discourse (Stendahl/Munck), the Shema (Lohmeyer), a concise narrative like a pronouncement story or apophthegm, as opposed to circumstantial narratives like tales (Dodd), a foundation myth (Perrin), a Hebrew Bible commission (Hubbard), a manifesto

(Trilling/Harnack), a legacy or testament or an Old Testament divine
address or *Gottesrede* (Trilling), an official or royal decree (Malina).[19]

The last named suggestion seems especially fruitful. Examples of
official or royal decrees are found in Genesis 45:9-11 (Joseph to his
brothers) and in 2 Chronicles 36:23 (Cyrus to the exiles). The pattern
consists of the following elements: (1) Message Formula, (2) Statement of Authority expressing the basis of the obligation to obedience,
(3) Command or Summons, (4) Motivation.[20]

So the royal decree of Cyrus (2 Chron. 36:23; cf. Ezra 1:2-4),
permitting and encouraging the Jews in Babylonian exile to return to
Jerusalem and rebuild the temple, can be analyzed as follows:

(1) Thus says Cyrus king of Persia,

(2) The Lord, the God of heaven, has given me all the kingdoms of
the earth,

(3) and he has charged me to build him a house at Jerusalem, which
is in Judah.

(4) Whoever is among you of all his people may the Lord his God be
with him.

Both in pattern and in content the final words of Matthew's gospel closely resemble the decree of Cyrus:

(1) And Jesus came and said to them,

(2) All authority in heaven and on earth has been given to me.

(3) Go therefore and make disciples of all nations, baptizing them
in the name of the Father and of the Son and of the Holy
Spirit, teaching them to observe all that I have commanded
you;

(4) and lo, I am with you always, to the close of the age.

The various efforts at defining the form of the passage have much
in common, pointing time and again to the threefold ordering of the
word of Jesus: claim to authority, commission, and promise. And the
whole is introduced by reference to the speaker and the setting.[21]

28:16-18a   The Setting

28:16   The narration of the meeting of Jesus with his disciples
is a marvel of reserve. No attempt is made to describe the resurrected
one or to draw his portrait. He is "Jesus" and that is all. The description of the appearance of the angel takes more words than this and is
more elaborate and impressive (vv. 2-3). Matthew says nothing about

Jesus' posture or gestures: nothing of whether he is walking, standing, sitting, taking food, displaying hands or feet or side. There is not a single word about the time, whether the meeting occurred in ·the morning or evening, on Sunday or a weekday, on Pentecost or at some other season. There is nothing about Peter, Thomas, or any other individual disciple. And Matthew is just as reticent about the setting or circumstances of the encounter. It is not described as having happened on a road, at table, in an upper or lower room, or in a village or town. It apparently happened in the open air on a mountain.

The eleven disciples left the city where Jesus had been rejected and assembled in Galilee, where Jesus had issued his initial proclamation (4:17) and had summoned his first disciples (4:18-22).[22] Galilee was literally "the circle of the Gentiles," open to the pagan world. Jesus has a word to speak regarding light for the whole world (5:14; 28:19) and Galilee is the right place for it (4:16). It is also a word about discipleship, and the mountain is the right place for that. Is it "the mountain to which he had commanded them" (supply: "to go"), or "the mountain where he had given them command" (or "set their lives in order" or "appointed them"), that is, the mountain of 5:1, where he had spoken the Sermon on the Mount, addressing the crowds of followers on the theme of the righteousness of the disciple?

The latter is tempting, but in either case Matthew conjures up the picture of an unnamed and mysterious place of revelation,[23] and the revelation is the most authoritative ordering of the life of the community.

28:17   The eleven gathered before him with mixed awe and doubt, faith and unfaith together. The church in Matthew's view is, to the end of the age, a mixed body consisting of good and evil (22:10) wheat and tares (13:24-30, 36-43), sheep and goats (25:32-33), and even "the good" are sometimes "men of little faith" (6:30; 8:26; 14:31; 16:8).[24]

28:18a   Mixed as they were, it was an act of grace for Jesus to come to them and speak to them. There is no interest in proving his physicality (Luke 24:36-40) or in interpreting his wounds (John 20:24-29), no talk of moving unhindered through doors (John 20:19, 26) or of eating at table (Luke 24:30, 41-43). The whole scene focuses on his word.

28:18b-20   Jesus' Decree

Jesus had entered the holy city meek and riding upon an ass and had been crucified beneath the placard, "This is Jesus, the King of the Jews" (27:37), but now he speaks from a throne higher than that of

Cyrus the Great, summoning the small band of followers to a task universal in space and time. The decree is a mere handful of words, a total of 50 in the Greek text, and yet nothing more and nothing greater could be expressed in so few syllables.[25]

28:18b   From the beginning of his gospel Matthew has been defining the authority of Jesus. He opens his narrative by naming him "Jesus Christ, the son of David, the son of Abraham" (1:1), by declaring that he is the "ruler who will govern my people Israel" (2:6), and by describing him as one whom foreign dignitaries worship (2:1-12). At the same time, Matthew defined that rule negatively by denying the inclusion of every trace of self-serving or secularity (4:1-11; 20:20-28).

It is remarkable that in this final paragraph titles are not heaped up to suggest the magnificence of the authority bestowed by the Father upon Jesus. He is not here called "the Christ," "the Son of Man," "the Lord," "the Son of God." In the formula referring to baptism he stands between Father and Holy Spirit as "the Son" (v. 19) and that is peculiarly appropriate, for if there is any one title or summary description of Jesus dear to Matthew's heart, it is "Son."[26]

He fulfills prophecy as the Son called out of Egypt (2:15), and at his baptism and transfiguration the voice from heaven acknowledged him as "my beloved Son" (3:17; 17:5). The temptations came as tests, probing the sonship: "If you are the Son of God . . . ." (4:3, 6; cf. 27:40). And in the last of the temptations, Satan offered to give Jesus "all the kingdoms of the world and the glory of them" (4:9). Jesus' obedience to the Father and trust in him led him through conflicts with the powers of this world all the way to the cross. But the Father has now raised up the obedient and faithful son and bestowed upon him "all authority in heaven and on earth."

The word behind "authority" *(exousia)* is sometimes translated in various parts of the New Testament as "power" or "freedom" or "right." The word is rich and provocative in connotation. Authority is what Hellenistic religion promised (cf. Acts 8:19; 1 Cor. 6:12; 8:9; 10:23; 2 Cor. 10:8; 13:10), and at the same time it is a quasi-technical term, used in Judaism of those teachers qualified to pronounce on legal matters. In Matthew, the authority of Jesus is bound especially closely, as compared with Mark, to his teaching (Matt. 7:29; cf. Mark 1:22). That Jesus has "all" authority is interpreted in part by the other three "all's" in 28:18-20: all nations, all I have commanded, all the days.

The writ of councils, kings and governors is severely limited (10:17-18, 28). But the wide expanse of heaven is the throne of God, and the length and breadth of the earth is his footstool (5:34-35). The Son's authority runs to the outer edges of the universe, summons all nations to discipleship, and endures to the end of all days.

All that teachers and scribes saw in Torah or Wisdom—existing before the foundation of the world, seated on the lap of the heavenly King, principle by which the world hangs together and makes sense, guide and light for the life of God's people—Matthew saw in Jesus (5:21-48; 11:28-30; 16:12; 18:20; 23:1-36). And all that the priests located in the temple—great ancient focal point and public symbol of God's presence and provision and of Israel's devotion and identity—Matthew likewise located in Jesus (12:6; 21:12, 23-27).

All the symbols and guides of Judaism are put in the shade, but so are all the leaders of the Christian community, whether renowned for their learning (23:8-12) or for their spiritual endowments (7:15, 22; 24:11, 24; cf. Rev. 3:22).[27]

Members of Matthew's community found security in tradition, race, or in the fact of their belonging to the right community, and appealed to the sanction of authoritative leaders, the sanctity of the law, or the authority of the personal experience of the Spirit. But here it is stated once more and most emphatically: One is your teacher, one your master (23:8-10).

Jesus, identified by all he taught, all he did, and all he suffered in the preceding chapters of the gospel, and nothing or no one else, is the foundation for the life of the church, and he is the touchstone for assessing all the speech and silence, all the action and passion of the church. He has neither peer nor successor.

28:19a   The "therefore" *(oun)* of 19a means that the command of verse 19 flows from the claim of verse 18. Indeed, the authority comes into clear focus in the command, for the command begins to reveal and describe the meaning of the authority claimed. Verses 19 and 20 together are the earliest commentary on the declaration of verse 18.

The word of command has given the entire saying its traditional name, "The Great Commission." And yet caution is necessary. In the first place, the saying lacks both the usual early Christian words for sending, apostleship, mission, and also the customary words for gospel, preaching, proclaiming, repentance, and forgiveness (contrast 10:7).[28]

Also lacking is any explicit reference to charismatic activity in any form: exorcism, healing, raising (contrast 10:8).

Then, in the second place, the word usually translated in English as "go" functions in the original as an auxiliary, underscoring the ac-

tion of the main verb, "make disciples." It means something like "get
started making disciples" or "hurry to make disciples." Jesus is not
saying that the hearers should do two things: (1) go to distant lands or
other peoples, and (2) make disciples out of them.[29]

The entire authority of Jesus is focused on the command to "make
disciples." The eleven (not "twelve," not "apostles"), the nucleus of the
people of God, are summoned on the basis of Jesus' unlimited and incomparable authority to get going in the business of making disciples
out of all the nations of the human family.[30]

Does "all nations" mean "all Gentiles" and so exclude the Jews, or
does the "all nations" include them? Matthew records hard words
against Israel: for its failure to receive the prophets and the son, the
kingdom would be taken away and given to another nation (21:43). On
the other hand, it was of course a Jewish scribe who came to Jesus
desiring to be a disciple (8:19; cf. 13:52), a Jewish woman who anointed
him (26:13) and a Jewish Joseph who buried him in his own tomb and
was called "a disciple" (27:57).

And then, too, the Gentiles are described as outsiders (18:17) and
receive their share of hard knocks (5:47; 6:7, 32), and Matthew has the
prophecy that "all nations" will exhibit enmity toward the church
(24:9).

In the end "all the nations" will be gathered before the Son of Man
in his glory and they will be divided into sheep and goats (25:31-33).
That parable of the last times appears to operate with the widest possible horizon—all humanity without any exceptions.[31] And so also the
summons to make disciples has all humanity in view (24:14), and the
Jews are not excepted or excluded.[32]

Why else does the genealogy go back precisely to Abraham, and
why is Jesus called "the son of Abraham" (1:1, 2, 17)? Is not Matthew's conception close to that of Paul: "In Christ Jesus you are all
sons of God .... There is neither Jew nor Greek .... If you are
Christ's then you are Abraham's offspring, heirs according to promise" (Gal. 3:26-29). Matthew might say "heirs according to the miracle
of grace," as if raised up from stones to be children of Abraham (3:9;
8:11-12).

And yet uneasiness remains. Perhaps the question whether "nations" includes Jews or not is a bad question. It presupposes that Matthew has worked out a theory on the relationship between Jews and
Gentiles or synagogue and church. But if Matthew has any theory or
conviction, it concerns discipleship. With his eye on the church, he
uses the story of Jesus in conflict with God's ancient people to warn

and encourage those who have come to call themselves God's people that discipleship is the heart of the matter. The charge to "make disciples" is aimed at the church not so much in relation to the world outside as in relation to the world inside. It is a word about the integrity of the church. Matthew reminds his readers that the will of Jesus is not just that more and more people be converted, but that people from all nations become a community of disciples, doing all that he commanded.

Matthew appears almost anti-Semitic or anti-Judaic if he is interpreted as writing his gospel in order to praise the church and sanction its existence, ideas, and activities. Then he seems only to fault the synagogue. But Matthew is writing to a church grown easy and smug and self-satisfied. His topic is not "the synagogue and the church" but "the people of God are summoned to discipleship."

28:19b Discipleship is closely related to Baptism (19b) and teaching (20a). These three are sometimes interpreted as coequal members of a triumvirate, named in no particular order, but simply listed this way because it is, after all, not possible to say three things simultaneously. And then the order is almost unconsciously altered and the series is interpreted to mean: "make converts by first preaching to them and then baptizing those who believe."

However, the order makes excellent sense just as it stands, especially if the issues in Matthew's community revolved precisely around Baptism and teaching. Matthew was addressing certain charismatics of an antinomian tendency. They understood and experienced Baptism, as also the Corinthians had, as infusion of divine energy, conferring rebirth on the human spirit and freedom from the bonds of mortality and the demands of custom and law. They regarded their Baptism as the occasion on which the Spirit's presence was first manifested in dramatic and charismatic utterance and act. And teachers in Matthew's community had a way of asserting themselves not only as guardians of the tradition and wisdom but as lordly dispensers of fresh truth and new wisdom (Chap. 23).

The way Matthew speaks of the Baptism of Christians at the end of his gospel is illuminated by the way he spoke of the baptism of Jesus at the beginning. Matthew has reordered the narrative of Jesus' baptism so that it becomes clear that the moment was for Jesus not an occasion of ecstasy or enthusiasm or only of the revelation of his sonship, but was rather his first step on the way of righteousness (3:15; 21:32). All Jesus' charismatic energy and prophetic power—he was conceived by the Spirit (1:18, 20) and the Spirit at baptism alighted upon him (3:16)—was focused on executing the Father's will and standing against demonic forces and obstructionist human authorities. In Jesus there is a new creation. The old evil foe is unsuccessful (4:1-11) and his rule is being overthrown (12:28). The kingdom of God and his righteousness (6:33) is breaking in.

And so also the Spirit named at the close of Matthew's gospel is associated with Baptism, but Baptism does not well up and issue in ecstasy, in freedom from the bonds of tradition or morality, or in pyrotechnic display of charismatic endowment. However highly Matthew may have respected and cherished those elements, he held righteousness and discipleship even more dear.

The way Matthew has linked the Spirit in a series with the Father and the Son leads in the same direction. His use of the triple formula has provoked a wealth of discussion. This is not the place to comment on the textual issues raised by the manuscript tradition, on the early Christian use of the trinitarian formula in Baptism, or on its use apart from Baptism in liturgical blessings. It is useful to note, however, that other early Christian traditions associate Baptism with Jesus and the Spirit differently from Matthew. In Luke-Acts, for example, Baptism is in or into the name of Jesus and bestows the Spirit.[33] Matthew's formulation is neither accidental nor merely traditional.

Matthew manages very deftly to make at least two points. In the first place, he proclaims the presence of God in the Son and in the Spirit, simultaneously confessing God to be not an abstract principle but a saving (1:21) and re-creating (12:28) personal power, reaching into human history to establish a new community out of all the nations.[34]

In the second place, Matthew manages to hold the Spirit on a tight rein. He has previously tied the Spirit to the Father (3:16; 10:20) and to the Son (12:18, 28) but now in a final brief formula he binds the three as closely as possible. They constitute one name. The Spirit has no fresh mission separate or distinct from that of Father and Son. Baptism is an act setting a person onto the way of discipleship, onto the path of righteousness as one in the possession and under the authority of the single reality of Father, Son, and Holy Spirit.[35]

28:20a   Jesus is not here talking about missionary preaching or kerygma to the unconverted aimed at gaining their assent and at winning them for faith and Baptism (contrast Luke 24:47). This is instruction inside the church among those who have already been initiated through Baptism. The whole book forms the subject matter they are to learn.

The gravitational center of the teaching of Jesus is not theories or speculative doctrines. All the law and the prophets add up, not to some Christological speculation, certainly not to some schematization of historical aeons or a theory about the relations between Jews and Gentiles, but to the command to love. The gift and deed of God in Jesus claims people as disciples.

The phrase "all that I have commanded you" echoes a number of Old Testament expressions which serve as sweeping summaries for the authoritative will of God, especially in Deuteronomy.[36] Jesus has spoken a warning against relaxing "one of the least of these commandments" (5:19),[37] and speaks very conservatively of the Sabbath (12:1-8, omitting Mark's statement about every man as lord of the Sabbath; see also 24:20 as compared with Mark 13:18). But here, at the conclusion of the gospel, Jesus is not binding his community to the letter of the decalog nor is he speaking simply of the new commandment of love in Johannine fashion. He places into the center of the life of the community the will of the heavenly Father as he has been expounding it from the beginning. The golden rule (7:12) and the double commandment of love (22:37-39) are summaries of the law and the prophets and therefore of the will of God, and his will can be summed up also as mercy (9:13; 12:7).

In a remarkable passage the book of Deuteronomy, much like Matthew, recognizes that there will arise prophets, dreamers of dreams, and doers of signs and wonders. It also offers ethical or moral criteria for assessing the validity of the teaching and claims of such inspired people (Deut. 13:1-5).

So God's movement into the world in Jesus has as its goal a community of disciples, gathered from among Jews and Gentiles, initiated through Baptism into the community and onto the way of righteousness, practicing the will of God as Jesus has interpreted it. And he is present wherever the call to righteousness is proclaimed and heeded.

28:20b   One further structure is built on the foundation of the authority of Jesus, or one further stream issues from that authority. The words describing it are connected to the preceding and given prominence by the solemn introduction, "And behold."

The authority of Jesus extends over time as well as over the space in which all nations live; for he is not confined to the past and is not merely the revered founder of the community or the ancient fountain of the teaching still flowing in the community. He has not cast his mantle upon successors, and so there is not a single word about his relatives nor about elders, shepherds, leaders, teachers, evangelists, prophets or apostles. There is nothing like Acts 20:18-35, Ephesians 4:11-14, or the Pastorals.

Furthermore, Matthew is completely silent on the topic of the coming of the Holy Spirit and Pentecost, and he breathes not a word about ascension. In Luke-Acts the Holy Spirit fulfills the promise of the divine presence and power in the community, and in the Fourth Gospel Jesus promises the Paraclete, but not so in Matthew.

Jesus himself is Emmanuel,[38] the place of the presence of God, and he continues with the community, indwelling the community wherever two or three of the pious gather in his name and lift their voices in prayer (18:20), just as the Shekinah or Presence of God dwelled in the temple of old (1 Kings 8; M. Yoma 1:5; Sifre Numb. 35:34), just as the Presence of God was believed to rest upon two or three who shared words of Torah together (M. Pirke Aboth 3:2).[39]

But "I am with you" is by no means confined to cultic or legal contexts. Everywhere in the Bible the phrase is God's solemn promise to be present with his people, guiding, helping, protecting and empowering them in all their historic struggles.[40]

Jesus' disciples need not look for any other teacher or teaching, any fresh revelations or instructions, any supplementary energizings or powers above or beyond what they have in him, their Master, their Teacher, the Son of God. Easter means the ongoing life of the one teacher, Jesus, in the time of the church.

As long as the stars hold their place and sun rises and sun sets, as long as the seas rush in and out, as long as the heavens above and the earth below endure, they are well supplied, with gifts and teachings to suffice them, for he himself continues with them as Lord and Teacher with his word. His disciples have all they require—all the blessing and rescuing and also all the demands they need—for all the days right up to the last day at the close of the age.[41]

The horizon of his authority is the end, the judgment day and its final accounting.[42]

Summary: Exalted Teacher of the Church

Matthew has nothing but scorn for the notion that Jesus is still dead and buried. Grave-robbing had been suggested to account for the empty tomb, but he does not bother to dignify the rumor with a thoughtful response. He does have a tale of his own to tell on the priests and soldiers, but he contents himself basically with ridiculing the rumor.

Moderns may sometimes find themselves regretting the fact that Matthew did not attempt to argue for the Christian faith, did not support Christian conclusions with reasons, but instead responded with words dripping with irony. And yet, on the one hand, it must be remembered that arguments for the truth of the resurrection are curiously unsatisfying, and on the other hand, Matthew's interest lies elsewhere than in those attacks thrown in from outside.

Shunning arguments for the empty tomb, Matthew also does not merely retreat from reasonings to a lapidary announcement of the resurrection, proclaiming it on a take it or leave it basis. He does indeed remind his readers of their shared tradition. Matthew incorporates the entire Markan tradition on the resurrection of Jesus, including not only Mark's brief resurrection narrative (Mark 16:1-8) but also the raising of Jairus' daughter (Mark 5:21-43; Matt. 9:18 emphasizes that she was already dead when Jairus approached Jesus), the passion and resurrection predictions (Mark 8:31; 9:31; 10:33-34; Matt. 16:21; 17:22; 20:17-19), the transfiguration (Mark 9:2-9; Matt. 17:1-9), the word about the rejected stone chosen to be head of the corner (Mark 12:10-11; Matt. 21:33-46), the rebuke of Sadducees ignorant of Scripture and of the power of God (Mark 12:18-27; Matt. 22:23-33), the prophecy of drinking wine new in the kingdom of God (Mark 14:25; Matt. 26:29), and the promise of going before the disciples once again after the striking of the shepherd (Mark 14:28; Matt. 26:31). All these are reported with minor editorial changes in the same contexts as in Mark.

In the body of the gospel before the final chapter Matthew adds precious little to the Markan tradition on the subject of resurrection. In the conclusion to the peculiarly Matthean parable of the wheat and tares, Jesus comments that "the righteous will shine like the sun in the kingdom of their father" (13:43; cf. 8:12; 22:13), borrowing imagery from the ancient near eastern tradition of astral immortality which enters the biblical stream at Daniel 12:3 (cf. Ecclus. 50:7; Eth. Enoch 39:7; 104:2). So disciples are pictured as destined to be transfigured gloriously just as Jesus was (17:1-8; 28:3; Phil. 3:21). However, Matthew is not interested in these traditional images for their own sake, but employs them in order to encourage the disciples' life of righteousness.

The beatitudes reveal more directly the heart of Matthew's concern as he meditates upon the world to come: mourners will be comforted, the meek will inherit the earth, the merciful will obtain mercy, the pure in heart will see God, and those who hunger and thirst after righteousness will receive satisfaction (5:4, 5, 7, 6; cf. Luke 6:21).

In a curious Matthean passage Jesus speaks of Peter and the church and then shifts to a promise of ultimate victory for the community of disciples: "On this rock I will build my church, and the powers of death shall not prevail against it" (16:18). "The powers of death" (RSV) are more literally "the gates of hades." The dead were popularly pictured as entering the shadowy underworld through great gates opening to admit them into the realm of death but never swinging open to permit their return to life (cf. 11:23). In the context of the first passion prediction and the summons to his disciples to lose their life for his sake and so find it, this word of Jesus is an announcement of his singular and irresistible authority, a foreshadowing of the awesome declaration at the conclusion of the gospel, and an assurance to the church that even death has met its Master.

Both in 16:18-19 and 28:18 Jesus claims for himself the same authority ascribed to the awesome figure of the Apocalypse: " I have the keys of death and hades" (Rev. 1:18; cf. 3:7; Is. 22:22). On the other hand, the context of the saying in the Apocalypse is persecution and martyrdom, whereas Matthew is encouraging disciples to live in faith and walk in the way of righteousness (21:32) less as a reaction against persecution, though that too may be present, than as a reaction against the tendency to laxity and a cooling of love, accompanying their fascination with spiritual endowments.

The Matthean Jesus calls Peter a rock and gives him certain powers. Clearly the power is that inherent in the correct interpretation and transmission of the teaching of Jesus (cf. 23:13). Living in the power of that teaching and in the presence of its author (11:28-30; 18:20) the church is safe. Matthew presents Jesus as having power to guard his community of disciples even from the final storm at the end of the world (7:24-27; cf. Luke 6:47-49; Matt. 8:23-27). Death has no power over the church of the resurrected Lord.

For Matthew, the resurrection of Jesus is the grand and climactic miracle at the end of the time of expectation and yearning, capping all his other great deeds on behalf of his people. His resurrection belongs to the last things. It is final in the sense that it is God's ultimate verdict rendered on Jesus as his agent for establishing his kingship, and it is the deed by which the powers of this present age are shaken and the new world begins to dawn.

And yet, Matthew does not isolate the resurrection and sunder it from the crucifixion, nor does he deal with these final events apart from all that preceded, but together they hold a kind of preeminence. Matthew alone has reported (27:51b-53) that at the moment of the crucifixion an earthquake (28:2; 8:24; 24:7) shook the land splitting the rocks and opening tombs, so that death yielded up some prisoners in a bizarre—and still only partial—fulfillment of Jesus's word to Peter at Caesarea Philippi (16:18). Many sleeping saints, raised from their slumbers, left their tombs, entered the city after Jesus' resurrection, and showed themselves to many. The report is offered as evidence of the cosmic significance and decisive character of Jesus' death and resurrection. Good Friday and Easter together, not either one in isolation from the other, constitute God's action inaugurating the new age and the rule of the Messiah. The power of death and evil (and of the evil one, 4:1-11; 6:13) begins to be overcome and the rule of God, integrally connected with righteousness and life (6:33; 19:16; 25:31-46), begins to dawn.

The shocks generated by the cross and resurrection effect changes not only in the heavens and under the earth but also on the earth. For Matthew, Jesus' death and resurrection signal the opening of a new age in world history. For him the rejection of Jesus in Jerusalem closes the book on the special privileges of "the lost sheep of the house of Israel" (10:6; 15:24).

The crucifixion was an act of surly disobedience on the part of people who resembled that son whose "yes" to his father's call was quick, but whose doing of the father's will was deficient or even non-existent (21:28-32). It was a rebellious and murderous deed like that of the tenant farmers denying to the master the fruits of his vineyard (21:43).

The work of Jesus roused stiff opposition from the first, when Herod's soldiers sought to take the child's life (2:16). And at last the inhabitants of Jerusalem assumed dread responsibility for his crucifixion (27:25) and denied his resurrection (28:15).

His death and resurrection close one age and open another. Matthew has no interest in promoting a displacement theory with the Jews totally cut off and the Gentiles elected to be the new people of God. He is not simple-mindedly anti-Jewish on the one hand, nor is he naively pro-Gentile on the other. While no Gentile bias marks his work, the author does exhibit a universalist perspective according to which Jesus is the son of Abraham (1:1), the one in whom the promise of universal blessing has been fulfilled (Gen. 12:1-3; Gal. 3:8, 29). Many are coming from east and west to sit at table with Abraham and Isaac and Jacob (Matt. 8:11). Particularistic restrictions against the inclusion of Gentiles in the household of God (10:5-6; 15:24) have been removed by his death and resurrection.

The house of Israel, the city of Jerusalem, and the splendid temple are revealed as having forfeited their ancient advantage, and the eleven are summoned on the mountain in Galilee to "make disciples of all nations" (28:19).

The gospel of the kingdom is to be proclaimed in the time before the end "in all the world as a witness to all people" (24:14). True Israel, the eschatological people of God, is in the process of emerging, formed out of believing and confessing people who are marked by the bringing forth of fruit. The old distinction between Jew and Gentile has lost its significance.

So his death and resurrection work a decisive turn in the history of salvation or a broadening, a great inclusive widening.

When " all the nations" are gathered before the throne of the Son of Man (25:31), they will be judged not on the grounds of national origin or religious tradition or pneumatic endowment but on the basis of their deeds. "The righteous," those of every race, nation and heritage, who have been disciples in deed and have walked in the way of righteousness, will enter the kingdom prepared for them from the foundation of the world (25:31-46).

Matthew knows that Christians—presumably quite orthodox Christians in terms of their confession of the resurrection event and their rejection of the slander of graverobbing—have their own peculiar difficulties with Jesus' resurrection. They found it easy to extol the mighty deeds of God including especially Jesus' resurrection by which he opened the new age, but, exulting in the powers of that new age, they also found it easy to neglect the call to discipleship and the way of righteousness.

As Matthew narrates the events surrounding Easter, he makes it clear that the central fact of Easter cannot be reduced to the phrase "the resurrection." People are not being called to believe in "the resurrection" but in "the resurrected Jesus."

But who is this resurrected Jesus? How does Matthew describe him? He is no cipher. Matthew sketches his essential features with a few swift strokes of his pen. Stated most provocatively, Matthew identifies the resurrected Jesus as the Teacher of the Sermon on the

Mount. For Matthew the resurrection means the vindication of that Teacher and his teaching. That may seem too narrow and reductionist, but if so, then it might be said that the resurrected Jesus is simply the one who spoke all the words and performed all the deeds and endured all the sufferings recorded of him in the preceding 27 chapters. For his part Matthew does focus in the final paragraph of his gospel on all that Jesus "commanded," and in the gospel, from beginning to end, Jesus is the Son and the Teacher. As Son he himself trusted and obeyed, and the sum and substance of his teaching was the kingship of God and the will of God. Jesus is, for Matthew, the messianic interpreter of the Torah, the will of God. The kingdom dawns where he becomes Lord, wherever people in faith take his yoke upon themselves (11:29).

Just as there is one Father, who is in heaven, so Christians have one master *(kathēgētēs)* and one teacher *(didaskalos)*, namely Jesus, who by virtue of his resurrection lives and is present in the midst of the church. That resurrected Jesus—teacher, Son, Lord—is Matthew's fulcrum, or his place to stand, as he deals with issues in his community and assesses tendencies in the church.

Matthew uses the Easter traditions to attack both the appeal to the letter and the appeal to the spirit. What are the signs and evidences of the blessed presence of God in the midst of human life? Who are the people of God and what are their essential marks? Where is the light of the dawning of the new age?

The essential mark of the people of God and sure sign of the dawning kingdom of God is not height of ecstasy, not splendor of cult, not rigor of legalism (possession and external observance of Torah), certainly not antinomianism, not an unbroken line of authoritative teachers or successors of Jesus (whether a chain of the relatives of Jesus in some kind of Christian caliphate or a series of teachers among whom Peter might count as first and chief rabbi interpreting the teaching of Jesus, Matt. 16:16-19; 18:15-18).

Matthew declares that discipleship is the one infallible mark of the presence of God and the kingdom of God. When people take upon themselves the yoke of Jesus, then God is praised as king and his will is done on earth as it is in heaven.

God has raised from the dead the teacher of the Sermon on the Mount. There is and there need be no other Lord than that one, no other teacher or master, no other guide for life and teaching, no other court of appeal.

luke

The Setting:
Roman Power and the Lordship of Christ

The third gospel and the book of Acts constitute the carefully planned work of a single, far-seeing author, and because of their manifest unity these two books commonly bear the handy designation "Luke-Acts" in modern discussion.

Questions outnumber answers regarding the place of writing. Ancient tradition offers no real help, but various clues lead some moderns to conclude that Luke-Acts was written near the center of the empire and close to the Western reaches of the early church, perhaps in Greece or even in Rome.

Luke sets the events of the life of John the Baptist, Jesus, and the church into a Roman chronological framework (2:1-2; 3:1-2), even though Sabbath, Passover, Pentecost, and the day of atonement also continue to be reference points to the very end (e.g. Acts 20:6, 16; 27:9).

Luke is the only New Testament writer who mentions a Roman emperor by name. He speaks of Augustus (2:1) and Tiberius (3:1) in the Gospel and of Claudius in Acts (18:2). Furthermore he refers to Nero (to whom Paul appealed) not by name but by three of his most characteristic titles: caesar, augustus, and lord (*kaisar, sebastos, kyrios:* Acts 25:8, 21, 26).[1]

Luke names with a stunning accuracy the titles of a whole array of officials of the towns, cities and provinces of the empire. He writes

93

with an insider's knowledge of the powers of Roman governors (whether proconsul, imperial legate, imperial procurator, or prefect) and magistrates in dealing with Roman citizens and with the native populations of their varied jurisdictions in civil and criminal cases, and he is in command of technical detail relating to Roman justice (crimes defined by statute and those falling outside the written letter of the law, change of venue, right of appeal, and rules of evidence).[2]

Luke took pride in Paul's Roman citizenship and was not at all embarrassed to portray Paul as invoking its protection and employing its benefits and privileges (Acts 16:37-39; 22:25-29; 23:27; 25:11-12; 26:32).

This does not mean that Luke was a citizen of Rome, but his consciousness was shaped and informed by the Roman reality. He writes with a kind of automatic presumption that the Roman empire with its system of government, its laws and officials, its cities and roads and sailing vessels, both is and will continue to be the context of the life of the church. Rome does not represent a demonic force marked for destruction (as in the book of Revelation) but is taken for granted as the environment in which the church is called to live.

The Lukan writings stand in marked contrast to the Johannine. John thinks of the world as a dark power allied with falsehood and death. For John the truth and the lie, the spirit and the flesh, Christ and the world are mortal enemies locked in combat. Luke wants rather to prepare the church for the long haul in the world and through history, and thinks the church does and must live responsibly in the world and under the Roman power that rules the world.

In this and other respects Luke-Acts resembles other early Christian literature associated with Rome and the west: Romans (ca. A.D. 55), the Gospel According to Mark (ca. A.D. 65-72), Hebrews (ca. A.D. 80), 1 Clement (ca. A.D. 96), 2 Clement (ca. A.D. 130), the Shepherd of Hermas (ca. A.D. 110-140). All these writings attempt to come to terms both with Roman hegemony and with the ongoing history of the world in a positive fashion. In spite of sporadic, popular, and sometimes officially sanctioned persecution of the church by Rome and her citizens, the authors of these writings perceive the relations between church and world as at least potentially harmonious.

Luke's mind does not operate in terms of sharply antagonistic positions. Trusting in the wise and omnipotent providence of God in history, he is inclined to be more positive than negative, more constructive than critical, designing harmonious mosaics out of disparate fragments. He stresses, especially in Acts, that the Pharisees believe in the resurrection, in spirits, and angels, and so are forerunners of the Christians rather than sinister opponents. The Jewish people as a whole looked with favor upon Jesus. The plot against Jesus was the scheme of the leaders, and even they acted in ignorance. The city of Athens may be full of idols but yet, without knowing his name, the Greeks worship the one true God and need only gentle leading and further enlightening. As Christ is the fulfillment of the promises of all the prophets, so Christianity is the fulfillment of Jewish and Greek piety. All human piety is preparation (rather than as in Paul the basis of obstinate self-assertion, the ground of striving for divine recognition and status in our own eyes), and every good and pious person in whatever nation is acceptable to God (Acts 10:34-35).

The style of Christianity exhibited in Luke-Acts (and in other early Christian writings associated with Rome) is neither mystic nor enthusiastic but is practical and pastoral. Oriented to history in a positive fashion, the outlook is free of gnostic, docetic or dualistic taint. Indeed, Luke views with dismay fanatical otherworldliness, whether it manifests itself as quietistic withdrawal from society or as revolution and zealotism. The positive themes of repentence and forgiveness on the one hand, and of a pious, obedient life on the other, come to the fore in Luke as in the other early Christian writings associated with Rome.[3]

A couple of subsidiary arguments for Roman or Western provenance may be mentioned. Some regard Luke's knowledge of Palestinian geography as so obviously deficient that he could not possibly have had any firsthand experience of the land. Whether or not that is so, it does seem that he looks eastward out across the Mediterranean and views Palestine from a distance. By no means is Palestine the navel of the universe for him. It seems to have shrunk in size and significance and for Luke the familiar body of water in Galilee is no "sea" but only a "lake."[4]

Furthermore, when he speaks of the cities and towns of the eastern Mediterranean, Luke frequently writes as though his readers require aid in locating them: "a city of Galilee named Nazareth," "Perga in Pamphylia," "Philippi which is the leading city of the district of Macedonia," "Myra in Cilicia." But he simply names as known and familiar such places in the West as Syracuse, Rhegium, Puteoli, the Forum of Appius and Three Taverns (Acts 28).[5]

Luke's view of the progress of the gospel is not that it fanned out or spread in concentric circles in all directions from Jerusalem but that the gospel ran from Jerusalem to Rome. He hides whatever he may know about progress to any other point of the compass. As Isaiah had seen a prophetic vision of a great future highway to be constructed by God himself, stretching from Babylonian captivity to Jerusalem and freedom, so Luke had a retrospective vision of another highway laid by God from Jerusalem to Rome. The news of Jesus' resurrection had risen like the sun in the east and traveled westward across the water to the capital of the world.[6]

Luke pondered the divine design he perceived woven into the gospel's eastern origin and its Roman, western destiny. If Luke-Acts was not written in Rome, it certainly was composed by an author deeply concerned about the relations between the Christian movement and Roman power.

The Purpose of Luke-Acts

The 52 chapters of Luke-Acts constitute about 27% of the New Testament, and one thing that means is that Luke has written a greater portion of the New Testament than any other single author. It is rich and varied, and without doubt Luke was involved at many levels with several issues. Almost everyone recognizes the reductionist error of imagining that Luke had only one simple motive or purpose in writing.[7]

Luke's work in whole or in part has been used to support the conclusion that he desired to do one or more of the following: write the climax to the history of God's people narrated in the Old Testament, preserve the early Christian tradition, add to Mark his other sources, continue the gospel-like narrative to the end of the life of Paul, describe the past, defend the community against the inroads of false teachers and false doctrines, encourage the truth in teaching and goodness in life, promote charity, combat misunderstandings, compose differences within the church, resolve questions concerning Christian hope raised by apocalyptic fervor or its waning, proclaim Jesus as Lord of all, promote admiration for Paul, stimulate the universal outreach of the church and its inclusion of Gentiles, provide Gentile-Christians especially with a sense of the providence of God, praise God for his own (Luke's) salvation and inclusion among God's people, encourage Christians in their confusions and tribulations by recounting the past triumphs of the word, defend Christians from Roman suspicions and commend the Christian gospel to Roman curiosity.[8] These are only some of the best known and most plausible of the suggestions made about Luke's intentions, and of course these need not be mutually exclusive.

Interpreters have ascribed widely differing aims to the author.[9] Nevertheless, any reading of Luke-Acts reveals that the author has written a tale of two cities and of two or more generations, and in what follows it will be assumed that Luke's treatment of the resurrection traditions is aimed especially—although not exclusively, to be sure—at confessing and clarifying Jesus' lordship both spatially (over those two cities and all they signify) and temporally (from generation to generation).[10]

Luke worried about Roman suspicions and misunderstandings of the church, and about radical Christian misconstruing of the lordship of Jesus. He was, furthermore, concerned about false teachers and leaders within the churches of his generation and about the rise of impiety, venality, and superstition among his contemporaries.

The Cities

Luke has an urban bias and he rehearses the movements of Christian missionaries through numerous cities, but he has meditated especially on the significance of Jerusalem and Rome and on the relationship of the Christian gospel and community to those two great centers. Jerusalem and Rome, even when they are off stage, exert a powerful magnetic pull in his narrative so that all the action in the gospel tends toward Jerusalem and the entire movement in Acts climaxes in Rome.

The fact that Luke focuses so intently on that movement towards Jerusalem and then towards Rome is not the result of any merely antiquarian passion for reconstructing the past. Jerusalem was the city toward which Jesus set his face (Luke 9:51). Necessity was laid on him to go there (13:33; 18:31). Then in his Easter narrative Luke has suppressed Mark's mention of a postresurrection march to Galilee (Mark 16:7) in order to picture the apostles' remaining in Jerusalem from Palm Sunday through Good Friday and Easter to Ascension and Pentecost and beyond at the command of Jesus (Luke 24:49; Acts 1:4; 8:1).

Nor may the fact that Luke-Acts concludes in Rome be taken for granted as simple historical reporting. Paul's goal, according to his own testimony, was Spain (Rom. 15:19-28). He had finished his work in the east and was heading west. Rome was not the end of his journeying, but was to serve him as launching platform for work to the west, as Syrian Antioch had served him during his labors in the eastern Mediterranean.

In Acts there is no hint that Paul was aiming at Spain. Rome, rather than being a staging area for forays westward, is itself the great goal toward which the action tends. Rome represents "the end of the earth" of Jesus' commission (Acts 1:8). It is the city Paul "must" reach (19:21; 23:11; 27:24). Rome is for Luke the prophesied and destined goal.

So Luke's sharp focus on Jerusalem and Rome is to a certain extent artificial, in the sense of artful and deliberate. For Luke, Jerusalem and Rome were more than major capital cities. Each was symbol of ancient exertions and traditions, each the focus of religious and political authority, of physical and metaphysical powers, of deep faith and hope.

Jerusalem was the holy city, home of priest and sage and prophet, goal of pilgrims, beloved daughter of Zion, place of David's throne and David's tomb (Luke 1:32; Acts 2:29), the keeper of the great temple whence the odor of incense and the smoke of offerings rose daily to God. Zechariah served there (Luke 1:8). Simeon and Anna waited there (2:25, 36). The infant Jesus was presented there (1:22; Acts 21:26), and the 12-year-old Jesus impressed the doctors of the law there (2:41-52). In his last days Jesus taught there daily (21:37; cf. Acts 3:12). It was the hub of earliest Christian activity (24:52-53; Acts 2:46), and Paul in Acts returned regularly to Jerusalem and the temple.

Rome was the first city of the empire, the residence of emperor and senate, seat of power, home of entrepreneurs, hub of commerce and finance, and magnet for taxes. The great city had been founded anew by Augustus, who had established order at the center, secured the borders, and inaugurated a period of unprecedented peace and prosperity, celebrated in cult, art, and literature.

Luke wanted to speak of the lordship of Jesus over both Jerusalem and Rome, and desired to do so in such a way that both cities and the great traditions they enshrined would be affirmed rather than merely denied or despised.

From Jerusalem to Rome

Too often the progress to Jerusalem and then from Jerusalem to Rome is taken to signify the passing of the torch from Jew to Gentile, the rejection of the Jews and their displacement as chosen people by the Gentiles. But such a view is a miscalculation of Luke's intentions, which center on celebrating continuity rather than conflict.

However they may differ over the identity of the author of Luke-Acts, ancient and modern students have found common ground in judging him to have been a Gentile rather than a Jew, living in the context of a Gentile-Christian community, writing from the perspective of one born a pagan outsider and subsequently adopted into the people of God, so that he came to be of the house and lineage of Abraham and Isaac and Jacob.[11]

The author of Luke-Acts reviews the historical progress of the word of God and marvels at the way it has penetrated the Gentile world all the way to himself and to people like himself. Luke-Acts is the author's own canticle of wonder and praise at the generosity of the God who had crossed boundaries to reach and embrace him. He had been lost and was now found and alive (Luke 15:24, 32; 19:10). God's redemptive purpose was expressed not only in the life of Jesus at work in Palestine, but also in the continuing life of the church and especially in the progress of the gospel among Jews and then among non-Jews. Luke exhibits a sense of the providential ordering of his own life and circumstances and in the sweep of history which had conveyed the word to him. His book is the doxology of one born not a Jew but a Gentile, not near but far off (Acts 2:39).

Luke aims to portray not the rejection of the Jews or Judaism but the origins in the Jewish people and Jewish scriptures of a new and universal people of God. The word of God embraces in its progress first Jews, then Samaritans, and finally Gentiles (e.g. Acts 8:5-40; 10:1—11:18; 13:46-47; 15:17; 17:26-28; 22:21), restricted only by human ignorance and bondage to traditional prejudice. Luke insists—perhaps he had to—that God himself thrust a reluctant body of disciples across one boundary after another through angels, pneumatic outpourings, visions, and prophecies (Acts 8:17-26; 10:1—11:18; 13:2; 16:6-10; 18:9-11; 22:21).

Rome and the Church

Luke's record of the progress from Jerusalem to Rome is even more apology than doxology. Nothing was more obvious than the fact that Jesus had suffered crucifixion at the hands of Pontius Pilate in Jerusalem, and that Paul had been jailed repeatedly and was then ultimately executed in Rome. On the surface it might appear that the Christian endeavor was inevitably, deservedly and tragically at odds with Roman imperial power. Christian insiders may have interpreted the claims of God's kingship as a call to overthrow the existing political order or to pray for its overthrow by God, and pagan outsiders may have been alarmed at all the Christian rhetoric about Lord and lordship, King and a kingdom, power and an eternal throne, putting down the mighty and exalting the lowly, and a final day of reckoning preceded by wars in a period of civil and cosmic disorders.

Luke's reiteration of the charges leveled against Christian figures throughout Luke-Acts and his examination of the grounds for those accusations seems to indicate that he was not simply setting straight the ancient record, but was addressing issues vital to his Christian and pagan contemporaries. The Christian movement of Luke's day was suspected of religious, moral, and political wrongdoing.

Jesus had himself been rejected as a political revolutionary threatening the peace of the city and empire (Luke 22:70-71; 23:1-5). The first Christians were tentatively compared with the rebel movements under Theudas and Judas (Acts 5:36-37). Stephen was charged with blasphemous speech against the Jewish temple and the law of Moses (Acts 6:11-14). At Philippi Paul was accused of disturbing the peace and advocating unlawful practices (16:20-21; cf. 18:13). At Thessalonica Christians were charged with fomenting political revolution, of acting against the decrees of Caesar, and of saying there is another king, namely Jesus (Acts 17:6-8). At Jerusalem the tribune thought Paul was the Egyptian who had recently stirred a revolt and led four thousand men of the assassins into the wilderness (21:38).

Luke works hard to show the groundlessness of the accusations of lawlessness and insurrection. He does not try to hush up the suspicions or ignore the allegations. Rather he features numerous trial scenes, scrutinizes the charges, and shows how magistrates and courts consistently returned verdicts of innocence or summarily dismissed the charges as patently fraudulent.[12]

Furthermore, Luke's portraits of Christian figures (and their predecessors like Zechariah and Elizabeth, Simeon and Anna) are studies in piety. They are blameless from the point of view of Jewish and Roman law.

Because of his apologetic intentions, Luke portrays Joseph in a manner quite different from the way Matthew does. Joseph is pictured as a law-abiding citizen of the great Roman empire, exemplary in his pious obedience to the decree of Caesar Augustus. At first, it seems surprising that Joseph did not travel to Bethlehem alone but was accompanied by Mary. What was the need of that? However, since she was with child (2:5), Luke is saying that Jesus himself traveled from Nazareth to Bethlehem as the decree required. There is in the scene no hint of rebellion, no odor of insurrection, not even a whisper of resentment at the length or hardship of the journey or at the prospect of taxation. Luke's Christmas story is full of peace and of civil obedience, and he follows it with scenes of pious obedience to ancient Jewish religious ordinances (2:21-52).[13]

Luke never misses an opportunity to focus on the piety of church life or the virtue of converts to the church (Luke 7:1-10; Acts 2:42-47; 4:32-37; 6:7; 10:1-2; 16:14; 17:4, 34), or on the misguided zeal, mercenary spirit, or downright nastiness of the opponents (Acts 12:1; 14:19; 16:19-21; 17:5; 19:23-27; 23:12-15; 24:26).

Luke desires to convince his readers that Christian missionary activity constitutes no danger to morals or to the tranquility of the state. In a comprehensive apology, Paul declared that he had not offended against the temple of God, the law of Moses, or the decrees of Caesar (Acts 25:8, 11; 28:19).

The growth of the Christian movement and the fact that it succeeded, against all odds and against all opposition, in arriving at Rome are for Luke signs that it is of God and enjoys his favor (Acts 5:39). More than that, the unhindered proclamation of Paul's gospel in Rome is Luke's way of announcing that Jesus is now enthroned in his word over Jerusalem and Rome and over all they stand for.

Luke enthusiastically accepted and repeated all the royal titles of Jesus and all the Christian talk about the kingdom of God. But as he proclaimed Jesus as Christ, Lord, and Son of God, eternal ruler over Jews and Gentiles, exalted to the right hand of God by resurrection and ascension, he was sensitive to the accusations and suspicions of his Roman contemporaries about Jesus' lordship. Luke emphatically rejected political apocalypticism, even as he rejected other forms of radicalism and enthusiasm.

He attempted to make it clear that the Christian movement is nothing like a Parthian invasion, and that it is incorrect to define it as a disruptive political movement or regard its leaders as dangerous agitators. It is true that Luke-Acts portrays the church as a kind of revolutionary movement. The coming of the kingship of Jesus entails the overturning of ordinary expectations and the transvaluation of values, and yet it is not the sort of ferment the Roman empire need fear. Uproars may punctuate the progress of the church in its march from Jerusalem through Syria, Asia Minor, and Greece toward Rome, but the movement is no dagger aimed at the heart of the empire. It is working neither to topple it violently nor even to undermine it quietly. Jesus is Lord and a kingdom is coming, but Luke believed the church could and should coexist peacefully with empire and emperor. In his vocabulary "power" is a synonym for "Holy Spirit." That is the power

Jesus promised his followers, and it alone is the power Luke cherishes for his readers.

The mass of political apologetic in Luke-Acts has led interpreters from time to time to suggest that Luke composed his two volumes as a kind of lawyer's brief to be entered on Paul's behalf at his trial before the tribunal of Caesar. Such a theory requires an impossibly early date for Luke-Acts and the sources behind them, and fails to account for page after page of material irrelevant to any judge in such a case. What is right about the theory is the perception of political argument in the author's book. One of Luke's purposes from beginning to end is to define for Christian insiders and for pagan outsiders the nature of Jesus' lordship and the kingship of God.

The Generations

Luke belonged to the third generation. In the preface to Luke-Acts (Luke 1:1-4) the author reveals that he stood not among the men and women of Jesus' own generation, eyewitnesses of his deeds and sufferings, and not even among the first writers to receive word from the eyewitnesses, but among the following rank of believers and reporters. He and his contemporaries were third generation Christians, and the Christian fellowship of his day was suffering from the circulation inside the church of false, inadequate, or misleading reports concerning Jesus and the Christian message.

Confronted by false witnesses, the author advertised his own accuracy and the dependability of his report, based on the ready availability of reliable testimony.

The forecasts in Paul's farewell sermon to the Ephesian elders (Acts 20:18-35) may reflect the conditions prevailing in Luke's own day: "fierce wolves will come in among you, not sparing the flock; and from among your own selves will arise men speaking perverse things, to draw away the disciples after them" (20:29-30). It is not possible to specify just exactly what perverse things Paul and Luke had in mind.

In part because the language of Paul's sermon to the Ephesian elders at Miletus resembles that of the Pastorals, and in part because the book of Revelation seems to testify to the inroads of gnosticizing teaching in the areas including Miletus and Ephesus around the end of the first century, many have identified the opposition Luke has in view as gnostic.[14] However, the sermon aims primarily to encourage sincerity and a spirit of selflessness in church leaders together with fidelity to the Lukan-Pauline tradition in a time of confusion.[15]

In his preface to his two volume work (Luke 1:1-4)[16] Luke expresses his hope that his readers come to know "the truth" *(asphaleia)* concerning the things of which they had been informed. He not only desired to tell the truth and to present the facts about Jesus and the kingdom of God in an era disturbed by conflicting accounts, inadequate reports, and perverse assertions, but he insisted that it was perfectly possible for a writer of his generation and place to know and to speak that truth.

The preface is only the first of many passages describing a chain of witnesses linking Luke and his contemporaries with the first Christian generation and with Jesus himself. Luke did not claim a special gift of revelation from the Holy Spirit, although a very few ancient manuscripts have him doing just that since they add the words "and to the Holy Spirit" after the phrase "seemed good to me" (Luke 1:3).

In support of his accurate knowledge Luke pointed to rather more ordinary and perhaps less spectacular credentials. He had "followed all things closely for some time past." Luke may be referring to research and reading but he is probably invoking his own personal involvement and experience. Luke, of course, would be the last one to separate verbal testimony and the Spirit's working. In Luke-Acts the Spirit's chief work is precisely the empowering and provoking of witnesses to bear testimony with boldness of speech.

The ego of the author, emerging briefly and tantalizingly from the wings in the preface, quickly recedes only to step forth again not only at Acts 1:1 but also in the "we-sections" (Acts 16:10-17; 20:5-16; 21:1-18; 27:1—28:16).[17]

The impression gained from the prefaces and the we-sections is that the author did indeed participate in some of the events of which he writes. He was a companion of Paul, who outlived Paul, and saw the fulfillment of Paul's prophecy that falsehoods and perverse teachings, inside as well as outside, would confuse and threaten the flock. He regarded himself not only as Paul's admirer, but as in a sense his successor and his spokesman against the errors disturbing the church. He is himself a "servant of the word" working in the tradition of Paul and his predecessors, and his book summons his contemporaries to proclaim Jesus and the kingdom in the same way that he does.

A large pattern is discernible in the narratives of Luke-Acts: a person or group is called and empowered by the Spirit, proclaims the good news, performs signs and wonders, confronts opposition, meets with fellow Christians in solemn assembly, suffers humiliation at the hands of enemies, and experiences divine rescue. This pattern is repeated in the case of Jesus (the Gospel of Luke), the Twelve (Acts 1-5), the Seven (6-8), Peter (9-12), and Paul (three or four cycles in Acts 13-28). The sections are skillfully interwoven, so that Paul, for example, is introduced already at the end of Acts 7, called in Chapter 9, and active in Chapter 11, even though his own story does not begin in earnest until Chapter 13.[18]

The shaping of the material signals something more than a biographical interest in the great personalities of the church's early days. Luke has expended considerable energy and ingenuity on the parallels among the chief actors of his story in order to encode a message about continuity through the generations: the Lord works providentially in each succeeding epoch as in the past. Paul (and the same is true of Luke and of his entire generation) was separated from Jesus and the eyewitnesses by a great gulf, but it was not unbridgeable.

The exalted Jesus binds generation to preceding generation by appearing in vision and audition, calling prophets or witnesses, bestowing the Spirit, confirming the proclamation by signs and wonders, empowering them in their Christian assemblies, and vindicating or rescuing them in the face of opposition.

Luke's work is both an argument defending the presence and availability of accurate testimony, and a digest of that correct teaching and proclamation. Luke advocates contact with Jesus not in mystical flight or gnosticism on the one hand, nor in crass institutionalism or traditionalism on the other. The exalted Jesus was himself prophet and teacher, and he sent prophets and teachers. The book of Acts is testimony, not to Luke's historicizing of the revelation, but to Luke's conviction that the word of the Lord continues to sound forth in the mouths of Christian witnesses in spite of the lapse of time and in spite of the distance in miles or culture.

Luke's careful patternings, his neat parallels and linkings, and his production of a continuation to the gospel, indicate his concern for the malaise and urgent questionings of his time: How are chronologically later generations connected with Jesus, the kingdom and salvation? Has the divine power and presence faded in time? Do later Christians suffer nearly fatal disadvantages in comparison with the first Christians? Where can contemporaries turn for the truth in the midst of conflicting reports and interpretations?

Luke has answered that there is a sure word from the Lord because the resurrected Jesus himself appeared to chosen witnesses and fully indoctrinated them (Luke 24; Acts 1). He bestowed on them the

Holy Spirit, so that they acted and spoke as his successors, just as Elisha went forth in the spirit and power of Elijah. Those apostolic successors are pictured as standing in their turn in direct continuity with still later witnesses. In an age disturbed by claims and counterclaims, Luke asserts that those of his contemporaries who stand with him in the tradition of Paul and Peter and the Seven and the Twelve are linked securely to Jesus. Thus they are the ones who have certainty and know the truth of the instruction they have received (Luke 1:4).

In his use of the traditions of Jesus' resurrection, Luke meditated upon the fact that the word of God had arrived in the heart of the empire with its power and its claim concerning the lordship of Jesus and the kingship of God, and he confronted confusion in the church regarding generation gaps and norms of Christian teaching. Luke has dealt with issues of the ecumenicity of the church in space and time, its mission and vocation, the claims of God and Caesar, the sources of the church's life, and the truth of its proclamation.

Luke 24 divides into its subsections naturally enough:[19]

24:1-11(12)	Angels at the tomb
24:13-35	On the Way to Emmaus
24:36-53	Farewell
	(a) Appearance at Table in Jerusalem (36-43)
	(b) Final Words and Commissioning (44-49)
	(c) Blessing and Departure near Bethany (50-53)

All the events of Luke 24 are embraced within the span of a single day (see the references to time in 24:1, 13, 33), and all run their course within the orbit of a single place, namely Jerusalem and its immediate environs.

Besides weaving the events together against a uniform background of time and space, Luke has employed a number of other readily apparent literary devices to link one part of the chapter to another and to connect this final chapter of the gospel to the rest of his story.

The women's discovery (24:1-11) is recapped in a flashback at verses 22 and 23, and verse 24 refers back to the visit by Peter (24:12) or others to the tomb. Cleopas and his companion return from Emmaus to Jerusalem, carrying the reader along with them to the next scene, in which Jesus appears to the eleven. Furthermore, the teaching Jesus conveyed to the Emmaus disciples (25-27) is repeated in verses 44-46.

Both the angel (24:6) and then Jesus himself (24:44) reiterate what Jesus had said previously during his ministry in Galilee. The women were told to remember (24:6) and they did (24:8).

The third section of the chapter, recounting Jesus' appearance to the eleven and his commissioning of them (24:36-49), prepares for the life of the church described in the book of Acts. The departure near Bethany, so tersely reported in 24:50-53, is expanded in the account of Jesus' ascension in the first chapter of Acts, and links the close of the gospel with the opening of Acts.

Luke 23:56b — 24:12: Angels at the Tomb

Luke 23:56b — 24:12   On the sabbath they rested according to the commandment.
¹But on the first day of the week, at early dawn, they went to the tomb, taking the spices which they had prepared. ²And they found the stone rolled away from the tomb, ³but when they went in they did not find the body. ⁴While they were perplexed about this, behold, two men stood by them in dazzling apparel; ⁵and as they were frightened and bowed their faces to the ground, the men said to them, "Why do you seek the living among the dead? ⁶Remember how he told you, while he was still in Galilee, ⁷that the Son of man must be delivered into the hands of sinful men, and be crucified, and on the third day rise." ⁸And they remembered his words, ⁹and returning from the tomb they told all this to the eleven and to all the rest. ¹⁰Now it was Mary Magdalene and Jo-anna and Mary the mother of James and the other women with them who told this to the apostles; ¹¹but these words seemed to them an idle tale, and they did not believe them. ¹²But Peter rose and ran to the tomb; stooping and looking in, he saw the linen cloths by themselves; and he went home wondering at what had happened.

As he edits and reworks Mark's account of the events at the tomb on Easter morning (Mark 16:1-8), Luke stresses the piety of Jesus' followers, the centrality of Jerusalem, the cross as divinely ordained and necessary prelude to Jesus' glory, and the natural human resistance to belief in the resurrection.

23:53b   The English chapter division cuts straight through a single Greek sentence, assigning the first part to Chapter 23 and the second to Chapter 24. But the words of 23:53b are an integral part of Luke's portrait of the women and indeed of the early Christian community generally. With a few quick strokes of the pen Luke depicts the piety and godliness of the women. They were like Zechariah and Elizabeth, "righteous before God, walking in all the commandments and ordinances of the Lord blameless" (1:6).

24:1   On Sunday morning after the Sabbath pause, the women went to the tomb in the last watch of the night just before dawn.[20]

Unlike Matthew and John, Luke follows Mark in ascribing to the women the intention of anointing Jesus' body with spices and ointments (23:56). Anointing a corpse on the Sabbath itself would not have constituted an infraction of the law (M. Shabbath 23:4, 5), but Luke recounts the basic story in Mark's terms and finds in their Sabbath rest an indication of special piety exceeding any legal demand (cf. Acts 8:2; Tobit 1:17-19).

24:2-3   Some ancient manuscripts add the phrase "of the Lord Jesus" to the end of this sentence, and that additional phrase is Lukan in style and may well be original.[21] Luke has Peter call Jesus "Lord" in 5:8 and he himself speaks of Jesus as Lord in editorial sections.[22]

The stone, such a problem in Mark's account, is passed over quickly by Luke in his brief sentence of discovery. The women did find the stone rolled away, but they did not find the corpse. They found what they did not expect, and they failed to find what they had anticipated.

The quest of the women is prefigured in the account of the disappearance of the 12-year-old Jesus and his subsequent discovery in the temple after three days by his parents (2:41-52).[23] The resurrection of Jesus is for Luke the central affirmation and fact of the Christian community, and the resurrection has left its impress on a number of traditions of the prior life and ministry of Jesus. Examples are noted below in the summary section.

24:4   The women are like Zechariah and Elizabeth not only in piety, but also in the way they were impressed by the weight of physical and historical facts and troubled at first by God's intervention. Their expectation of finding the corpse and intention of anointing it were rudely contradicted, and the women were plunged into puzzlement *(aporia)*.

This is the first in a series of descriptions in this chapter of the inner disposition of Jesus' followers. One of Luke's chief concerns is to trace the odyssey of the first Christians from sorrow to joy, from perplexity to understanding, from unbelief to faith.

As the women stood perplexed within the tomb, two figures suddenly appeared to them.[24] They are there like a flash of lightning (9:29; Acts 9:3; 22:6; cf. Luke 10:18), clothed brilliantly (Acts 1:10; 10:30; 2 Macc. 3:26), and the language indicates that Luke connects transfiguration, resurrection, and ascension. The flashback reference in the Emmaus conversation (verse 23) will remove any doubt that Luke means angels.

That there are two figures, not one as in Mark and Matthew, emphasizes the reliability and adequacy of their message. It is established in legal fashion in the mouth of two or three witnesses (Deut. 17:6; 19:15; cf. John 8:17), just as Moses and Elijah bore witness to Jesus at the mount (9:28-36), as the disciples went out witnessing in pairs (10:1), and as the two messengers spoke at the ascension of Jesus' lordship and return (Acts 1:10).[25] The two angels in John's account of Easter function quite differently (John 20:12).

24:5   Awestruck (24:37; Acts 10:4; 24:25), the women averted their faces and prostrated themselves before the heavenly messengers (cf. Acts 9:4; Matt. 28:9-10; cf. Ezek. 1:28; Dan. 10:9, 15).

The question put to the women by the angels was designed to expose the inadequacy and indeed the faithlessness of their behavior, as pious as their intention to anoint him certainly was. In similar words the prophet Isaiah had mocked the people who visited witches and mediums in an effort to contact the departed concerning the will of God: "Should they consult the dead on behalf of the living?" (Isa. 8:19). According to rabbinic tradition Moses and Aaron had mocked Pharaoh: "You fool! Does one seek the dead among the living or the living among the dead?"[26]

Luke's central testimony is that Jesus lives (24:23; cf. 15:32; Acts 4:2; 17:18). Martyred, he is dead no longer but now reigns in paradise (23:43), has entered into his glory (24:26), has gone through the portal of death into the kingdom of God (Acts 14:22). He lives triumphant from the grave and is therefore both alive and the source of life or leader to life (*archēgos tēs zōēs*, Acts 3:15).[27] But the affirmations regarding Jesus are unfolded gradually. Luke first establishes the fact that he is alive and ridicules the notion that he can be found in a cemetery.[28] Where Jesus is and how he lives or how he now interacts as the living one with the community of disciples are large questions which he does not yet address in this paragraph.

24:6a   The words, "He is not here but has risen," found in some ancient manuscripts, are nearly identical with Mark 16:6 and Matt. 28:6 and appear to be a later, post-Lukan insertion into the text designed to bring the angels' words in Matthew, Mark, and Luke into closer harmony.

24:6b-7   The angels speak like a pair of schoolteachers rehearsing a lesson, but the lesson is taught in words that are characteristically Lukan and diverge from Mark considerably. Jesus had be-

gun his public ministry in Galilee and had gathered his first followers
there (23:49; Acts 13:31). From the very beginning Jesus had encountered opposition there (4:16-30), reckoned with it, and interpreted it
for himself and his followers in the light of Scripture.

The description of the Son of man betrayed into the hands of men
is poignant (cf. 9:44). The use of the active verb "rise" (*anastēnai*, aorist active infinitive) is unusual. The more ordinary picture is that of
Jesus acted upon in the resurrection by the power of the heavenly
Father.

But the heart of this summary of the career of Jesus is the word
"must" *(dei)*. The word is found in Mark (Luke's source) on one important occasion (8:31) but it is used so many times in Luke and Acts that
it is practically Luke's possession and certainly it is his hallmark.[29]

No cold or heartless fate rules the affairs of earth, but history
proceeds rather according to the will of a good and gracious God who
has announced his intentions in Scripture and whose ways can be
found out by the trusting hearer. "Must" means the same as the
phrase in the primitive creed, "according to the Scriptures" (*kata tas
graphas*, 1 Cor. 15:3-4). Luke's convictions about God's providence run
deep, and his vocabulary is correspondingly rich as he speaks repeatedly of the will and word and counsel and plan of God.

Galilee is mentioned differently in Mark's version of the angel's
message. The women are there told that the disciples are to proceed
to Galilee. Both Matthew 28 and John 21 record appearances of the
resurrected Jesus in Galilee. But Luke most emphatically locates all
the appearances of the resurrected Jesus in and around Jerusalem,
suppressing the reference to any movement to Galilee. Indeed the
disciples are specifically instructed not to leave Jerusalem (24:49;
Acts 1:4).

24:8-9   The women had been with Jesus from Galilee (8:1-3) all
the way to the end (23:49), and they did "remember." Luke does not
say that they came to faith or believed, but is there any difference in
his mind? It would ruin the suspense and spoil the dramatic progress
of the chapter if Luke placed any stress on their faith so early in his
recital.

Luke's view is that God has shaped the history of his people by his
words of promise and by his deeds of visitation. He has acted and he
will act. Remembering his past utterances, counting on his promises,
and taking him at his word are all part and parcel of living as his sons
and daughters. Luke theologizes by telling the story, calling to mind
the past, and declaring the mighty acts of God on behalf of his people.

For him the Old Testament is not a book of law or a set of legal prece-
dents but a great, unfinished historical narrative, a movement
rushing to a climax, as the sermons in the book of Acts clearly demonstrate. His theology takes the form of confessional narrative or doxo-
logical report.

The women returned from the tomb and announced the capstone
of all God's deeds to the eleven and the others. For Luke the eleven
constitute a definite group within the larger body of disciples. They
alone are "the apostles" (v. 10). But the apostles are not alone (see 10:1;
23:49; Acts 1:14, 21).

The talk about Galilee and memory looks back in time, while the
reference to the eleven and the wider circle of followers is preparing
for a new stage of history in the immediate future.

24:10   Mary Magdalene is the one woman reported by all four
gospels as having been at the tomb on Easter morning. Joanna is
named with Mary Magdalene in 8:2-3 as an early follower of Jesus. In
that passage Joanna is described as the wife of Chuza, administrator
(see Matt. 20:8) in the employ of Herod Antipas. Luke also knows another and higher ranking official of Herod's court, namely Manaen
(Acts 13:1). Mark in his Easter narrative mentions Mary Magdalene,
Salome, and a Mary whom he describes variously as "the mother of
James and Joses" (15:40), "the mother of Joses" (15:47), and "the
mother of James" (16:1). John records that at the cross with the
mother of Jesus and Mary Magdalene there stood a "Mary the wife of
Clopas" (19:25). If John's Clopas and Luke's Cleopas (24:18) are the
same person, then Luke may have had reason to remember the name
of this Mary who was both "mother of James" and "wife of Clopas/
Cleopas."

Luke defines the Twelve or the eleven as apostles, chosen out of
the larger body of disciples (6:13-16). For him they constitute a fixed
body of first generation Christians, eyewitnesses, with unique status.
They are the first link in the chain connecting later generations to
Jesus by means of their testimony (cf. Luke 1:1-4). The qualifications
of an apostle are recited on the occasion of choosing a replacement for
Judas (Acts 1:21-22).

24:11   Luke has at least two interests in declaring that the
apostles discounted the women's report as foolishness or humbug[30]
and greeted it with disbelief. In the course of this chapter he means to
trace the difficulty attending the birth and growth of Christian faith
in the resurrected Jesus, and he is exploring the basis of Christian testimony to what he regards as the central affirmation of that faith.

Luke knows from the response of his contemporaries that the message of the resurrection runs counter to the wisdom of the world and the evidence of mind and senses (Acts 17:32; 26:8; cf. 2:12; 4:2). He is at pains to make it as clear as he possibly can that Easter faith is not a mindless conviction, easily achieved or lightly held, and it rests on something far more substantial than emotion, visions, or mere hearsay. He testifies that it arose in spite of the native inclination of the first generation to doubt the initial reports. It was forced upon them by the evidence and does not rest upon rumors of angels or idle chatter. The apostles were anything but gullible or quick to believe.

By emphasizing the perplexity of the women and the disbelief of the apostles and the others with them, Luke depicts those earliest Christians as unsentimental and hardheaded realists in need of proof before they would believe and proclaim the resurrection of Jesus from the dead. So he defends Easter faith and portrays the resurrection as worthy of a respectful hearing.

24:12   The verse obviously has some sort of relationship with the tradition of Peter's dash to the tomb together with the Beloved Disciple recorded in John 20:3-10. Some of the same words appear in both passages: Peter, ran, to the tomb, stooping and looking in, saw the linen cloths, went home.

It is difficult to imagine that this verse was written into Luke's gospel by a scribe working on the basis of John's report. He would have had to omit the Beloved Disciple, change the reaction from belief to amazement, and leave out the comment regarding knowing the Scriptures (a constant theme of Luke's in this chapter). On the other hand, it is easy enough to imagine John using a tradition found also in Luke and editing it to include the Beloved Disciple and the alacrity with which he came to faith.[31]

The fact that Luke's resurrection narrative, including verse 12, exhibits a number of parallels with the birth narrative in Chapter 2 may also argue for the authenticity of 24:12.

Birth	Resurrection
Shepherds went in haste (2:16)	Peter ran
They found the child lying (2:16)	He saw cloths lying
Swaddled in cloths (2:7, 12)	Linen cloths
Parents wondered (2:18; cf. 2:33)	Peter wondered
What had happened	What had happened

Furthermore, the manger (*phatnē*, 2:7, 12, 16) was probably cut out of rock and located in a cave as was the tomb of Jesus (23:53).

Beyond verse 12, the resurrection narrative seems to echo some elements of the birth narrative: an angel or angels appeared (*epestē/ epēstēsan*, 2:9, 13; 24:4), the names Mary and Joseph are prominent in both, and the people bearing those names shelter Jesus and care for him. The author himself marvels at the birth of Jesus and at his resurrection, at the beginning and the climax of his earthly life, at his entrance and his exit. Gregory of Nazianzus said that the one who was bound in swaddling cloths at birth was unbound at the resurrection.[32]

Nevertheless, the opening paragraph, with or without verse 12, ends on an inconclusive and incomplete note.

Luke 24:13-35: On the Way to Emmaus

Luke 24:13-35   [13]That very day two of them were going to a village named Emmaus, about seven miles from Jerusalem, [14]and talking with each other about all these things that had happened. [15]While they were talking and discussing together, Jesus himself drew near and went with them. [16]But their eyes were kept from recognizing him. [17]And he said to them, "What is this conversation which you are holding with each other as you walk?" And they stood still, looking sad. [18]Then one of them, named Cleopas, answered him, "Are you the only visitor to Jerusalem who does not know the things that have happened there in these days?" [19]And he said to them, "What things?" And they said to him, "Concerning Jesus of Nazareth, who was a prophet mighty in deed and word before God and all the people, [20]and how our chief priests and rulers delivered him up to be condemned to death, and crucified him. [21]But we had hoped that he was the one to redeem Israel. Yes, and besides all this, it is now the third day since this happened. [22]Moreover, some women of our company amazed us. They were at the tomb early in the morning [23] and did not find his body; and they came back saying that they had even seen a vision of angels, who said that he was alive. [24]Some of those who were with us went to the tomb, and found it just as the women had said; but him they did not see." [25]And he said to them, "O foolish men, and slow of heart to believe all that the prophets have spoken! [26]Was it not necessary that the Christ should suffer these things and enter into his glory?" [27]And beginning with Moses and all the prophets, he interpreted to them in all the scriptures the things concerning himself.

[28]So they drew near to the village to which they were going. He appeared to be going further, [29]but they constrained him, saying, "Stay with us, for it is toward evening and the day is now far spent." So he went in to stay with them. [30]When he was at table with them, he took the bread and blessed, and broke it, and gave it to them. [31]And their eyes were opened and they recognized him; and he vanished out of their sight. [32]They said to each other, "Did not our hearts burn within us while he talked to us on the road, while he opened to us the scriptures?"

³³And they rose that same hour and returned to Jerusalem; and they found the eleven gathered together and those who were with them, ³⁴who said, "The Lord has risen indeed, and has appeared to Simon!" ³⁵Then they told what had happened on the road, and how he was known to them in the breaking of the bread.

In the first part of the chapter (24:1-12) Luke had Mark before him both as source and model. And towards the end of the chapter (24:36-49) he worked with traditions shared with Matthew and John. The Emmaus story is distinguished not only as uniquely Lukan, without parallel in the other gospels, but also as the centerpiece of the entire chapter.³³ It is the longest of the units—indeed it is the longest Easter narrative in the entire New Testament—and it clarifies issues vital to Luke and his first readers.

24:13-27   Part One of the Emmaus Narrative

The scene has shifted from the holy city of Jerusalem to a road leading to an obscure village named Emmaus, from early morning to late afternoon, from mourning women to a pair of depressed male disciples, and from the word of angels to teaching by the resurrected Jesus himself.

24:13-14   Luke here as elsewhere introduces a new episode or announcement with words omitted in the RSV: "And behold!" (*kai idou,* 1:20, 31, 36; 2:25; 5:12, 18; 7:12, 37; 9:39 etc.)

Two out of "the eleven and all the others" (v. 11) who had greeted the women's report with disbelief and mockery on that same day, the first day of the week, were abandoning Jerusalem. The disciples were beginning to scatter, like sheep without a shepherd in the wilderness (15:3-7). Their drifting apart expressed their conviction that he was dead and that their hope in him had been mistaken. They were leaving Jerusalem and leaving Jesus. They resemble the crowd of 5000 just before the feeding: ready to disperse to the villages round about, going their separate ways (9:12).

The location of Emmaus is disputed and it is hard to tell exactly what place is denoted by the name.³⁴ The obscurity and difficulty move the reader to inquire why it is that Emmaus is named. What were the connotations of Emmaus for Luke and his readers? At least two of the suggested locations bore military and political overtones and were symbols of victory and defeat. Emmaus is certainly an appropriate place for a conversation on the topics of liberation and messiah.

As they walked, the two engaged in warm conversation (*homileō*, 24:14, 15; Acts 20:11; 24:26), regarding the meaning of the recent events involving their lives, their hopes, and Jesus.

24:15-16   The RSV does not translate the archaizing Biblical phrase with which the Greek introduces the next stage in the narrative: "And it happened that" *(kai egeneto)*. As they were conversing and in fact debating with one another (*syzēteō*, 22:23; Acts 6:9; 9:29; cf. Acts 15:2, 7; 28:29), Jesus himself overtook them *(eggizō)* and joined them, becoming their companion on the way (*symporeuomai*, cf. 7:11; 14:25).

Their inability to recognize him is a special condition of this particular encounter and does not imply that Luke has some theory about a change in Jesus' appearance brought on by resurrection. Mark 16:12, "in another form," is an early comment on this passage, and its author does think of a transformation, but nowhere in the Emmaus narrative does Luke betray any interest in Jesus' body, his corporeality, or his wounds. Non-recognition plays no part in Mark or Matthew, but John employs a similar device in Jesus' appearance to Mary Magdalene (20:14; cf. 21:4).

That the disciples did not recognize Jesus renders the ensuing conversation possible and builds suspense into the narrative, as the reader is compelled to ask what it will take to open the disciples' eyes. In terms similar to those employed here, Luke has elsewhere emphasized the inability of the disciples to understand the suffering and service of Jesus (9:44-45; 18:31-34) and of the inhabitants of Jerusalem to appreciate the conditions of true peace (19:42) or to grasp the meaning of Scripture (Acts 13:27). Their eyes are held; something is wrong with them; they do not yet have the capacity to know who or what Jesus really is or to penetrate to the secret of the kingdom of God.

24:17   Without greetings (cf. John 20:19, 21, 26), salutation (cf. John 21:5), or overture of any kind Jesus drove directly to the heart of the matter, asking (literally), "What are these words?" (cf. 4:36).

Once again Luke vividly describes the feelings of the participants in the Easter drama: they stopped in their tracks and turned their faces, sad and sullen (*skythrōpoi*, cf. Matt. 6:16), to the stranger. For Luke such sadness is as much a mark of the old age as joy is of the new (see on 24:52).

24:18   Cleopas[35] answered for both of them, and he speaks for Luke. The ministry and death of Jesus were known and notorious events. These things happened, not in a corner, but in the public arena

(Acts 26:26). Even this much of Cleopas' response is already part of Luke's defense of the Christian movement. It is no closed and secret society but an open and respectable fellowship.[36]

Only a stranger in town, ignorant of current events, would have to ask who Jesus was and what had happened to him.

24:19-21a   The two describe Jesus as being "of Nazareth," and the naming of the home town conjures up the image of Jesus' appearance in the synagogue, where he had aroused both admiration and fiercest anger in his inaugural sermon, setting forth the platform for his ensuing public ministry in terms of a liberation transcending narrow political hopes (4:16-30).

The Emmaus disciples call Jesus "a prophet," and that description also echoes the sermon at Nazareth. Jesus had there spoken of himself as fulfilling the vision of Isaiah: at the end of the ages a prophet anointed not by oil only but by the Spirit of God will arise to bring good tidings to the afflicted and to proclaim liberty to the captives (Isa. 61:1-2; 58:6). Jesus continued in the same synagogue sermon by comparing his program of inclusive ministry with the work of Elijah and Elisha. And like one or the other of that ancient pair he subsequently healed the sick, raised the dead, fed the hungry, and ascended into heaven. According to Luke, Jesus furthermore was the great prophet of the last times promised by Moses (Deut. 18:15, 19 is used of the Messiah in Acts 3:22-23; 7:37). The Emmaus disciples apply to Jesus a phrase used elsewhere of Moses: "mighty in word and deed" (24:19; Acts 7:22; cf. 1:1, "all that Jesus began to *do* and *teach*").

Jesus is like Moses, Elijah-Elisha, and the anointed prophet announced by Isaiah. He is in their train and fulfills their promise. He leads the people of God to freedom and to service of their God, and the Spirit of God rests upon him so that he inaugurates the year of Jubilee.

Cleopas and his companion, therefore, express one of Luke's most cherished and characteristic convictions about Jesus, when they describe him as a "mighty prophet" (7:16, 39). At the end his enemies had mocked him, taunting him to play the clairvoyant and "prophesy" (22:64; Mark 14:65; Matt. 26:67-68). That trial scene is heavy with irony: the enemies of Jesus all unwittingly expressed the truth as Luke sees it. Jesus really is God's prophet and spokesman, and Jesus suffered a prophet's fate, perishing in Jerusalem as had many prophets before him (11:49-51; 13:33-34; cf. Heb. 11:36-38).

Having called Jesus a prophet, the Emmaus disciples immediately proceed to tell the stranger "how our chief priests and rulers delivered him up to be condemned to death and crucified him" (v. 20). Luke is very sensitive to the fact that Jesus suffered crucifixion as the legal execution of the verdict of state officials.[37] He confronts the offense not only by declaring that Jesus' death was imbedded deep in God's plan but also by saying that it happened against the will of the people. It was the plot of high officials, and even they acted in ignorance.

Luke almost always discriminates between the people on the one hand and their leaders on the other. The crowds are almost always described as friendly toward Jesus in Luke-Acts (but see Luke 23:13, 18), and the condemnation of Jesus is depicted as the work of Jewish and Roman leaders and not of the general populace. For example, at 23:35 Luke omits Mark's report (15:29) regarding passersby or crowds mocking Jesus at the cross. Instead, the multitudes stand by, watching. Then they return home, full of sympathy for Jesus (Luke 23:35, 48).

Luke even begins to discriminate among the various leaders. Pharisaic leaders render friendly verdicts, especially in Acts (cf. Gamaliel in 5:33-40). Roman officials time and again call Jesus and the Christians innocent (Luke 23:4, 14; Acts 26:30-32). Opposition toward Jesus and the Christian movement is concentrated especially in the Sadducean and high-priestly families (Acts 4:1, 5-6; 5:17-18; 9:1-2; 23:6-10).

So Luke portrays Jesus and his Christian followers as enjoying broad popular support (Acts 2:47). That they arouse antagonism and end up as defendants in courts is the result of jealousy and enmity among a determined minority, and even they can be excused as having acted in ignorance (Acts 3:17). Luke explicitly says that Herod and Pilate found in Jesus' favor (Luke 23:6-17), and yet he also notes that willy-nilly they fulfilled scripture by convicting Jesus (Acts 4:24-27). Their eyes and ears and hearts have been dulled or hardened, but they need only repent to be healed and saved (Acts 28:26-27).

The Emmaus disciples were mistaken, not in thinking Jesus was a mighty prophet, but in believing that his martyr's death disqualified him as redeemer of Israel and fulfiller of Israel's hope.

The contemporaries of Jesus had been looking for the redemption of Jerusalem (2:38) or of Israel (1:68), for the consolation of Israel (2:25; cf. 6:24), for the kingdom of God (23:51) or the restoration of the kingdom to Israel (Acts 1:6), for rescue from all their enemies (1:71), and for real and lasting peace (1:79; 2:14; 19:38, 42).[38]

How could Jesus be Savior, Christ, and Lord (2:11) if he went in weakness to the cross? What kind of liberation could such a one possibly bring? Luke in his use of the Easter traditions is struggling to clarify Christian hopes and expectations regarding the sovereignty of God and the role of Jesus in God's strategy.

24:21b-23   When Luke records the disciples' lament that it was the third day since he had died, he may be indulging in a piece of irony, since the third day is the day of rescue and deliverance, and Jesus had prophesied his triumph on the third day (9:22; 13:32; 18:33; cf. Acts 10:40).[39]

The mention of the women at the tomb early in the morning binds the Emmaus narrative to the opening paragraph of the chapter (24:1-12) and offers Luke the opportunity to repeat the information that the tomb is empty, that the women saw a vision of angels (cf. "men" in 24:4), and that Jesus is alive.

The word "vision" *(optasia)* does not betray a Lukan judgment upon the encounter with the angels as merely subjective occurrence. For Luke, a vision is an extraordinary event in which angels and the resurrected Jesus, belonging to the heavenly realm and ordinarily invisible, step across the deep, primeval boundary (16:26) and really present themselves in the world of sense perception (1:22; Acts 26:19).

Paul, however, in his epistles distinguishes between visions and revelations on the one hand and the appearances of Jesus on the other (2 Cor. 12:1; 1 Cor. 9:1; 15:8). The former are private experiences and only the latter form the basis of his proclamation and ministry.

Attributing life to a corpse, as the women had done, involved a great contradiction. Cleopas and his companion reveal their opinion of the women's message as mere hearsay in the repeated "saying . . . who said" (v. 23). For their part the men did not believe but were only astonished (v. 22).

24:24   The verse implies that more than one of the apostles and the wider circle visited the tomb, but verse 12 speaks only of Peter. Whatever the difficulties, the storyteller manages to keep the reader's attention fixed on the contradictory pair of ideas that forms his theme: a grave and life, crucifixion and a kingdom. The suspense builds. In the presence of the resurrected Jesus the Emmaus disciples discussed the absence of Jesus and the death of their hopes. Conversing with him and looking directly at him, they failed to see him. What does it take to generate faith?[40] What kind of savior and liberator is he?

24:25   Cleopas and his companion, in their words to the stranger, announced the topic of the entire narrative: how can the redemption of Israel possibly be achieved by one who suffered crucifixion? Jesus chided them as foolish, that is, ignorant of the ways of God (*anoētos*, Gal. 3:1, 3), as too slow of heart to grasp the drift of the Scripture which in its totality is a prophetic voice testifying to him (John 5:39).

24:26   On the basis of the same Scriptures the contemporaries of Jesus had drawn a portrait of a powerful Messiah and a triumphant nation. But what scripture has prophesied was the suffering (meaning death, 22:15; 24:46; Acts 1:3; 3:18; 17:3) of the Messiah as the necessary prelude to his peculiar glory and lordship (cf. 1 Peter 1:11).

Luke does not say that the crucifixion and resurrection of Jesus is the key opening all the seals and locks of scripture, but that the Bible, plainly and prophetically, substantiates the Christian claim that the crucified and resurrected Jesus is the Messiah of Israel and Savior of the world.

"All the prophets" and "it was necessary" are central Lukan themes, employed in connection with Jesus' suffering to indicate that his death is part of God's mysterious providence, the door through which Jesus was exalted to power at the right hand of God (2:9, 14; 9:32; cf. Acts 3:13; 14:22).

24:27   Luke everywhere stresses the continuity between the great ancient figures of Jewish history (Abraham, Isaac, Jacob, Moses, Joshua, Samuel, David, the prophets) and Jesus. Luke thus argues for the great age and antiquity of the Christian movement. It is no novelty but is legitimated by time and durability and by its fulfillment of prophecies written in an ancient sacred book.

24:28-35   Part Two of the Emmaus Narrative

A transition in the Emmaus narrative occurs here, signalled by a series of shifts: from the road to the town, from walking to sitting at table, and from conversing to eating. Many commentators seem oblivious to the shift. They fasten their attention almost exclusively on the recognition of Jesus in the breaking of the bread, regarding the walk to Emmaus as a kind of teasing prelude or suggestive introit, and they interpret the entire passage liturgically and eucharistically.[41]

The shift is real and not imagined. But what is happening? Has Luke lost control of his material? Is he suddenly jumping to a new topic—from the necessity of Messiah's suffering to the abiding presence of Jesus or personal enlightenment in the breaking of the bread? Such themes may have been integral to some earlier form of the narrative,[42] but it does not seem possible to recover the exact contours and significance of the Emmaus story before Luke received it, meditated upon it, and retold it in its present form, language, and context.

But in its present shape and place, it makes excellent sense as a complex unity of two neatly meshed segments. Part two (the meal at Emmaus) is a further expression of the conviction voiced in part one (the conversation on the way) that in the crucified and resurrected Jesus the Scriptures of Israel and the hopes of Israel for redemption are not frustrated but fulfilled, and furthermore, the redemption or liberation is not the sort that Rome needs to fear.

24:28-29   Why does the narrative picture Jesus as ready to part from them and continue on his way? Does it belong to the storyteller's art, designed to provoke hearers to cry out, "No! Don't leave them yet!"?

The move allows Luke to picture the inner turmoil of the disciples, their dawning comprehension, and their struggle to throw off their apathy and unbelief. It prompts them to beg Jesus, to beseech him as in prayer (see the use of the same verb in Acts 16:15), to remain or abide with them.

Eucharistic interpretations fasten on that prayer and on the fact that abiding *(menō)*, mentioned twice in v. 29, focuses attention on the presence of Jesus.[43] Caution is required, however, since repetition is a feature of the chapter as a whole: "talk" in 14 and 15; "prophet" in 25-27; "go" in 28; "declined" and "reclined" in 29-30.

Later the disciples spoke of their hearts burning within them in reference to the conversation leading up to that climactic moment (v. 32). Faith is thus pictured as a slow growth, developing through successive stages (almost as in Mark 8:22-26). The move on Jesus' part leads to the offer of hospitality and serves as transition to the second part of the narrative.

24:30   The action of Jesus at the table in Emmaus recalls other times and other scenes, especially the feeding of the five thousand (9:10-17).[44] At that time Jesus had spoken to the vast throng in the wilderness about the kingdom of God (9:11, different from Mark 6:4; cf. "redeem Israel" 24:21). Then, when the day was turning dark *(klinō, 9:12 and 24:29, but different from Mark 6:35)*, they reclined *(kataklinō, 9:14-15; 24:30)*. Jesus then took bread, blessed it, broke it, and gave it to them (9:16; 24:30). The actions in the two meals are described in nearly identical terms, and the themes of bread and kingship dominate (cf. John 6:1-15).

The scene at Emmaus also echoes the Last Supper. What distinguishes Luke's account of Jesus' Last Supper most sharply from Mark's is Luke's collecting of sayings scattered through Mark to form a compact farewell discourse. One of the fundamental themes of the Lukan discourse is the contrast between pagan politics and the servant style of God's kingship (see especially Luke 22:24-30).

Bread and kingship are again paired in Luke's summary description of Jesus' activity during the 40 days between Easter and Ascension. He says that Jesus ate with his disciples (*synalizō;* cf. Acts 10:41) or stayed with them *(synaulizō)* and taught them about the kingdom of God (Acts 1:4). For Luke the Emmaus narrative is a concrete instance both of that teaching and of that eating or abiding.

Luke pictures at least two reversals of roles, as Jesus switches from questioner to teacher and from guest to host. For their part the Emmaus disciples at the beginning sound like worldly wise and well informed citizens, quite in charge of their own lives. But very rapidly their ignorance is exposed, they receive elementary teaching, and they sit like children at table in their own home. These role reversals mirror Luke's theme of the transformation of messianic hope.

24:31 At the meal their eyes were opened. Indeed, the opening of their eyes is the climax of the narrative and of the entire story of Jesus and his disciples. Previously Luke has ransacked his vocabulary to find language adequate to their blindness, heaping up phrases describing their lack of understanding, their fear, and their want of perception. Meaning was hidden from their minds and eluded their grasp (9:45; 18:34). Like the crowds and their leaders, they had hard hearts, deaf ears, and blind eyes (Acts 7:51; 28:26-27), but at Emmaus the scales fell from their eyes and they began to see (cf. Acts 9:18).

But in what sense is this a recognition story?[45] What did they see? Luke describes no display of hands or feet or wounds, and the story concludes without any confession of Jesus by name or title.

What they saw is not just that the stranger is Jesus, or that Jesus yet lives, or even—and this is the most common and almost universally accepted interpretation—that the eucharistic feast is the vehicle of his enduring presence. They suddenly saw the truth of his teaching about the Scriptures and Israel's hope, that kingship belongs to one exalted from the grave, that the kingdom of God is not horses and chariots but the favor of God (2 Kings 6:15-17; Luke 2:14).

The kingdom does not come with the traditional, observable signs of military might or moral victory. The kingdom is present with its peace and salvation where Pharisee and prostitute, righteous and unrighteous, easterner and westerner, northerner and southerner, prodigal and responsible, rich and poor, tax collector and prophet sit at table and break bread with one another. Those who believe that the kingdom comes by military might, political power, or forceful insistence upon the rightness of one's own person and the brutal submission of the other see the cross as depressing defeat and the sharing of bread as an equally impotent and meaningless gesture. Nevertheless, the Emmaus narrative teaches that the cross and the breaking of bread are the most eloquent expressions of the power of the one who said, "I am among you as one who serves" (22:27) and "The kingdom of God is in the midst of you" (17:21).

24:32 Luke focuses on the feelings and human reactions of the disciples throughout the chapter. Here he testifies to the power of Scripture, once it is properly understood, to kindle in the heart a burning at once consuming and yet benign (3:16; 12:49), which cannot be contained but flares up in speech (Jer. 20:9; Ps. 39:1-3; Test. Naphtali 7:4; Acts 2:3; 4:20).

24:33-35 Immediately they left Emmaus and set out for Jerusalem. Their movement builds a bridge to the next paragraph, but it also expresses graphically that their lostness is at an end. They have been found and are returning to the community with haste and joy.

They need not repeat their whole story, for the Lord has sought out the others as well. An initial appearance (*ōphthē*, cf. 22:43) to Peter is reported without being narrated, just as at 1 Cor. 15:5.[46]

Luke probably has two chief concerns in naming Simon. One is to prepare for the role Peter plays in the early chapters of Acts. The other is to satisfy the reader that the story of Peter has reached the conclusion for which Jesus prayed: Peter had nearly been separated like chaff from the grain as he (and the others) acted with swords (22:35-38, 49-51) in an attempted defense of Jesus, and then he balked at the threat of physical harm to himself and denied involvement with Jesus. But Peter remembered the Lord's word, and his self-reliance collapsed (22:61-62). Therefore, with the brief statement that the Lord had now appeared to Peter and gathered him, the Lukan narrative of Peter reaches a satisfactory conclusion, and the way is paved for the beginning of Acts.

So the Lordship of Jesus is not known or manifested in acts of war or vengeance or in dreadful and mighty signs, but is attained through a cross and expressed in a meal—an act of hospitality, peace, brotherhood and sisterhood. His kingship is known in the time of the church, as in the time of his earthly life, in acts of service and in the reception of the sinner, the straying, the poor, the outcast, the despised, the wanderer, and the stranger. Luke pictures the promised liberation or redemption in nonviolent, nonmilitary terms. He rejected fire and sword (9:51-56; 22:38, 50) and healed the slave whose ear was severed (22:51). Jesus traveled the way of peace (2:14; 19:38, 42).

Jesus saved and liberated people by fellowshipping with them.[47] He entered the house of Zacchaeus, accepted his hospitality, and said, "Today salvation has come to this house" (19:9; cf. 23:43). In such fellowship he is made known with the power of his kingship.

Luke 24:36-53: Farewell

Luke 24:36-53   [36]As they were saying this, Jesus himself stood among them. [37]But they were startled and frightened, and supposed that they saw a spirit. [38]And he said to them, "Why are you troubled, and why do questionings rise in your hearts? [39]See my hands and my feet, that it is I myself; handle me, and see; for a spirit has not flesh and bones as you see that I have." [41]And while they still disbelieved for joy, and wondered, he said to them, "Have you anything here to eat?" [42]They gave him a piece of broiled fish, [43]and he took it and ate before them.

[44]Then he said to them, "These are my words which I spoke to you, while I was still with you, that everything written about me in the law of Moses and the prophets and the psalms must be fulfilled." [45]Then he opened their minds to understand the scriptures, [46]and said to them, "Thus it is written, that the Christ should suffer and on the third day rise from the dead, [47]and that repentance and forgiveness of sins should be preached in his name to all nations, beginning from Jerusalem. [48]You are witnesses of these things. [49]And behold, I send the promise of my Father upon you; but stay in the city, until you are clothed with power from on high."

[50]Then he led them out as far as Bethany, and lifting up his hands he blessed them. [51]While he blessed them, he parted from them, and was carried up into heaven. [52]And they returned to Jerusalem with great joy, [53]and were continually in the temple blessing God.

As at the beginning of the chapter, the scene is once again Jerusalem, now apparently in the early evening (vv. 29, 33). No individuals are named, but the passage has about it the air of a summary, and

Luke probably intends readers to understand that all Jesus' friends and disciples (Luke 23:49; see Acts 1:13-14 for a partial list), including all those named earlier in the chapter, have gathered together.

If the Emmaus narrative were excised, the transition from verse 11 or 12 to 36 would not be especially rough. A phrase or two would connect the passages neatly. By inserting and indeed highlighting the Emmaus narrative, Luke has filled the entire day. The Emmaus material mirrors the passage of time from morning to midday and on into late afternoon and evening. But, more importantly, Luke has provided the present passage and the farewell of Jesus with both introduction and interpretation.

The scene includes two of the most prominent features of the Emmaus material: teaching about his death and resurrection in fulfillment of Scripture and a meal. But these are dealt with in reverse order, so that the material in verses 13 through 46 is structured chiastically: ABBA (necessity of suffering/eating/eating/necessity of suffering).

New elements are the declaration regarding the proclamation to all nations (24:47-48) and the promise of power from on high (24:49).

24:36-43   At Table in Jerusalem
24:36   Paul (1 Cor. 15:6), Matthew (28:16-20), and John (20:19-29) all testify that the resurrected Jesus appeared not only to select individuals but before assemblies of his followers. In their reports of the event Luke and John are closest to one another. Both locate the appearance in Jerusalem on Easter night. Both use the phrase "stepped into their midst" (Luke: *estē en mesō autōn;* John: *estē eis to meson*). Some manuscripts of Luke 24:36 have the words: "and he said to them, 'Peace be with you'," exactly as in John 20:19. Only in Luke and John are there assurances and a display of parts of the body with the invitation to touch him. Furthermore, both connect the appearance with mission and the gift of the spirit.

24:37   Luke stresses the physical reality of the body of the resurrected Jesus in a manner different from John 20 but reminiscent of the first two epistles of John. The resurrected Jesus is no "spirit" (RSV) or ghost (*pneuma;* a variant reading in some ancient manuscripts is *phantasma,* cf. Mark 6:49). Luke understands the resurrection realistically and may be fighting docetic, gnostic, or spiritualizing misinterpretations, as Paul also did on Hellenistic soil (1 Cor. 15:35-55).[48]

But Luke is even more intent upon asserting the fact of the resurrection as fulfillment of Scripture: Jesus was not abandoned to Hades and he did not see corruption (Acts 2:24-31; Ps. 16). And he will come as really and as surely as he was seen to depart (Acts 1:11), an assertion designed to bolster sagging Christian faithfulness and perseverance.

The agitation and indeed terror of the disciples are surprising after the Emmaus story. There Jesus seemed anything but frightening.

24:38   Interpreted in the present sequence, following the Emmaus pericope, Jesus is rebuking his followers for their failure to grasp the necessity of his suffering. They were troubled by his evident lack of success.

24:39   Jesus displayed his hands and feet, inviting their inspection by touch (*psēlaphaō*, 1 John 1:1; Ign. Smyrn. 2:1-3; 3).[49]

In Biblical fashion Luke speaks of the bones. If they were destroyed, then all hope of resurrection would be lost. It was thought that there existed in every person one indestructible bone from which God could and would refashion the entire person at the resurrection. When Moabites killed the king of Edom, took his bones and burned them, reducing them to limestone and whitewash, they committed an unimaginably great insult.[50]

Luke's words are not meant primarily as a comment on the nature of Jesus' resurrection body. He is saying as clearly as possible that death could not hold the crucified Jesus (cf. Acts 2:24). He conquered death completely. God has defeated death in its accustomed realm of "flesh and bones," the visible world of sensation and temporality.

It is worth noting that this massively realistic way of describing the resurrected Jesus characterizes only the 40 day period between the resurrection and the ascension. After the ascension the exalted Jesus appears from heaven in blinding light or strange sound, comprehensible to some but not to all (Acts 9:3-7; 22:9; 26:13). He also appears in dreams, visions or trances (Acts 7:56; 9:10; 18:9; 22:18).

24:40   Verse 40 ("And when he had said this, he showed them his hands and his feet") is found only in a few manuscripts. It adds nothing to the narrative and is redundant, whether it is original, or was derived by a scribe from John 20:20.

24:41   Luke is fascinated by the inner as well as the outer condition of the people of whom he writes, but he does not search around in their psyches in hopes of dredging up dark materials to display or condemn. Rather he seems tolerant and great-hearted. He excuses the disciples' drowsiness in Gethsemane by saying they fell asleep "for grief" (22:45). Here the disciples are still disbelieving, but it is "for joy" (cf. Acts 12:14).

They marvel at the sight of Jesus, regarding his return as too good to be true. Luke treats the tradition of the disciples' disbelief far more generously than the longer ending of Mark. John devotes careful attention to the same problem in his own unique fashion in the narrative about Thomas (20:24-29).

That Jesus ate and drank with his disciples after the resurrection is a curious part of the early traditions of Easter (Acts 1:4; 10:41; John 21:9-13). Luke describes the meals of Jesus as occasions of joy because Jesus broke taboos and offered fellowship to sinners (see on v. 30), and he chronicles the church's struggles to keep its breaking of bread from deteriorating into a private ritual reserved for the initiated alone (see Acts 10:48; 11:3; Gal. 2:11-12).

24:42-43   They gave him a bit of fish (see John 21:9-13), and some ancient manuscripts add that they also offered him "a piece of honeycomb."

Because of its proverbial sweetness (Judg. 14:18) honey became a symbol of the Word of God (Ps. 119:103), and because it is food ready for human consumption without human labor, it was a widespread ancient symbol of paradise. Honey came to signify the eucharist in parts of the early church, and that may account for its introduction into the present narrative by some early scribe.[51]

Jesus accepted the food and ate in their presence. The eating may be part of the demonstration of his return to life and conquering of death (cf. Luke 8:55), although Raphael's eating in the presence of Tobit was an illusion and did not prove anything about the angel's corporeality (Tobit 12:16-22). Luke pictures Jesus as eating not only in the sight of the disciples but also in their company and as their guest (cf. Gen. 18:8). Giving and receiving hospitality established enduring bonds between people formerly strangers or enemies. Jesus saved them by entering into fellowship with them (cf. Acts 27:33-38). In one sense Paul was correct when he wrote, "The kingdom of God does not mean food and drink but righteousness and peace and joy in the Holy Spirit" (Rom. 14:17), but for Luke the common meal was the one observable sign of the advent of the Messiah's rule; and where the Christ rules, there is peace and joy.

24:44-49   Final Words and Commissioning

A second part of the narrative of Jesus' meeting with all his disciples in Jerusalem on Easter night opens here. The focus shifts from the meal to teaching, the mirror image of the movement in the Emmaus story.

The teaching is cast in the form of a farewell speech: Jesus on the eve of his departure gathers his followers and especially those chosen as his successors, celebrates a final meal, delivers his last words (offering reassurances, rehearsing the past, giving instructions for the future) and then blesses the gathering and departs. Thus considered, the scene is full of echoes of other biblical farewells.

It exhibits a number of parallels to Isaac's blessing of Jacob: nonrecognition, feeling of hands, eating, speech about peoples and nations, blessing (Gen. 27:1-40). Furthermore, it is similar to Luke's prior account of the Last Supper (22:14-38). The form of a farewell is familiar and the biblical tradition contains numerous examples.[52]

24:44   The beginning of Jesus' address is reminiscent of the opening phrases of Deuteronomy, which in its entirety is Moses' farewell discourse: "These are the words which Moses spoke ... " (Deut. 1:1).

Jesus here describes himself both as an inspired prophet (cf. 24:19) and as the subject of scriptural prophecy. The reference here at the end of the chapter to his words previously spoken echoes the saying of the angels at the beginning (24:6) and contributes to the symmetry of the chapter.

Speaking in this chapter previously about the Scriptures, Luke had named "the prophets" (v. 25) and "Moses and all the prophets" (v. 27). Here he speaks of the Scriptures in language that was, at the end of the first century, becoming the standard mode of describing the totality of the Hebrew Bible: the Law (Torah), the Prophets (Nebiim) and the Writings (Ketubim). Luke apparently speaks here of "the psalms" as chief representatives of "the Writings."[53]

Scripture in its totality points to Jesus, and Jesus fulfills the Scriptures completely. God's will finds fullest expression in him, so heeding the word of Jesus (and of his witnesses) leads to salvation, but disregarding his word results in being cut off from the people (cf. Deut. 18:18).

24:45   Luke has previously noted the disciples' lack of understanding (9:45; 18:34; 24:25). Now once again Luke displays his psychological perspective. Instead of saying Jesus opened the Scriptures, he says he opened their minds (cf. Acts 16:14, the Lord opened Lydia's heart).

Jesus had been blindfolded by his enemies, and his powers as seer had been mocked and denied (22:64). But aged Simeon (2:32), the Baptist (3:6) and Jesus himself (4:18) had been correct: he came to open eyes and to enlighten, that all flesh might see God's salvation.

He gave sight to the blind (7:21-22; 18:35-43) and opened the eyes of the Emmaus disciples (24:31). Now at the end he opens the minds of all his gathered friends to understand the will of God, and he proceeds to spell out the content of that will.

24:46-47   The summary clearly reveals Luke's own mind regarding the sum and substance of the Scriptures. God has willed these two things: 1) the Messiah's suffering *(pathein)* and subsequent resurrection on the third day (Acts 2:23, 30, 31; 3:18; 13:27-32; 17:3) and 2) the universal call to repentance with a view to the forgiveness of sins.

Again, the end of the book recapitulates the opening. Turning, repentance, and coming home were stated as the goal of John's proclamation in the midst of Israel. His preachment was designed to ready people for the advent of their king (1:16-17, 76-77; 3:4). The exact words "repentance for the forgiveness of sins" appear in Luke's description of John's baptizing (3:3). In the time after the resurrection, the disciples call people to repentance and bid them concretize their penitence in baptism. To the penitent baptized they offer God's forgiveness, the Holy Spirit (Acts 2:38; 3:19; 5:31), and inclusion in the community of believers. They work not among Jews only but among "all the nations" *(panta ta ethnē,* Matt. 28:19; Dan. 7:14), as the promise is to those near and to those far off (Acts 2:39; 11:18; 13:47-48; 28:28).

Luke adds the note that the proclamation is to begin in Jerusalem.[54] That too was prophesied: "For out of Zion shall go forth the law, and the word of the Lord from Jerusalem" (Micah 4:2; Isaiah 2:3).

24:48-49   At the end of his gospel Luke prepares for the beginning of Acts: the friends and disciples of Jesus are commissioned as witnesses *(martyres,* Acts 1:8; 2:32; 3:15; 5:32; 10:39, 41; 13:31). They had been with him from the beginning in Galilee and could testify concerning his life and teaching, his passion and his resurrection.

Paul called himself a witness not only of the things he himself personally had seen and heard but also of the passion and resurrection of Jesus, the truth of which he had experienced in his own sufferings and escapes (Acts 22:15; 26:16).

The mention of witnesses not only paves the way for Acts but recalls the preface to the entire work, where the author had cited his chain of authorities and announced his intention of enabling his readers "to know the truth" about the message they had heard (Luke 1:1-4).

The Holy Spirit, here called "the promise[55] of my Father" (Acts 1:4; 2:16-18, 33, 39) and "power from on high" (Luke 1:17, 35; 4:14; Acts 1:8; 8:19; 10:38) will "clothe" the disciples, as Elijah clothed Elisha by casting his mantle upon him (see Acts 1:8-11).

Verses 48 and 49 illumine one another and reveal a key Lukan conviction. He understands the work of the Holy Spirit not in terms of morality and sanctification of personal life but in terms of prophetic deeds (healings, exorcisms, raisings) and especially prophetic speech and powerful testimony.

The disciples are commanded not to leave Jerusalem (contrary to what is said in Mark 16:7; Matt. 28:17; cf. John 21:1) but to sit tight in the holy city (Acts 1:4), which has been Jesus' announced goal ever since 9:51 (13:22, 33; 17:11; 18:31; 19:11, 28). There in Jerusalem they will experience the fulfillment of all the promises and fill the city with their proclamation, and from the city the word will be launched on its triumphal course toward Rome.

Talk of testimony and witnesses has a judicial ring and seems appropriate in a work so full of accusations, trials, courts, and judges. Luke strove to impress the innocence of Jesus and of the Christian movement on his audience. But the language of testimony is also prophetic. Isaiah called the Lord's people both his servant *(pais)* and his witnesses *(martyres,* Isaiah 43:10-12; 44:8). The servant of the Lord is to be a light and lighten the nations (Luke 2:32; Acts 13:47; cf. Isaiah 49:6).

24:50-53   Blessing and Departure

24:50   The shift in place from Jerusalem to Bethany seems to signal a break in the narrative, and verses 50-53 are often detached from 36-49 and viewed as an independent piece. The section does function as the conclusion to the entire chapter, but it should nevertheless be taken very closely with 36-49. The unit (24:36-53 begins when Jesus "appeared" *(estē,* 36) and closes when he "disappeared" *(diestē,* 51), and as a single whole constitutes Jesus' farewell (see on v. 36).

Jesus led the disciples—presumably the eleven and all the other men and women as well—out of Jerusalem a short distance in the direction of Bethany, previously identified as near Bethphage on the (eastern) slope of the Mount of Olives, the place from which he had begun his approach to the temple and holy city (19:28-37).

Luke apparently feels that the short distance ("a Sabbath's day journey," Acts 1:12; "fifteen stadia" or about two miles is the distance from Jerusalem to Bethany, John 11:18) to Bethany beyond the city walls does not contradict the command to remain in the city. The most direct route from Jerusalem towards *(heōs pros)* Bethany would take them to the summit of the Mount of Olives.

There Jesus lifted his hands in benediction, and many ancient manuscripts describe his disciples and friends as bowing or prostrating themselves *(proskyneō)* before him.

Luke here paints Jesus in priestly colors. On the Mount of Olives, in full view of the temple, Jesus performed the act left undone by Zechariah's dumbness at the opening of the gospel. The people had waited in vain for him to emerge from the sanctuary and pronounce the blessing (1:21-22; M. Tamid 7:2). With the work of salvation completed (4:18-21; 19:9; 23:43), blessing is bestowed.[56]

The disciples are by no means abandoned at the ascension of Jesus; they are commended to the Father's care and promised the inspiration of the Holy Spirit.

24:52   Having pronounced the benediction, Jesus then disappeared. The appearance that began in v. 36 is over. He had left the company of the Emmaus disciples by becoming invisible or disappearing (v. 31), but the ascension carries with it the connotation that the appearances are at an end and the disciples ought not expect Jesus to continue appearing visibly to them (see on Acts 1:12).

Some ancient texts here include that he "was carried up *(anephereto)* into heaven." The reference to the ascension may have offended an ancient copyist, who, judging it inconsistent with the chronology offered in Acts 1, omitted it. But Luke is schematizing and telescoping here as he rounds off his narrative, and the reference to being carried up into heaven may well be original. On the other hand, at a time when the third gospel and Acts were separated in the canon, a copyist may have inserted the verse to bring the gospel to a neat conclusion.

24:51   The scene is free of any trace of sadness, sorrow, or pain of parting, perhaps to some extent because these verses (50-53) belong closely with the preceding (36-49). Terror and disbelief (37-41) have yielded to faith and rejoicing, which form the climax of the entire passage. Furthermore, the joy is a sign of the new age inaugurated by the work of Jesus, and it marks the life of the community which calls him Lord and Christ.[57]

The gospel closes where it opened, in Jerusalem. Luke focuses on Jerusalem more than the other synoptists do. It is for him the link between the history of Jesus and Israel on the one hand and the life of the church of Jews and Gentiles on the other.[58]

Jerusalem is the place where the people of God are to be found, performing acts of worship in the temple. And so the chapter closes as it began, with descriptions of Christian believers as devout and pious worshipers of God. The ground has been laid for the book of Acts.

Summary with Comments on Acts 1–2: This Jesus—Lord and Christ

Luke's whole story concerns the resurrection. Every page speaks of resurrection at least proleptically or parabolically. Luke was constantly defining the resurrection and lordship of Jesus, and one of the chief aims in his work of definition was to display to any Roman reader the utter baselessness of the suspicion that the Christian faith in Jesus as exalted Lord was politically dangerous. To his Christian readers Luke was, in addition, defining authentic or true Christian existence as discipleship on the path of hope in the footsteps of Paul, Peter, the Seven, the Twelve, and Jesus. Walking in those steps on that path—and only on that path in that particular tradition—they were assured that the link to salvation was secure.

In Luke-Acts the resurrection of Jesus is more than one fixed element in a larger set of repeated themes and more than one moment among many in the career of Jesus.[59] It is the heart of Christian teaching and believing, and not even the crucifixion has anything like equal prominence and weight.

Of course, Luke has a moving passion narrative, portraying Jesus as a martyr in the noble succession of persecuted prophets. Nevertheless, when Luke reflects on the meaning of the crucifixion, he speaks of it ordinarily, although not exclusively, as a miscarriage of justice, proof of the people's ignorance, evidence of the hardness of the human heart and the blindness of human eyes. By way of contrast to the crucifixion as the act of human beings, Luke declares that the resurrection is God's verdict and action. Typical of Luke's rhetoric are the formulations indicating that human beings killed Jesus but God raised him from the dead (Acts 2:23-24, 36; 3:13; 4:10; 5:30; 10:39-40; 13:29-30).[60]

However, closely associated with that essentially negative view of the crucifixion is the statement that the death of Jesus, together with the resurrection, occurred by the will of God. They "had" to happen. Even his death was "necessary." It was foretold, prophesied, in accord with the word of God, part of the counsel and will of God. All unwittingly the crucifiers advanced the plan of God.

The truth in the old cliché that Luke has no theology of the cross[62] is the fact that Luke has done very little in the way of exploiting the positive riches of the cross of Jesus for Christian existence. However, Luke, through his lengthy passion narrative, seeks to draw readers close to Jesus and to stir them to sympathy for Jesus. Luke desires that they relate to Jesus as the one malefactor did (23:40-42), confessing their own sin, declaring Jesus innocent, and seeing in that righteous sufferer the King of paradise. Furthermore Luke incorporates the Markan interpretation of discipleship or Christian existence in terms of following the crucified, taking up one's cross "every day," and walking the path toward the kingdom through many tribulations (Luke (9:23; Acts 14:22). When Luke describes Simon of Cyrene as carrying Jesus' cross "behind him" (Luke 23:26; cf. Mark 15:21), he is portraying Simon as a prototypical disciple. Thus Luke is at times not far from a theology of the cross after all.[63]

Nevertheless, whatever prominence is granted the nativity, the miracles, the teaching, or even the death of Jesus, it remains true that the resurrection has unique weight. The resurrection of Jesus is God's own miraculous deed, and resurrection can and frequently does stand alone in Luke-Acts as a summary of the entirety of the Christian proclamation. So the priests and Sadducees were annoyed that the apostles were "proclaiming in Jesus the resurrection from the dead" (4:1-2). At Athens Paul preached "Jesus and the resurrection" (17:18, hr 32). Both before the Sanhedrin and before governor Felix, Paul summed up his teaching in a reference to resurrection (23:8; 24:15, 21), and Festus explained to Agrippa that Paul spoke "about one Jesus, who was dead, but whom Paul asserted to be alive" (25:19).

In fact, the basic function of the apostles is described as bearing witness to the resurrection (1:22; 2:32; 4:33; 10:41; 13:31; 22:15). Of course, the apostles had witnessed the entire career of Jesus "beginning from the baptism of John" (1:21; 10:37-39) and they bore testimony to that career, but his resurrection is their real theme and focal point. The prior words and deeds serve to identify the one who has experienced resurrection and to define the character of his present lordship.

Luke regards resurrection as a central biblical teaching held by the Jewish people and their leaders with the exception of the Sadducees (Luke 20:27; cf. Mark 12:18; Matt. 22:23; Acts 4:1-2; 23:6-10; cf. 24:15).

For Luke, the Scriptures are primarily prophetic writings, straining forward full of the promise of light and glory, liberty and redemption, power and a kingdom. They bring hope of victory over all darkness and ugliness, over all perverse and demonic powers in rebellion against the heavenly Father. Devout and zealous Jews disagreed about the shape and the time of the awaited fulfillment. According to Luke, religious patriots, even while they held a doctrine of resurrection, were captivated by the dream of the early defeat of Israel's political oppressors and of splendor restored to a resurgent nation (Luke 19:11; 24:21; Acts 1:6; 5:36-37; 21:38). Luke rejected that dream as the dangerous brainchild of people who do not know the things that make for peace (Luke 19:42) and do not recognize the time of visitation (19:44).

The Sadducees pinned their hopes neither on resurrection nor on political rebellion. They believed that Israel's glory resided in her temple and ritual and that their continuation and security depended on a policy of accommodation to Roman power. Luke rejected the Sadducean program just as he rejected that of the Zealots and rebels. In the book of Acts he voices a sense of spiritual kinship with the Pharisees, whom he portrays as pacifistic and anti-Saducean believers in the resurrection (5:33-39; 23:6-10).

For Luke, the resurrection of Jesus or of the Messiah is a synonym for "the hope" or "the hope of Israel" (Acts 23:6; 26:6-8, 23; 28:20). Jesus' resurrection is exactly what God had promised, and Luke finds the resurrection or exaltation of Jesus in numerous individual passages as well as in Scripture as a whole.[64]

When Luke summarizes Christian testimony as the proclamation of "the kingdom of God" (Luke 4:43; 8:1; 9:2, 11, 60; 10:9, 11; Acts 1:3; 8:12; 19:8; 20:25; 28:23, 31) and of Jesus as "Lord" and "Christ" and "Son" (Acts 2:36; 5:42; 9:20; 16:31; 17:3, 7, 18; 20:21; 24:24), he is not introducing additional topics alongside resurrection but is rather paraphrasing his understanding of the resurrection. God has established his own rule by raising Jesus from the dead and exalting him to sit at his right hand. By the resurrection God has revealed Jesus to be great David's greater Son, Son of God, and has made him king, Lord, and Christ of the people of God. He sits upon David's throne (Luke 1:32; Acts 2:30) and of his kingdom there will be no end (Luke 1:33). He has passed through tribulation to kingship (Luke 19:11-27; 23:42-43; 24:26; Acts 14:22). Speaking of the kingdom of God and announcing the royal titles of Jesus are Lukan ways of explicating the content and consequences of Jesus' resurrection.

In addition to direct speech about resurrection and exaltation, various themes and materials in Luke-Acts exhibit a structure analogous to that of the death and resurrection of Jesus: the conception and birth of John the Baptist and Jesus in impossible circumstances (Luke 1-2); all the miracles of healing and exorcism and especially the raisings from the dead (Luke 7:11-17; 8:40-55; Acts 9:36-42; 20:7-12); the numerous accounts of narrow escape (Luke 4:18, 30; Acts 5:19, 23; 7:34, 36; 9:23-25; 12:6-10; 14:19-20; 16:25-26; 21:30-33; 27:1; 28:10); the finding of the lost (Luke 2:41-52; 15; 19:1-10); the exaltation of the humble (Luke 1:46-55; 2:34; 13:30; 14:11; 15:24, 32; 18:14).

One lesson Luke was teaching is that the God we relate to in the world is the one who gave Mary a Son and has now exalted him from death to his right hand. The way he acted in raising Jesus is the way he always acts. The resurrection is not so much a strange and unique event as it is the most stunning and electrifying example of how God is continually acting. At the resurrection the power of God everywhere present was most strongly focused.

Luke wrote as he did of God's visiting his people and of his resurrection of Jesus in part to encourage readers who were in danger of misjudging their own sufferings or tribulations (Acts 14:22). The people of God fall ill or arouse opposition, but God will overrule the enmity. Perhaps he will engineer an escape in history, or it may be that he will rescue them eschatologically. In any case, Luke wrote to encourage them in perseverance, hope, and joy.

Moreover, all those scenes of births, cures, narrow escapes, recoveries, findings and exaltations, just because they are structurally related to resurrection, provide further definition of the meaning of Jesus' resurrection and of his new status as Lord and Christ. God is at work in the world in nonpolitical, nonrevolutionary, nonviolent and yet powerful fashion, freely bestowing life and liberty, granting reunion and fellowship, wholeness and joy. The beneficiaries of the kingdom are not the members of any one nation or class but consist of all who repent and believe. Accusations of rebellion against secular authority are rejected as baseless slander, law and order are praised, the innocence of Jesus and his followers before Jewish and Roman law is asserted repeatedly, and over all there is written the word "peace" (Luke 1:79; 2:14; 19:38, 42; Acts 10:36).

Luke's portraits of Jesus and all his company from Luke 1 through Acts 28 show that those who confess the resurrected Jesus are pious, upright, moral and law-abiding persons.

By extending his story of healings, escapes, and exaltations beyond the ascension and up to the sojourn of Paul as a prisoner at Rome, Luke testified to his conviction that the power active in the resurrection of Jesus continues in the church from generation to generation.

One of the peculiarities of Luke's treatment of Easter is the way he has spread over an extended period of fifty days and many scenes what the other evangelists pack into a single report (Mark) or into three or four brief pericopes (Matthew and John). To put it another way, Luke sometimes (not always) divides resurrection, exaltation, and giving of the Spirit into discrete moments, whereas the other evangelists tend to assign to the resurrection or to Easter itself all the various motifs of vindication, triumph, exaltation, presence, commissioning, and empowering.

A treatment of "Luke's Easter narrative" must take account of the opening chapters of Acts. Only a cursory reading of Acts 1-2 can be offered here, but it reinforces the impression gained from the closing chapter of the gospel that Luke was fundamentally concerned about a correct apprehension of Jesus' lordship and about the question of continuity and the right tradition.

Acts 1:1-5   In the first book, O The-ophi-lus, I have dealt with all that Jesus began to do and teach, [2]until the day when he was taken up, after he had given commandment through the Holy Spirit to the apostles whom he had chosen. [3]To them he presented himself alive after his passion by many proofs, appearing to them during forty days, and speaking of the kingdom of God. [4]And while staying with them he charged them not to depart from Jerusalem, but to wait for the promise of the Father, which, he said, "you heard from me, [5]for John baptized with water, but before many days you shall be baptized with the Holy Spirit."

In the opening paragraph of Acts the author views the career of Jesus from a distance and speaks of the apostles as revered figures of the past.

Jesus no longer shows himself alive as he had to the twelve disciples in the days immediately before the ascension. Nevertheless, the connection with the past is secure. Jesus not only chose the Twelve (Luke 6:13) through the Spirit, led them as witnesses from Galilee to Jerusalem, and appeared to them alive after his crucifixion, eating with them and demonstrating that he was no ghost (Luke 24:36-43), but also instructed them about the kingdom of God himself for 40 days. In ancient Jewish tradition a teaching repeated 40 times is full instruction qualifying the student to become a teacher (see 4 Ezra 14; 2 Baruch 76:1-4). Jesus' disciples were readied for their own ministry of teaching.

Jesus commanded the apostles to stay in Jerusalem (Luke 24:49; Acts 1:4) and to await the fulfillment of the Father's promise, and that promise is described as the Holy Spirit to be poured out upon them.

Acts 1:6-8 ⁶So when they had come together, they asked him, "Lord, will you at this time restore the kingdom to Israel?" ⁷He said to them, "It is not for you to know times or seasons which the Father has fixed by his own authority. ⁸But you shall receive power when the Holy Spirit has come upon you; and you shall be my witnesses in Jerusalem and in all Judea and Sa-mari-a and to the end of the earth."

Verse 6 seems at first to portray the apostles as uncomprehending in spite of the lengthy instruction, but verses 1-5 are prefatory and anticipate what follows. Verses 6-8 really describe the key question addressed by Jesus during the entire forty days of teaching. Luke is here and everywhere contrasting hopes of political empire with the promise of the Spirit of God. It is the author's intention to address his readers' questions and clarify for them the meaning of the kingdom.

(1) When will it come (Luke 19:11; Mark 13:32; Matt. 24:36; 2 Peter 3:4-10)? Not only is the consummation not imminent but all date-setting is discouraged. God has his own schedule.

(2) What is the nature or character of the kingdom? It does not advance with signs to be observed (Luke 17:20) and hence is no political phenomenon. The kingdom is being defined in terms of the coming of the Spirit. The Spirit of God is the promise and power delivered to the church by the resurrection of Jesus.

(3) Who are beneficiaries of the coming kingdom? Israel only? The restoration of David's empire is too narrow. God's plan is to "re-

store" all things (Acts 3:21; Malachi 3:23), and the human recipients of the Spirit are Jews, Samaritans, and Gentiles. The good news and the kingdom or salvation are for those near and for those far off at the ends of the earth in distant lands (2:39; 1:8; 13:47; Isa. 49:6). All the nations will be blessed through Abraham's seed (3:25) in a kingdom not just wider than, but fundamentally different from, that of David.

Power and the Spirit (cf. Luke 24:21) are practically synonyms in Luke. The Spirit is divine power enabling people to bear bold testimony, and that witness has been summarized in Luke 24:46-47 as focusing on 1) the passion and resurrection of the Christ (through suffering to glory) and 2) repentance in his name to all the nations. People are summoned to acknowledge Jesus as Lord not by the conquest of arms but by the testimony of bold proclamation. All those in any nation who call on his name in faith will be saved (Acts 2:37-40; 10:34-35; 16:30-33). Clearly the power is nonpolitical and thoroughly respectable and pious.

Acts 1:9-11   [9]And when he had said this, as they were looking on, he was lifted up, and a cloud took him out of their sight. [10]And while they were gazing into heaven as he went, behold, two men stood by them in white robes, [11]and said, "Men of Galilee, why do you stand looking into heaven? This Jesus, who was taken up from you into heaven, will come in the same way as you saw him go into heaven."

Luke's account of the ascension, the only narrative report of the ascension in the New Testament, is full of oddities and difficult to interpret, until it is seen that the entire opening chapter of Acts echoes the ascension of Elijah. Elijah had chosen Elisha as successor to continue his prophetic witness in Israel.[59] For his part Elisha voiced a desire for a "double measure"—the share of inheritance allotted to a firstborn son—of Elijah's spirit, power that would clearly designate him as heir and successor (2 Kings 2:9; Deut. 21:17). The condition for reception was strange: he would have to have eyes that could see Elijah as he ascended (2 Kings 2:10). Luke emphasized with five different nouns and verbs that the apostles beheld the ascension. Then Luke proceeded to narrate Jesus' bestowal of the Spirit upon the apostles at Pentecost, indicating the status of the apostles as in some sense the prophetic successors of Jesus and emphasizing the source of their power and adequacy as witnesses.

One of the chief ways Luke portrays Jesus is as a prophet (Luke 13:33; 24:19). He is the anointed prophet of the last times (4:16-21; 7:18-23), a prophet like Elijah, Elisha (Luke 4:24-27; 7:11-16), and

Moses (Acts 3:22-23; 7:37), and his disciples/successors are prophets also.

Having witnessed the ascension they are assured that he will return at the end (1:11). Nothing is said of the presence or activity of Jesus in the time of the church. Luke lacks the Pauline notion that the church is one organism with Jesus as members of a body or the Johannine picture of Jesus as indwelling the believers. Jesus seems distant, if not altogether absent, from the life of the church in Acts. He reveals himself in dream or vision (Acts 7:56; 9:3-7, 10-16; 10:19; 22:17-21), intervenes through an angel (8:26; 13:7-11), or produces results by his hand or name (3:16; 4:10). Nevertheless, Luke's picture of Jesus should be contrasted not with those of Paul and John but with those drawn by suspicious Romans or by Christians inspired by false, zealotic, or apocalyptic and political hopes. Luke portrays Jesus as the one enthroned at God's right hand. He has poured his Spirit upon the disciples, and in the power of the Spirit the disciples act as Jesus' successors carrying forward a mission of peace and salvation as Jesus had.

Acts 1:12-14 ¹²Then they returned to Jerusalem from the mount called Olivet, which is near Jerusalem, a sabbath day's journey away; ¹³and when they had entered, they went up to the upper room, where they were staying, Peter and John and James and Andrew, Philip and Thomas, Bartholomew and Matthew, James the son of Alphaeus and Simon the Zealot and Judas the son of James. ¹⁴All these with one accord devoted themselves to prayer, together with the women and Mary the mother of Jesus, and with his brothers.

In the next scene of the day of ascension Luke again emphasizes the theme of continuity. Jesus' chosen apostles (Luke 4:14-16), the women (Luke 8:1-3), and his family (Luke 8:19-21; 1:38; 2:51) are all together, never having forsaken him. Luke has no parallel to Mark 3:21 and 14:50 (cf. also Luke 23:49). The company prayed as Jesus himself had prayed on the eve of his selection of the Twelve (Luke 6:12).

Acts 1:15-26 ¹⁵In those days Peter stood up among the brethren (the company of persons was in all about a hundred and twenty), and said, ¹⁶"Brethren, the scripture had to be fulfilled, which the Holy Spirit spoke beforehand by the mouth of David, concerning Judas who was guide to those who arrested Jesus. ¹⁷For he was numbered among us, and was allotted his share in this ministry. ¹⁸(Now this man bought a field with the reward of his wickedness; and falling headlong he burst open in the middle and all his bowels gushed out. ¹⁹And it became known to all the inhabitants of Jerusalem, so that the field was called in their language A-kelda-ma, that is, Field of Blood.) ²⁰For it is written in the book of Psalms,

> 'Let his habitation become desolate,
>   and let there be no one to live in it';
> and
>   'His office let another take.'
> [21]So one of the men who have accompanied us during all the time that the Lord Jesus went in and out among us, [22]beginning from the baptism of John until the day when he was taken up from us—one of these men must become with us a witness to his resurrection." [23]And they put forward two, Joseph called Barsab-bas, who was surnamed Justus, and Mat-thias. [24]And they prayed and said, "Lord, who knowest the hearts of all men, show which one of these two thou hast chosen [25]to take the place in this ministry and apostleship from which Judas turned aside, to go to his own place." [26]And they cast lots for them, and the lot fell on Mat-thias; and he was enrolled with the eleven apostles.

Lots were cast so that the Lord might choose a replacement for Judas Iscariot and raise the number of authoritative witnesses once more to twelve (Acts 1:15-26). Everything is designed to impress readers with the closeness of the ties between Jesus and the first Christian community led by his prophetic successors. The witness to the resurrection must know the entire career of Jesus from his baptism till the moment when he was "taken up" (Acts 1:2, 11, 22; Luke 9:51; 24:51).[60] Luke is here carefully defining the kingship of Jesus by reference back to all the words and deeds of Jesus recorded in the gospel and summarized in Acts. His is a reign of peace (Luke 2:14; 19:38, 42; Acts 10:36-38).

Acts 2:1-4   When the day of Pentecost had come, they were all together in one place. [2]And suddenly a sound came from heaven like the rush of a mighty wind, and it filled all the house where they were sitting. [3]And there appeared to them tongues as of fire, distributed and resting on each one of them. [4]And they were all filled with the Holy Spirit and began to speak in other tongues, as the Spirit gave them utterance.

The promise of the Father through John the Baptist (Luke 3:16) and Jesus (Acts 1:4-5) about the outpouring of the Spirit began to be fulfilled 50 days after Easter (Acts 2:1-4). Pentecost, one of the three great pilgrimage feasts, was originally an agricultural festival celebrating the offering of the firstfruits of the grain harvest (Lev. 23:15-16; Num. 28:16; Deut. 16:9-12; Jos. *Ant.* 3:252). Sometime during the first century it began to mark the giving of the law through Moses to Israel, and Exodus 19 was the portion of the Scripture prescribed for reading.[61]

It is not clear whether Luke intended his readers to see the 3000 converts as the firstfruits of a greater harvest or to note the parallels and contrasts between the Spirit and the law as identity symbols of church and synagogue.

Acts 2:5-13 ⁵Now there were dwelling in Jerusalem Jews, devout men from every nation under heaven. ⁶And at this sound the multitude came together, and they were bewildered, because each one heard them speaking in his own language. ⁷And they were amazed and wondered, saying, "Are not all these who are speaking Galileans? ⁸And how is it that we hear, each of us in his own native language? ⁹Parthians and Medes and Elam-ites and residents of Mes-o-po-tami-a, Judea and Cap-pa-doci-a, Pontus and Asia, ¹⁰Phrygi-a and Pam-phyli-a, Egypt and the parts of Libya belonging to Cy-rene, and visitors from Rome, both Jews and proselytes, ¹¹Cretans and Arabians, we hear them telling in our own tongues the mighty works of God." ¹²And all were amazed and perplexed, saying to one another, "What does this mean?" ¹³But others mocking said, "They are filled with new wine."

A favorite interpretation of the listing of the nations (2:5-13) points to the parallels with Genesis 10 and 11, the table of nations and the tower of Babel. Against such a background Pentecost seems to indicate a fresh deed of God, a removing of the curse and a reuniting of peoples. Other parallels are possible.[62] Nations are named in similar lists in patriotic documents celebrating military conquests, and Jewish authors in similar listings made propaganda for the invincibility of Rome or for the marvelous spread of Jewish religion (Jos. *Wars* 2:358-389; Philo, *Embassy to Gaius* 8-10 and 281-284).

In any case, Luke declares that God has in these last times released energy sufficient to unite divided peoples in a universal kingdom of divine and godly peace.

Acts 2:14-21 ¹⁴But Peter, standing with the eleven, lifted up his voice and addressed them, "Men of Judea and all who dwell in Jerusalem, let this be known to you, and give ear to my words. ¹⁵For these men are not drunk, as you suppose, since it is only the third hour of the day; ¹⁶but this is what was spoken by the prophet Joel:
¹⁷ 'And in the last days it shall be, God declares,
    that I will pour out my Spirit upon all flesh,
    and your sons and your daughters shall prophesy,
    and your young men shall see visions,
    and your old men shall dream dreams;
¹⁸ yea, and on my menservants and my maidservants in those days
    I will pour out my Spirit, and they shall prophesy.
¹⁹ And I will show wonders in the heaven above
    and signs on the earth beneath,
    blood, and fire, and vapor of smoke;
²⁰ the sun shall be turned into darkness
    and the moon into blood,

before the day of the Lord comes,
the great and manifest day.

21 And it shall be that whoever calls on the name of the Lord shall be
saved.' "

Luke manages to draw a picture of an enthusiastic and ecstatic
moment charged with pneumatic energy and at the same time to
guard against misinterpretations of the Christian movement as wild,
frenzied, or orgiastic. The outpouring of the Holy Spirit resulted in
powerful but sensible rhetoric and in reasoned speech.

Apocalyptic imagery is the pet of oppressed groups and margina-
ted peoples and easily breeds revolutionary talk and deeds. But Peter
like the rest of the Twelve is sober, and he used apocalyptic images not
to describe a future cosmic or political cataclysm but to define the
present moment as prophesied by God and as decisive for the destiny
of humankind.

Acts 2:22-36   22"Men of Israel, hear these words: Jesus of Nazareth,
a man attested to you by God with mighty works and wonders and
signs which God did through him in your midst, as you yourselves
know—23this Jesus, delivered up according to the definite plan and
foreknowledge of God, you crucified and killed by the hands of lawless
men. 24But God raised him up, having loosed the pangs of death, because it was not possible for him to be held by it. 25For David says concerning him,

'I saw the Lord always before me,
for he is at my right hand that I may not be shaken;

26 therefore my heart was glad, and my tongue rejoiced;
moreover my flesh will dwell in hope.

27 For thou wilt not abandon my soul to Hades,
nor let thy Holy One see corruption.

28 Thou hast made known to me the ways of life;
thou wilt make me full of gladness with thy presence.'

29 "Brethren, I may say to you confidently of the patriarch David that he
both died and was buried, and his tomb is with us to this day. 30Being
therefore a prophet, and knowing that God had sworn with an oath to
him that he would set one of his descendants upon his throne, 31he
foresaw and spoke of the resurrection of the Christ, that he was not
abandoned to Hades, nor did his flesh see corruption. 32This Jesus God
raised up, and of that we all are witnesses. 33Being therefore exalted at
the right hand of God, and having received from the Father the promise
of the Holy Spirit, he has poured out this which you see and hear. 34For
David did not ascend into the heavens; but he himself says,

'The Lord said to my Lord, Sit at my right hand,

35 till I make thy enemies a stool for thy feet.'

36 Let all the house of Israel therefore know assuredly that God has
made him both Lord and Christ, this Jesus whom you crucified."

Three Lukan pericopes speak of Jesus' ascension, each from a different perspective. The departure scene in Luke 24:50-53 portrays Jesus as priest blessing the people. The narrative of the ascension in Acts 1:9-11, written in terms of an Elijah-Elisha scheme, focuses on the church as continuing Jesus' prophetic work. In Acts 2 the ascension of Jesus is defined in political and royal imagery as exaltation and enthronement.

By way of contrast to the crucifixion, which is described as the act of mistaken human beings, the resurrection is God's verdict and action. Typical of Luke's rhetoric is the formulation " you killed/God raised." With God all things are possible, and it was not possible for death to hold Jesus. God had sworn to enthrone one of David's descendants. In Psalm 16 David spoke of life beyond death, referring not to himself, since he had died and his flesh had long since decayed in a tomb still visited by the pious. The descendant of whom David prophesied was none other than Jesus, as the apostles testify. His resurrection is his vindication by God and his exaltation to the right hand of God. Furthermore, he has received the gift of the Spirit to dispense to his people.

Elsewhere David called this descendant his Lord (Ps. 110:1), and Peter declares that Jesus has by his resurrection been enthroned as Lord and Christ. God sent him and God raised him, but the Jerusalemites had crucified him.

Acts 2:37-41   37 Now when they heard this they were cut to the heart, and said to Peter and the rest of the apostles, " Brethren, what shall we do?" 38 And Peter said to them, "Repent, and be baptized every one of you in the name of Jesus Christ for the forgiveness of your sins; and you shall receive the gift of the Holy Spirit. 39 For the promise is to you and to your children and to all that are far off, every one whom the Lord our God calls to him." 40 And he testified with many other words and exhorted them, saying, "Save yourselves from this crooked generation." 41 So those who received his word were baptized, and there were added that day about three thousand souls.

Peter's audience was moved to repentance, defined as a radical reversal of attitude toward Jesus. They dissociated themselves from the posture of rejection and the act of crucifixion, and were baptized in the name of Jesus, calling upon his name and submitting to his lordship. Proclamation, repentance, confession, Baptism, laying on of hands, and reception of the Spirit are regular elements of initiation into the Christian community in Acts.

Acts 2:42-47   [42]And they devoted themselves to the apostles' teaching and fellowship, to the breaking of bread and the prayers.

[43]And fear came upon every soul; and many wonders and signs were done through the apostles. [44]And all who believed were together and had all things in common; [45]and they sold their posesssions and goods and distributed them to all, as any had need. [46]And day by day, attending the temple together and breaking bread in their homes, they partook of food with glad and generous hearts, [47] praising God and having favor with all the people. And the Lord added to their number day by day those who were being saved.

Luke concludes by drawing a sketch of the Christian community. At least two sinister interpretations were placed on the Christian movement at an early date by outsiders: 1) it is politically subversive and 2) it is morally loose and licentious.[63] Furthermore Christian insiders in Luke's day were divided by conflicting teaching (20:29-30).

In briefest possible compass Luke portrays the community gathered around the apostles in the way the Emmaus disciples clung to Jesus (Luke 24:13-35). Luke's summary statement pictures a community at once peaceable and pure, innocent of any grasping for power or possessions, neither revolutionary nor blasphemous. Under their Lord they conducted themselves in devout, pious, and law-abiding fashion.

Conclusion

In his Easter narratives Luke aimed to do more than confound gnostics or other spiritualizers by asserting that the resurrection really happened in the world of space and time, and that the resurrected Jesus has flesh and bones capable of being seen, felt, and fed.

For him the resurrection was current lively report as much as it was past factual reality. It was the fundamental and founding report in the Christian community, parallel to the ancient words reporting God's deeds in the midst of his people in the days of patriarchs, kings, and prophets. It was handed down in the community from chosen eyewitnesses through reliable channels to him and the people of his own time. It was reliable report and thoroughly good news.

The cross appeared to nullify hopes for redemption and salvation and to confirm and deepen the impression that the world drifts and is tossed by chance winds blowing on capricious waters. He who came to seek and to save the lost (Luke 19:10) and who was in the world as one who serves (22:27) was rejected and put to death. But news of the resurrection serves to arouse and undergird Christian faith in Jesus as exalted Lord in spite of his crucifixion. That deed of evil and ignorant humans was overruled by God's raising of Jesus to life, glory, and kingship.

As Luke proclaimed the lordship of Jesus, he took care to display his fixed opposition to naive and dangerous political interpretations of the resurrection as the installation of Jesus as a secular rival to Caesar. Luke proclaimed a kingdom as peaceful as paradise (23:43), in which the king breaks bread with his subjects, even serves bread to them, reassuring outsiders and reminding insiders that this kingdom does not trumpet its advent or pave its way with the usual political and military signals of violence and arms. The news of his resurrection has been and is to be passed from teller to hearer. Luke's narrative of Easter portrays the angels, the women, Cleopas and his companion, the eleven, and all the others in Jerusalem as successive witnesses of the resurrection. By means of their testimony all peoples and nations are invited to become subject to Jesus and the kingdom.

John

The Setting: Excluded and Orphaned

Three distinct clusters of evidence have led interpreters to at least three different hypotheses about the situation of the author of the Fourth Gospel and of his community.[1]

Excommunication from the Synagogue

One hypothesis is that the Fourth Gospel was born in the context of a struggle with Judaism. The basic clues supporting this hypothesis are as follows: the sharply polemical edge to the evangelist's talk about "the Jews," the hostility of the chief priests and Pharisees, the deflating of the significance and achievements of Moses, the bite in the arguments about the messiahship of Jesus and the prominence of those debates, the appropriation of the scriptures of the Old Testament and the blunt declaration that "the Jews" do not listen to them, the insistence on Jesus' oneness with the Father (eliciting the charge that he has a demon, is mad, or is a Samaritan), the high visibility of Jewish and Semitic terms and of rabbinic exegesis, and parallels with the terminology and conceptions of the Dead Sea Scrolls.

The dialogue between Jesus and Nicodemus (Chap. 3) has long been perceived as, on some level, a conversation between the Johannine community and the synagogue of the late first century, but the situation of the Johannine community (at least at one stage in its life) seems to be most clearly mirrored in the drama of Jesus' healing of the blind man (Chap. 9). The Jewish parents of the Jewish blind man are afraid to get involved in defending their son or in identifying Jesus as his healer, because "the Jews" had already arrived at a solemn decision that confession of Jesus as the Christ was an act punishable by formal excommunication.

Following is a kind of composite portrait of the history of the Johannine community, pieced together from the writings of a number of interpreters who agree on the centrality of the phenomena listed above.[2]

In the very earliest period the Johannine group was at home within the synagogue, observing the Torah, not involved in debates about admitting Gentiles, experiencing no social dislocation and little alienation from their Jewish heritage, but insisting that Jesus is God's long awaited eschatological prophet-messiah, who had come to grant genuinely new deliverance to his people. The signs source (or signs gospel)—primarily a collection of the miracles of Jesus assembled as evidence of his messiahship—is the basic document of the group at this period.[3]

Perhaps Jews of an antitemple bias (like Stephen, Acts 6-7) were then attracted to the fellowship, and they in turn may have made converts among Samaritans (John 4, Acts 8).[4] The Johannine circle continued to sharpen its focus on the plenitude of God's gifts in Jesus.

The disastrous war with Rome (A.D. 66-70) resulted in the double catastrophe of the destruction of Jerusalem and the razing of the temple, resulting in the scattering of the priesthood and cessation of sacrifice and cult. The assembly of scholars at Jamnia under Johanan ben Zakkai and Gamaliel II reorganized Judaism on a Pharisaic platform around the institutions of synagogue, study of the Torah, and prayer. They also defined the identity of Judaism against aberrant and heterodox Jewish movements, including the Christian movement.[5]

Around A.D. 90 the Pharisees at Jamnia incorporated into the prayer known as the Eighteen Benedictions a new petition against Christians and other heretics. The new benediction was deliberately designed to detect Jews who desired to hold dual allegiance to Moses and to Jesus and to remain within the synagogue as members of a messianic fellowship. Some of the Christian Jews were unveiled and formally excommunicated (9:22, 34; 12:42; 16:2) and some Christian evangelists may even have been executed as worshippers of two Gods (Jesus and the Father), guilty of seducing people away from monotheism (16:2; cf. 5:18; 7:1; 8:44; 10:31-39; 15:18-20).

Driven from the synagogue, the outcasts concluded that they had actually gained more than they had lost and focused their hearts on the great promises of God realized in Jesus.

In the period following expulsion from the synagogue, the Evangelist—a loyal follower of the Beloved Disciple—produced the Fourth Gospel, expressing not only the theological convictions but also the social identity of the Johannine community. The gospel pictures (1) the Johannine community itself, (2) the parent synagogue from which it is sharply differentiated (3:11; 15:18-22), (3) Christian Jews remaining within the synagogue (8:31-32; 12:42-43) from whom the Johannine community is even more sharply alienated, and (4) other communities of Jewish Christian outcasts from the synagogue ("other sheep") with whom there is still hope of unification (10:16). Finally there is evidence of a separate body (5), consisting primarily of Gentile converts (5:35; 12:20; 21:7-19), who represent the emerging Great Church.

Some versions of this history picture the Johannine community as part of Jewish Christianity, while others imagine that it moved increasingly away from Judaism and from Jewish Christianity, alienated from the latter because it rejected the high Johannine christology.

The three epistles of John, later products of the Johannine community, not written by the Fourth Evangelist, indicate that the community split around A.D. 100 into (1) spiritualizing secessionists who were followers of Diotrophes (3 John 9), and (2) adherents of "the elder," who authored the Johannine epistles (2 John 1; 3 John 1). In the second century the secessionists (the larger of the two groups) continued to "go ahead" instead of abiding in the doctrine of Christ (2 John 9), developed their denial that Jesus Christ had come in the flesh, and moved into gnosticism, while the followers of "the elder" assimilated into the mainstream of the great or orthodox, and ultimately victorious, church.[6]

Hellenistic, Gnostic, or Mystic Connections

A minority view, once more widely held, is that John's is "the gospel of the Hellenists," produced as a kind of missionary tract in an effort to woo to the Christian faith the kind of sophisticated, cosmopolitan, educated people of the upper classes who were attracted to gnosticism and to the eclectic religious philosophies current at the end of the first century and the beginning of the second.[7] That audience found the synoptic gospels not at all suited to their tastes. In them

Jesus seems excessively partial to the poor, the unwashed, the ignorant, the outcasts, women of ill repute, slaves, and children.

It is very striking that John's gospel mentions no poor people, no
tax gatherers, no widows, no children, no demoniacs, no lepers, no
prostitutes, no Sadducees, no Herodians, and certainly no Zealots.
Thus Jesus in the Fourth Gospel never embraces infants, touches
lepers, utters exorcistic phrases, permits women to accompany him,
eats with tax collectors, or encourages revolutionaries. Also absent
are any pronouncements on charity toward the poor or taxes to
Caesar, any advice regarding the reciprocal obligations of husbands
and wives or parents and children, any proverbs featuring birds of the
air, leaves of the trees, or the grass and flowers of the hillside, or any
homely parables of finding a lost sheep or a lost coin. The worlds of
nature and of ordinary social life are nearly swept aside, as the talk
focuses on the identity of Jesus and on his mission. And the Fourth
Gospel, as it talks about Jesus, uses ideas and images (above and
below, light and darkness, spirit and flesh, life and death, truth and
falsehood, creative Word, rebirth) which reflect an international
rather than a strictly Palestinian background.[8]

John's gospel may be an example of the early church's laboring to
explain itself in relation to what were widely regarded as serious
handicaps: Jesus' Jewish parentage, peasant background, and Palestinian rootage; the prominence of women in his company, and the flavor of superstition and magic (exorcisms and ritual) in his ministry;
his role as a savior clearly subject to human limitations, executed by
Roman authorities.[9]

And yet for all the differences between John and the Synoptics,
John is structured like the others, running basically from Jesus' baptism to his death and resurrection, and the drama of his life is played
out on the same Palestinian landscape and in the same Jewish milieu.
John's gospel is not one of those fabulous romances of the life and
times of Jesus during the "lost" or "hidden" years between the ages of
12 and 30, nor is it an account of otherwise unknown or esoteric teaching offered by Jesus in a protracted postresurrection career of 18
months or 12 years before his ultimate departure. And the gospel is
not set in Egypt or India but in Palestine.

Nevertheless, the Fourth Gospel was apparently welcomed in
gnostic circles before it was accepted by those Christians now regarded as orthodox. Only from the middle of the second century
onward do clear allusions to John's gospel begin to be found among
the orthodox. Melito of Sardis (A.D. 160-170) used it, and Irenaeus

(A.D. 180) championed the inclusion of the Fourth Gospel alongside the synoptics.[10]

In spite of early acceptance by gnostics and tardy recognition on the part of the Great Church, the Fourth Gospel clearly does not belong in the same category as the Gospel of Thomas or the Valentinian Gospel of Truth. It holds a middle ground between the synoptics and the later gnostic gospels. In John's gospel Jesus is still Jewish and lives in the land of the Jews, but John records no genealogy linking Jesus to a Jewish past (instead his prologue presents Jesus as the Eternal Word), no praise of John the Baptist (or of Baptism, the Lord's Supper, or any other sacramental or cultic acts), no scribes, Sadducees, or Herods in conversation with Jesus (the setting is altered in a universalizing fashion), no use of "Gentile" as synonym of "heathen," no recommendation of Jewish law or custom by Jesus (but instead a "new" commandment and the assertion that the law came by Moses but grace and truth came through Jesus). Also Jesus seems less bound by human limitations. John presents no temptation in the wilderness, no agony in the garden, no seizure and arrest in the synoptic manner, no mocking at the cross, and no cry of dereliction. Talk of eternal life nearly supplants that of the kingdom of God (lest the gospel be suspected as anti-Roman propaganda).

John's gospel unfolds the cosmic drama of the Savior of the world (4:42). It is the story of a particular Jew of first century Palestine and, simultaneously, the account of a divine being beyond all nationality and earthly limitation. His peasant proletarian origins tend to recede into the dim background so that he is not really or ultimately from Nazareth or from Bethlehem but from above, and his lineage is not simply of Mary and Joseph but of the Father.

The author of the Fourth Gospel perceived in his target audience a hunger for immortality and redemption from the world of clinging flesh and inevitable change, a disdain of superstitious myth, exotic ritual and crude ecstasy, a yearning for light and life, and a faith in the liberating power of revealed knowledge and truth.[11]

While the Fourth Gospel is still faithful to the earliest traditions about Jesus in a way that the early apocryphal Gospel of Truth for example is not, it seems to some interpreters to be voicing its appeal to the same kind of people who were drawn by gnosticism, Hermetism and the mysteries of Isis. In this regard it is interesting to note that in the Fourth Gospel disciples come to Jesus not from fishing vessels, tax offices, or hearth and home, but from rival religions, other bearers of salvation, John the Baptist, or false theological loyalties.[12]

Christian Experience of Abandonment

The Fourth Gospel is remarkable in the amount of space it devotes to the Farewell Discourse of Jesus (Chap. 13-17). In featuring so prominently the valedictory words of Jesus, it appears to some modern investigators that the author has pictured his readers as standing in the place of children, heirs, or successors, and that he has ascribed to them the sentiments common to such people on the occasion of the departure of the father or leader: sorrow at the announcement, confusion about its significance, and anxiety about their own future (14:1, 5, 22, 27; 16:6, 20-22). Above all, the author has focused on their sense of being forsaken, orphaned, abandoned, and desolate (*orphanous*, 14:18).

Jesus announced that he was departing, that for a time they would not see him, and that even though they would still be in the world, he would no longer be in the world (13:33, 36; 14:3, 12, 28; 16:5, 7, 16, 19; 17:11). His going away was in one sense the result of the world's opposition (14:30; 15:18, 20, 24) and the world rejoiced at his departure (16:20), but the disciples expressed dismay and bewilderment; they were troubled, full of questions, and void of answers (13:6-9, 36; 14:1, 5, 8-10; 16:17-18).[13]

As the person uttering the farewell frequently does in such valedictory speeches, Jesus focused not only on their present bewilderment and the hazards of the future, but also on their equipment for dealing with their challenges and tasks by reason of what he had given them and would yet bestow upon them. He predicted betrayal and warned that they would all be scattered (16:32), and in the Fourth Gospel being scattered means being divided by unbelief from him who is the shepherd, the light, the life. Nevertheless, the farewell is fundamentally consolatory and full of promise. Jesus reminded them of his previous instructions, promised them the Paraclete and the gifts of peace and joy, and commended them to the Father in prayer (Chap. 17).[14]

In the Prologue (1:1-18) the author uses the first person plural pronoun three times to express his sense of solidarity with his community of readers (1:14, 16) and reminds them of what it is that constitutes them as a community against the outsiders. In the final two chapters of the gospel, the readers are again addressed directly. And in these chapters (in addition to the Farewell Discourses) the gospel deals at length with the sense of separation and distance and with the provisions of Jesus for bridging the gap between himself and his own.

In Chapter 20 Mary Magdalene wept because she could not find her Lord and then, when she was granted the sight of the resurrected Jesus, she clung to him and was rebuked for being satisfied prematurely. Peter stood dumb within the empty tomb, and Thomas seemed stoically resigned to accepting death as an insurmountable barrier to fellowship with Jesus. But the Beloved Disciple, believing without benefit of sight or touch, is portrayed as the very model of Johannine faith.

Chapter 21 climaxes in the discussion of the words spoken by Jesus about the Beloved Disciple: "If it is my will that he remain until I come, what is that to you?" (21:22-23). The author declares plainly that this saying of Jesus was misquoted and misunderstood as a promise that the Beloved Disciple would not die before the parousia. He then comments directly on the saying and indirectly offers insight into the situation of his community.

As time passed in the years following the death and resurrection of Jesus, more and more of the original eyewitnesses of Jesus died. Like Paul, many of the first generation of believers at first expected to be alive at the coming of Jesus (1 Thess. 4:15). But then Stephen was martyred (Acts 7), followed by James the brother of John (Acts 12), by Peter (John 21:18-19), and then by Paul (in the 60s of the first century at the hand of the Roman government). James the brother of Jesus was killed in Jerusalem in A.D. 66. Time passed, and still the coming of Jesus was delayed.

Some in the community apparently thought that at least the Beloved Disciple would remain alive as faithful witness and therefore as reliable and authoritative link backwards to the historical Jesus. Surely he would survive all the way to the parousia. But then he too died. So all the earliest disciples, eyewitnesses, authoritative apostles, and members of Jesus' own immediate family were swept away. The Johannine community suffered an acute sense of abandonment and felt cut loose, adrift, orphaned, dumped on the doorstep. John's readers were in danger of losing "life in his name" (20:30) or of not having it in anything like the fullness God intended for them.

The Farewell, the Prologue, and the resurrection chapters are devoted to a subtle discussion of the nature and genesis of Christian faith by which the ugly ditch between the past of the incarnate and crucified Jesus and the present of the Christian community is able to be bridged. All this material is evidence for describing the situation of the publisher and first readers of John's gospel as one of abandonment.

The Situation

So the Johannine community is variously described as consisting of Jewish Christians recently expelled from the synagogue, or as a circle of Jewish and Gentile Christians appealing to educated religious pagans, or as a Christian community depressed by the delay of the parousia, confused by the death of the last eyewitness, and torn by dissension.

These three suggestions about the situation of the author and his community do not exhaust all the possibilities. But how are even these three related? One or another may be a construct resulting from faulty modern perceptions. Or perhaps the situation of the Johannine community changed over the years. More will be said below in the comments on 21:23-24 about the relationship among the Beloved Disciple, the evangelist, and the editor or redactor of the gospel. Perhaps the experiences of the evangelist were not those of the Beloved Disciple, and the context in which the redactor worked may have differed significantly from that of the evangelist. The experiences of different persons and times may have left their impress on the gospel.

A solution acknowledging a certain amount of accuracy in each of the three basic suggestions can be worked out following the tack of historical change and development in the community.

In the second half of the first century, both in Judaism and in Christianity, apocalyptic hopes were waning. God had not miraculously intervened on behalf of Israel in its struggle with Rome nor had Jesus returned suddenly and triumphantly as Savior and Judge in a flash of lightning visible from east to west. History continued without the expected dramatic intrusion. As the apocalyptic fires were banked, gnosticism and mysticism, with their accent on the present inward appropriation of divine life and light, advanced significantly both in the Jewish and Christian communities. Simultaneously, both religious movements exhibited the marks of progressive institutionalization, with the development of official leadership, a list of authoritative books, the revision and fixing of liturgies, and other crystallizations of the tradition designed to safeguard the identity and existence of the community.[15]

This was the general background for the Fourth Gospel, which was probably published in Ephesus in western Asia Minor toward the end of the first century. Sharp struggles between church and synagogue certainly lay in the past for this community as for others, but the Johannine community had struggled on more than one front. Salvation is from the Jews (4:22), and so Judaism is the mother religion, but the daughter is by no means dependent nor does she live any longer in her mother's house. Indeed the evangelist and his community had very early discovered that the independent life of the daughter religion is healthy and right.

As the evangelist and his community pondered their experience, they developed their peculiarly daring positions regarding Jesus' unique person and status. The evangelist came to proclaim the superiority of Jesus over every other revealer or savior, whether Jewish, Greek, or Roman. Then he and his community found themselves in conflict not only with Jews and the adherents of various Greco-Roman cults and movements but also with other Christians.

The author was an evangelist, propagandist, inspired leader, and teacher, and he earnestly reached out to Jew, pagan, and fellow Christians of non-Johannine communities. But dialogue was not his gift. The experience of excommunication, disappointing contacts with pagans, and the beginnings of struggles within the Johannine community strengthened the author's habit of thinking antithetically in terms of ultimate contrasts and confirmed him in a kind of siege mentality.

His contrasts are of course not those of politics or apocalyptic. Another member of the community apparently composed the Apocalypse. His are the religious or spiritual dualisms of the Hellenistic synagogue and of the higher pagan religions.

The past struggle with the synagogue continued to live in the present of the Johannine community in the form of a powerful historical lesson, reflected upon and generalized, a piece of the past raised to the level of a symbolic event. For this author the company of believers is a circle of light and love in a dark world. They are called to love one another and can expect to be hated by the world.

In the vocabulary of the Fourth Gospel sin is not personal immorality or social injustice. As in Philo and the higher Hellenistic religions, it is paraphrased as dwelling in error or darkness, abiding in slavery under the ugly dominion of death, or as being scattered, fragmented, and lost. The gospel promises not so much the forgiveness of sins and moral renewal as the heavenly vision (1:14, 18; 14:8-11), regeneration (Chap. 3), and oneness with the divine (15:4; 17:22-23).

The Fourth Gospel focuses with unique power on Jesus as the one revealer and savior, who alone has descended and ascended, the sole mysterious source of truth and light, freedom and life. Therefore the gospel insists that sin has only the one fundamental meaning of unbelief, and true knowledge *(gnōsis)* is to know the one sent by the Father (17:3, 25). To know the Father and Son is to know love *(agapē,* 3:16), to dwell in love (13:35), and to have life (10:10; 20:31).

The pivotal difference between the gospel and Judaism, as well as between the gospel and current Hellenistic and gnostic religions and philosophies, can be defined as Jesus; and what was most offensive about the human, fleshly Jesus was his cross. To the Jews it was axiomatic that the Christ remains forever (12:34), and the adherents of Hellenistic religions and philosophies, far from looking to the flesh for deliverance, sought deliverance from the flesh and everything transitory and mortal.

To the Jew, John insisted that salvation is present now, in time and history, and to the Greeks he declared that salvation is present here, in the space below the skies.[16] To fellow Christians inside and outside his community the author offered the boldest statements of any evangelist on the dignity of Jesus.

The evangelist was a daring, penetrating thinker who had meditated long on the career of Jesus in the days of his flesh. He had seen the divine glory precisely in the flesh, and even in that which is most fleshly about Jesus, namely his dying. The evangelist declared that Jesus' dying was in reality his glorification. His cross was the first rung on the ladder of ascent. He took the shared tradition about Jesus and opened it up to make its burning center transparently visible. He labored to display the decisive, universal significance of Jesus.

When the evangelist died, the community was badly shaken. Death in its varied forms—the cross of Jesus, the persecution of the community whether by synagogue or world, the martyrdom of Peter (21:18-19), and finally the death of the Beloved Disciple—raised most acutely the question of the community's connection with the Father and the Son. A sense of abandonment and uncertainty gripped the community.

Sometime after the death of the evangelist, and in response to that death, a member of his community edited the entire work, added other fragments of the evangelist's legacy, composed Chapter 21, and issued the gospel. The redactor was a pupil and admirer of the evangelist and shared his views of Jesus, although his own outlook was more irenic and not so sharply dualistic as the evangelist's. He apparently regarded the evangelist as the Beloved Disciple, whether he really was or not.

In publishing the gospel the editor disseminated the evangelist's bold message about Jesus and also directly addressed the matter of abandonment as a religious theme.

Chapter 20 (the first of the two resurrection chapters) offers primarily the evangelist's word about the glorified Jesus as the sole "Lord and God," about faith as the proper form of relationship to him, and about true life as the blessing bestowed upon the faithful of every time and every place. Opposition to faith, false faith, and unfaith are all dealt with in Chapter 20.

Chapter 21 clearly reflects the redactor's concerns in a situation of abandonment and of anxiety about the community's connection with the revealer in the days after the death of the last eyewitness. Perhaps it also addresses a word to members of Petrine communities unfortunately somewhat pleased at the passing of the Beloved Disciple. More is said about the situation of the editor in the introduction to the comments on Chapter 21.

To members of his own community—confounded by the power of death and by the passing of the last eyewitness, tempted to seek security and identity by stoking up apocalyptic hope, by adherence to an ecclesiastical system of leaders and sacraments, or by mystic meditation, gnostic contemplation, or charismatic experience—he extolled the glory and triumph of the cross (chapters 1-20). He also declared the wonder of the works of Jesus performed through the community and especially praised the potency of the word of testimony enshrined in the community's book.

Together the Johannine resurrection narratives (Chap. 20-21) speak eloquently of the cross of Jesus and his followers, the fruitfulness as well as the offense of the cross, the blessedness of faith in the one glorified upon the cross, the crucified and resurrected one as Jacob's ladder, the vacated tomb as the new inner sanctum and holy of holies, and the sufficiency of the word of testimony entrusted to the community and of its power to provoke faith and so produce life.

John 20

The Johannine narratives of Easter are remarkable for the intensity of their concentration on individual persons and their varied responses to Jesus. The synoptic gospels share with John an interest in the discovery of the empty tomb on Easter morning by a group of women and in the appearance of the resurrected Jesus to the whole body of disciples, among whom Peter is prominent. John has selected three individual figures for special comment: Mary Magdalene (singled out from all the other women), the Beloved Disciple (here as usual in tension with Peter), and Thomas (over against the rest of the Twelve). Through each one of these persons John bears witness to some aspect of the meaning of Easter faith.[17]

John 20:1-18: Three Disciples

John 20:1-18   Now on the first day of the week Mary Magdalene came to the tomb early, while it was still dark, and saw that the stone had been taken away from the tomb. [2]So she ran, and went to Simon Peter and the other disciple, the one whom Jesus loved, and said to them, "They have taken the Lord out of the tomb, and we do not know where they have laid him." [3]Peter then came out with the other disciple, and they went toward the tomb. [4]They both ran, but the other disciple outran Peter and reached the tomb first; [5]and stooping to look in, he saw the linen cloths lying there, but he did not go in. [6]Then Simon Peter came, following him, and went into the tomb; he saw the linen cloths lying, [7]and the napkin, which had been on his head, not lying with the linen cloths but rolled up in a place by itself. [8]Then the other disciple, who reached the tomb first, also went in, and he saw and believed; [9]for as yet they did not know the scripture, that he must rise from the dead. [10]Then the disciples went back to their homes.

[11]But Mary stood weeping outside the tomb, and as she wept she stooped to look into the tomb; [12]and she saw two angels in white, sitting where the body of Jesus had lain, one at the head and one at the feet. [13]They said to her, "Woman, why are you weeping?" She said to them, "Because they have taken away my Lord, and I do not know where they have laid him." [14]Saying this, she turned round and saw Jesus standing, but she did not know that it was Jesus. [15]Jesus said to her, "Woman, why are you weeping? Whom do you seek?" Supposing him to be the gardener, she said to him, "Sir, if you have carried him away, tell me where you have laid him, and I will take him away." [16]Jesus said to her, "Mary." She turned and said to him in Hebrew, "Rab-bo´ni!" (which means Teacher). [17]Jesus said to her, "Do not hold me, for I have not yet ascended to the Father; but go to my brethren and say to them, I am ascending to my Father and your Father, to my God and your God." [18]Mary Mag´dalene went and said to the disciples, "I have seen the Lord"; and she told them that he had said these things to her.

John has arranged the first 18 verses carefully so that the narrative about Mary Magdalene, together with the material on the Beloved Disciple and Peter, forms a sandwich. John begins with Mary, interrupts her story to focus on the Beloved Disciple and Peter, then returns to complete the narrative regarding Mary:

20:1-2 Mary Magdalene
20:2-10 Beloved Disciple and Peter
20:11-18 Mary Magdalene

By means of this structuring John has found a way to keep Mary's encounter with Jesus and confession of him from overshadowing the faith of the Beloved Disciple. He keeps his priority over Mary as well as over Peter. The author has also found his own way of integrating the fluid and multiform Easter traditions of the early church. The synoptics say that women were the first at the empty tomb, and Matthew goes on to record that the women saw Jesus himself on their way back to the city. Paul lists Peter as the first to whom Jesus appeared and mentions no women as recipients of appearances (1 Cor. 15:5-9). Luke apparently agrees with Paul (Luke 24:34).

According to John, a woman was first at the tomb and first to encounter Jesus. Peter may have been the first of the Twelve to lay eyes on the resurrected Jesus—John does not say so, but at least allows for the possibility. Nevertheless, the Beloved Disciple is first of all, not in discovering the tomb, nor in beholding the resurrected one, but in coming to faith; and there is neither greatness nor priority which exceeds that in the mind of John.

In the contrast with Mary Magdalene, the Beloved Disciple not only retains his priority but has his faith further described. Mary first thinks Jesus is still a corpse, mislaid, carried off, absent. When she encounters the living Jesus, faith begins to stir in her but her faith is described as inadequate and out of focus. One of the strong themes of Mary's story is her search for the body and her desire for bodily contact with that visible and tangible body. The Beloved Disciple, however, relates to the resurrected Jesus appropriately and believes without either seeing or touching the resurrected Jesus. In that he illustrates, already at the beginning of the chapter, the attitude blessed by Jesus at the end.

20:1-2   Mary Magdalene

20:1   Mary arrived at the tomb "while it was still dark." The other gospels offer notes of time which on the surface contradict John. Mark, for example, says that the women came to the tomb "after the sun had risen" (Mark 16:2). Furthermore, according to John, Mary Magdalene arrived alone and made the discovery of the empty tomb all by herself.

20:2   A first person plural pronoun survives in the "*we* do not know." That is the only trace, if indeed it is that, of the other Marys (Luke 24:10; Matt. 28:1; Mark 16:1) and Joanna (Luke 24:10; 8:3) and Salome (Mark 16:1) and the rest of the women (Luke 24:10).

John's account is spoiled if it is harmonized at the historical and chronological level and read as a scene occurring in a sequence including events recited in the synoptists. It does John a disservice to read him as describing what happened first, before sunrise and arrival of the other women. It distracts from John's point to ponder whether Mary Magdalene, having discovered the tomb empty, went to summon not only Peter and the Beloved Disciple but also the other Marys, Joanna, and Salome, who then brought spices and arrived after dawn.

John has both sifted the tradition and elaborated upon it.[18] He has transmitted a spare, lean portrait of the events of that day, cutting away everything extraneous to his purpose. He does not mention tampering with the tomb, and countering rumors about grave-robbing or fraud is not his intention.

Mary Magdalene is the only woman named in the Easter narratives of all four gospels. According to the synoptic gospels seven demons had been cast out of her (Luke 8:2). She was among those women who followed Jesus from Galilee, ministering to him (Luke 8:1-3; Mark 15:40-41 par.), and she witnessed the crucifixion and burial (Mark 15:40-41 par. and 15:47 par.). John has placed her in two scenes only: at the cross (19:25) and at the tomb. In the former scene she stands with Jesus' mother and with "his mother's sister, Mary the wife of Clopas" and with the Beloved Disciple. Nothing further is reported of her at the cross than that she was there, but her presence at cross and tomb serves to bind the two scenes together into one indissoluble whole. John tells the stories of crucifixion and resurrection in temporal sequence, of course, but he clearly wants his readers to grasp the inner connection between cross and glory.

John's Mary is the very picture of attentiveness and devotion. She is by no means numbered among the enemies of Jesus. She is no plotter, no interrogator, no crucifier. But is she a believer? Her attitude and position seem curiously similar to those of Nicodemus, who admired Jesus and came to him by night (John 3). She calls Jesus "the Lord" (20:2), indeed "my Lord" (20:13), but she went to the tomb with the conviction that her Lord was quite dead. John may be critiquing a form of Christian belief, one that regarded Jesus as Lord but was overwhelmed by a sense of his distance or absence and their own abandonment.

It is not said that she brought spices to anoint him, as the women are said to have done in Mark and Luke. In John's narrative, Jesus had been anointed by Mary of Bethany before his entry into Jerusalem (John 12:1-8), and after his death Jesus was anointed by Joseph of

Arimathea and Nicodemus, who brought 100 pounds of spices and gave to the corpse of Jesus the kind of lavish respect befitting royalty in their death (see 2 Chron. 16). Even without spices Mary's devotion is precisely like that of the women in the synoptic accounts. She focused on his mortal remains. She counted on his remaining dead. When she saw that the tomb was empty, she wanted the corpse back again. The empty tomb did not impress her as signifying anything but loss, and John with a few quick strokes of the pen portrays her agitation as she sets off in her quest for the dead Jesus. So far Mary is still in "the dark" (cf. 6:16-17; 8:12; 12:35, hr 46; 13:30).

20:3-10   The Beloved Disciple and Peter

20:3   But before completing Mary's story, John breaks in with his unique report concerning Peter and the Beloved Disciple (cf. Luke 24:12).

Because the Beloved Disciple and Peter almost always appear not merely together but in contrast with one another, it is only fair to say that they are in some sense rivals, pictured in tension with one another.[19] The tradition pointed to Peter as the first to see the resurrected Jesus and therefore as the first to come to faith. John's narrative is not a flat contradiction of that tradition. It does not say that the Beloved Disciple was granted the first appearance and came first to Easter faith. The account is shaped in such a way that the priority of the Beloved Disciple is of a different order of magnitude altogether. It has a different content.

And so the narrative speaks not only of the two disciples but of the nature of Christian faith.

20:4   The two disciples set out running together toward the tomb. The Beloved Disciple outran Peter and arrived sooner, but he did not enter.

20:5   He did bend over and peer into the tomb. The author focuses attention in this scene and the next on what these visitors beheld in the tomb. The Beloved Disciple saw the grave cloths lying there.

20:6-7   Simon Peter followed in the footsteps of the Beloved Disciple (cf. 18:15), in some way coming behind him in priority. The Beloved Disciple waited for him to arrive and enter. The author does not imply respect but simply employs a device ensuring the fullest contrast between the two. Simon Peter entered the tomb ahead of the Beloved Disciple and spied the linen cloths and, rolled up by itself, the napkin which had been on Jesus' face.

20:8   The Beloved Disciple is then described for the second time in this brief paragraph as "first at the tomb" (vv. 4 and 8). He went in, and of him alone is it said that he came to faith. His faith, based not on the word of angels nor on the sight of the resurrected Jesus, is the climax of the paragraph. He is an encouragement and example for all the multitudes of generations afterwards who do not have the opportunity of sight.

He saw empty cloths in an empty tomb and came to faith. John has constructed the Lazarus account (Chap. 11) in such a way as to help the reader make some connections and contrasts between Jesus' resurrection and the raising of Lazarus. When Jesus commanded Lazarus to emerge from his tomb, "The dead man came out, his hands and feet bound with bandages, and his face wrapped with a napkin. Jesus said to them, 'Untie him and let him go' " (John 11:44).

Lazarus was bound, Jesus unbound. Grave cloths and napkin circled and bound Lazarus, but cloths were left behind by Jesus. Lazarus would need the cloths again, for he was still in the grip of death. Jesus laid aside the cloths and the grave, for in dying he had triumphed over death. What the Beloved Disciple "saw" when he beheld the cloths in the tomb was that the death of Jesus was the death of death, that the dying of Jesus was the source of life.[20]

20:9   Then and only then does the evangelist picture the Beloved Disciple as understanding the meaning of the Scriptures. Not until then did he understand that the Scriptures promise God's victory and God's glory on the earth not by an act of power or of mere unveiling, but through the crucifixion of Jesus. The Beloved Disciple "knew the Scriptures" when he heard them saying that life emerges from the death of God's Son, and eternal life is irrupting into the world already now through the incarnate, crucified, and resurrected Jesus.

20:10   Once that climax is achieved, the account is swiftly rounded off and closed with the remark that the two disciples went home again.

20:11-18   Mary Magdalene

20:11   Without further ado Mary Magdalene is reintroduced. Nothing is said of any contacts between her and the two who had just left, and to ask why they did not meet or why, meeting, they did not speak, is beside the point and misuses the account. She is pictured once more as a devoted and distressed mourner. While still weeping, she goes through precisely the same motions as the two men. She bent over and peeked inside the tomb.

20:12   But she saw something different from what the other two had seen. At least the vision seems to be entirely different; but because the author has set the two sights into deliberately parallel positions, they can best be taken as parallel in content and import, so that the one throws light on the other.

Mary had a vision of two angels in white seated on the slab or shelf along the wall of the cave-tomb where the body of Jesus had lain. One sat at the head of the shelf and the other at the foot. Mark writes that the women, including Mary Magdalene, saw "a young man sitting (in the tomb) on the right side" (Mark 16:5). Matthew pictures the women conversing with "an angel of the Lord" who "rolled back the stone and sat upon it" (28:2), while Luke portrays "two men" standing by them inside the tomb (24:4).

20:13   For beings whose task is communicating messages for God, these emissaries are strangely tight-lipped. They have little to say, compared with the angels in the synoptic gospels. Two angels carry a message that is only three words long in Greek: *gynai, ti klaieis:* "Woman, why are you weeping?"

They are kept from saying too much lest they anticipate the conversation with Jesus and steal his scene. Yet their words are indirect testimony to the resurrection, for they are a criticism of mourning. The message borne by the angels is actually conveyed best by their posture, which speaks louder than words.

Ask an audience of ordinary Christians what Old Testament scene comes to mind as they picture two angels in a small dark space stationed one at the head and one at the foot of a shelf or slab, and almost immediately someone will respond, "The ark of the covenant in the Holy of Holies." That response is naive, uncomplicated, and correct.[21]

John is declaring that the crucified and resurrected Jesus is himself the place of most intimate and gracious meeting with God. He is the place where heaven and earth meet in holy and creative communion.

This interpretation of the scene is corroborated not only by the parallel vision of the Beloved Disciple in verses 3-10 but by numerous passages in the earlier sections of the gospel. Difficult at first, but finally illuminating, is the promise of Jesus at the beginning of the gospel. To Nathanael and the other disciples impressed by his display of more than earthly knowledge he said,

You shall see greater things than these ... Truly, truly, I say to you, you
will see heaven opened, and the angels of God ascending and descending
upon the Son of Man (1:50-51).

That word was not fulfilled by the production of wine at Cana in
the immediately following narrative. As impressive as that was as a
demonstration of his glory, it stands under the declaration, "My hour
has not yet come" (2:4).

What else inside this gospel might serve as fulfillment of that
promise of "greater things" and of the vision of angels ascending and
descending? The angel mentioned by bystanders in 12:29 does not offer any real help. If the promise of 1:50-51 has any fulfillment within
the boundaries of the gospel, it may very well be recorded in the scene
involving Mary Magdalene. Where the Beloved Disciple had seen a
tomb empty except for the mysteriously abandoned linen cloths and
napkin, she saw angels upon the "ascent" and "descent," upon the
head and the feet, or rather upon the places where his head and his
feet had rested.

Furthermore, all through his gospel "the greater things," "the
heavenly things," or the really difficult things, are the death and
resurrection of Jesus or rather the coincidence of exaltation and
humiliation, triumph and defeat, life and death (2:20; 3:12; 6:60). The
ultimate revelation is the gift of life through his death, the triumph
bestowed in his crucifixion, the victory achieved through his wounds.

So 1:50-51, presenting Jesus as the new Bethel, the place of the
dwelling of God, is to a certain extent balanced and also fulfilled by
20:12, depicting Jesus' tomb as the new Holy of Holies. And it is not
just Jesus with his signs of power or demonstrations of supernatural
knowledge but Jesus with his real death, the living Jesus who was
crucified, who is the place of meeting with God. The "greater things"
are his glory and triumph gained at the cross and empty tomb, and the
evangelist declares that these are the foundation of true and spiritual
worship.[22]

The reader should understand that, but Mary Magdalene does not
yet. She answers the question regarding her weeping by repeating her
conviction that he is still dead.

20:14   The scene shifts as Mary straightens up and turns her
back on the tomb and the angels, as though they had made no impression on her at all. The narrative is hastening to its climax. She sees
Jesus without recognizing him.

20:15　Jesus asks Mary, exactly as the angels had, "Woman, why are you weeping?" And he adds, "Whom are you seeking?" The latter question is very much like the first words out of the mouth of Jesus in this whole gospel. He put the question to the disciples of John—and to the readers—in 1:38 (see also 18:4, 7 and 13:33); "What are you seeking?"

Mary's mistaking Jesus for "the gardener" is puzzling. Is it a simple case of mistaken identification? Or is the author reminding the readers that the place of both the crucifixion and the resurrection was a garden (19:41)?

The death and resurrection of Jesus occurred in a garden. In this gospel, which opens with words echoing Genesis, "In the beginning," it is difficult to shake the conclusion that the author is intending to signify that God, through the death and resurrection of Jesus, is calling into being a new creation. A new world has emerged with the possibility of new life. Ironically there is truth in Mary's identifying Jesus as the gardener, but a truth she could utter without herself understanding. Mary was not yet thinking of life. In almost comical fashion she assured the "gardener" that if he would only tell her where the corpse of Jesus had been laid, she would go herself, hoist it up, and carry it back safely to the tomb where it belonged.

To her the empty tomb was still only a negative sign. Mary is marked by respect for the familiar reality of death coupled with a touching concern for the departed. She exhibits an impressive devotion to the memory of the departed Jesus, but that is not Christian faith according to John.

20:16　Mary was drawn closer to what John regards as faith when Jesus addressed her by name, "Mary." The shepherd who had laid down his life and taken it up again knows his sheep by name (10:3). He called to her and she heeded his voice and responded: "Rabboni!" or "Teacher!" (see 1:38; also Mark 12:51). With that confession, Mary had moved to a new and higher level of comprehension. He was not dead but alive and yet the title is still inadequate and backward looking.

20:17　Overjoyed to see him, Mary grasped him, as the women who fell in adoration at his feet are described as doing in Matthew 28:9. But Jesus rebuked her. John uses a negative participle with a present imperative, indicating that an action in progress should be broken off. Thus, literally translated, Jesus' words were, "Cease touching me" or "Do not keep clinging to me." Then he continued by declaring that he still had to ascend to the Father (see 3:13; 6:62).

Jesus' difficult words are easily misunderstood. They have been taken to mean that temporarily Jesus cannot be touched but later he will be able to be grasped, as if he had said, "Do not touch me now but soon you may touch me." That line of thought ignores the force of the present imperative and leads to speculation on precisely what was going to happen to render Jesus touchable. The ascension is then ordinarily located sometime between this scene and the one involving Thomas a week later, and his ascension is regarded as adding something to Jesus to remove his non-touchable character.

But the passage is not addressing a deficiency in Jesus but a deficiency in Mary's faith or attitude. She is represented as thinking that the goal of her life and of her relationship with Jesus had been achieved in the confrontation outside the tomb. Christian life to her meant abiding with the living, visible, audible, tangible Jesus. But John rejects that notion as surely as he rejects her quest for the corpse of Jesus.

When Jesus and Mary stand face to face, communicating audibly and tangibly like a sheep and a shepherd, their fellowship has not yet achieved its intended goal. That is the meaning of Jesus' words about ascending. Those words comprehend everything the gospel has previously said of his ascent, when he would draw all to himself. He was going away in order that he might come once again to his disciples. John is offering something different from what is offered by Matthew and Mark, who speak of Jesus' going up to Galilee (Mark 16:7 par.), and John thinks of ascension in terms which differ from Luke's understanding (Acts 1:9-11).

The promises uttered by Jesus in John's gospel about ascending and drawing people to himself and about coming again to his disciples did not mean that he would physically and geographically attract many out of the world's population to himself at Jerusalem. The oneness and fellowship between Jesus and his own would be totally different from the picture of Mary clinging to Jesus' feet. That cannot serve as a paradigm. "I have not yet ascended" means "I, the one standing here talking with you and touched by you, being in this form and fashion, am not the one with whom Christians have to do; this manner of contact is not the goal."

The goal of Jesus' crucifixion and resurrection is his complete oneness with the Father and his oneness with his brothers and sisters in fellowship with the same Father and God.[23] His whole earthly path had been a going to the Father (7:33; 13:3; 14:12, 28; 16:5, 10, 17, 28; 17:11, 13) in order that people might become the children of the Father

(1:12-13), that the scattered children might be gathered (11:52), and that the Spirit might be sent (7:39; 16:7). He was on the way to oneness with the Father. Then the Father and the Son will come and make their home with the disciple (14:23). " I in them and thou in me" is the way Jesus expressed the goal in his prayer (17:23). Mary must cease clinging to Jesus' feet. She must relinquish the old physical and social contact and exchange it for the new mutual indwelling.

20:18   When that has been said, Mary Magdalene's story can come to an end. She ran off to announce to the disciples what she had seen and heard. The first readers of the gospel needed to be reminded of Jesus' words to Mary and to hear Jesus call them "brother." There were those in the community who felt cut off, abandoned, orphaned by their distance from the historical Jesus, especially since the Beloved Disciple, the last historical link with the historical Jesus, had died.

John 20:19-23: He Breathed on Them

John 20:19-23   ¹⁹On the evening of that day, the first day of the week, the doors being shut where the disciples were, for fear of the Jews, Jesus came and stood among them and said to them, "Peace be with you." ²⁰When he had said this, he showed them his hands and his side. Then the disciples were glad when they saw the Lord. ²¹Jesus said to them again, "Peace be with you. As the Father has sent me, even so I send you." ²²And when he had said this, he breathed on them, and said to them, "Receive the Holy Spirit. ²³If you forgive the sins of any, they are forgiven; if you retain the sins of any, they are retained."

Like Matthew (28:16-20), Luke (24:33-49) and Paul (1 Cor. 15:5-7), John knows of an appearance of the resurrected Jesus to his gathered disciples. John's account seems especially close to Luke's: both locate the scene on Easter night in Jerusalem in a private place, emphasize the marvelous character of his appearing, and focus on the display of his body.[24]

20:19   John first sets the scene. The disciples of Jesus had closeted themselves behind locked doors. Doubt and fear are standing features of the tradition of Jesus' resurrection appearances to his disciples (Matt. 28:17; Luke 24:11, 25, 37, 41; cf. Mark 16:14), but John has his own peculiar interpretation of the disciples' behavior and mood. They acted as they did "for fear of the Jews" (7:13; 9:22; 19:38). Did the disciples fear that they would be hunted down and treated as Jesus was? Such an explanation imagines that John is rummaging around in the psyches of Jesus' first followers. But John has a larger agenda. By his reference to locked doors and fear of the Jews, he sketches a setting of enmity and unbelief. He means that the world is organized in powerful contradiction of God, and the message of the crucified and resurrected Jesus has to make its way against strong opposition. It is light and life engaged in struggle with death and darkness.

The disciples, locked in fear and unbelief, were for the moment "scattered" and "lost" in John's technical sense of those words. They were not in fellowship with Jesus but were overcome by the power of the inimical world, overwhelmed by the might of death, separated from Jesus and his Father, just as Jesus had predicted in 16:32. Yet the glorified Jesus did not leave them "orphans" and "desolate" (14:18). As he had promised, he came to them, calling and gathering them to himself and bestowing his peace upon them (14:27; 16:33; cf. Luke 24:36, alternate reading). "Peace" (Shalom) was and still is the word used by Jews for ordinary greetings. But the word is used also of significant moments of revelation (Judges 6:23; Daniel 10:19; see Paul's use of "peace" together with "grace" in the salutations of many of his letters). Jesus came to his disciples with his peace, penetrating the solid wall of their fear and lack of faith.

20:20   Jesus showed them his hands and side, not as in Luke to impress on them his solidity and corporeality and to reopen table fellowship with them (Luke 24:36-43), and not merely to establish his identity as Jesus of Nazareth their erstwhile teacher and leader. He does it to exhibit to them the wounds by which he had overcome the world (John 19:36-37; Zech. 12:10) and so to remove their fears and replace them with joy (16:21-22, 33; Luke 24:41).

Verses 19 and 20 seem to operate with contradictory assumptions about Jesus' body. Verse 19 (appearance in their midst in spite of a solid door barring entrance to the room) may be designed in part to guard readers from crassly materialistic conceptions of the body of the resurrected Jesus, a danger present precisely in this context in which Jesus displays his body and offers it to the disciples' touch. John is not indulging in speculation on the mysterious properties of the transfigured body, capable of moving through solid objects (see on Matthew 28:2) and at the same time able to be seen and felt. He wants to fasten attention not on the nature of the body but on the fact of wounds in the hands and side of the glorified Jesus.

20:21   Jesus repeated his greeting because it was to be more than an opening salutation or piece of common courtesy. Peace was his gift to them for all the days ahead. When they were at peace, at home with him, united with one another and abiding in him and he in them, then and only then could he send them into the world (17:18, 21,

23), because then they were one as he and the Father are one. Jesus was the sent one and the Father is "he who sent me." Jesus sends them forth with a task like that given to him by the Father. They continue his work.

20:22   The gift of his peace is paralleled by the gift of the Holy Spirit (also in 14:25-27), narrated quite differently from Luke's account of Pentecost in Acts 2. The Greek verb behind "he breathed out" upon them is found in the Greek Old Testament in the account of the creation of Adam (Gen. 2:7; Wisdom 15:11) and in the report of the vision of the valley of dry bones (Ezek. 37:9).[21] By his breath and Spirit God breaks the invincible grip of death and creates life (cf. Matt. 16:18).

The disciples received a share in the life of the crucified and resurrected Jesus, in fulfillment of 7:39 and the promises of the coming of the Paraclete (see also John 5:21). They receive the Spirit and are sent. Their being sent parallels the sending of the Paraclete into the world, and as the world comes into view, so does sin.

20:23   The disciples—every Christian is in view—received with the Spirit a commission that took aim on sin (cf. Luke 24:47-49; Ezek. 36:25-27; 1 QS 4:20-21). The vocabulary of that commission seems strange in John but at home in Matthew (16:19; 18:18).[26] Matthew defines sin as transgression, trespass, lawlessness, bearing evil fruit. John thinks not so much of the deeds as of the heart—believing or unbelieving—out of which all deeds proceed (see John 8 and 9). The gospel begins (1:29) and ends (20:23) with traditional sounding words about dealing with sin. The author tells his story, comments on the tradition, and deepens its reference. Here as elsewhere he is intensifying, radicalizing, and making fresh applications.

In the Baptist's testimony to Jesus (1:29-36), Jesus' bestowal of the Spirit goes hand in glove with his power to remove sin, and the Baptist pictured Jesus as the charismatically endowed giver of the Spirit (1:33) and as the Lamb of God who takes away the sin of the world (1:29, 36). That he takes away or destroys the sin of the world means that he overcomes the sinful world (16:33) and gains the victory by refusing to falter in his obedience to the Father, by persevering in his absolute and unbroken oneness with the Father all the way to glorification at the cross. By his total love for those the Father has given him (13:1) and by his doing the will of the Father, the prince of this world is condemned (16:11) and Jesus becomes the Savior of the world (4:42).

Jesus opens the eyes of the blind so that they see and believe (Chap. 9), and since unbelief is the heart of sin for John, coming to faith means nothing else than the destruction of sin. The believer's vocation is the sharing of the life-creating word (17:20). The disciples on Easter night received the Spirit and were sent with authority to forgive or retain sins, to bring people to faith, and to open their eyes (see John 12:36-50; Isa. 6:9-10).

Through them the Paraclete will convict the world of sin, which is unbelief (16:8-11). They had the opportunity to begin exercising their vocation almost immediately with Thomas.

John 20:24-31: My Lord and My God

John 20:24-31 ²⁴Now Thomas, one of the twelve, called the Twin, was not with them when Jesus came. ²⁵So the other disciples told him, "We have seen the Lord." But he said to them, "Unless I see in his hands the print of the nails, and place my finger in the mark of the nails, and place my hand in his side, I will not believe."

²⁶Eight days later, his disciples were again in the house, and Thomas was with them. The doors were shut, but Jesus came and stood among them, and said, "Peace be with you." ²⁷Then he said to Thomas, "Put your finger here, and see my hands; and put out your hand, and place it in my side; do not be faithless, but believing." ²⁸Thomas answered him, "My Lord and my God!" ²⁹Jesus said to him, "Have you believed because you have seen me? Blessed are those who have not seen and yet believe."

³⁰Now Jesus did many other signs in the presence of the disciples, which are not written in this book; ³¹but these are written that you may believe that Jesus is the Christ, the Son of God, and that believing you may have life in his name.

20:24 Only in John is one of the twelve disciples (besides Judas) absent on the occasion of the appearance of Jesus to the gathering of disciples. Matthew says "the eleven" were on the mountain when they first met the resurrected Jesus (28:16), and Luke counts "eleven" in the room on Easter night (24:33).

As John has focused earlier in the chapter on Mary Magdalene and the Beloved Disciple, so now he turns the spotlight on Thomas as he explores yet another facet of faith. John has need of Thomas. In peeling him off from the rest he is able to put Thomas into the shoes of all later generations, all people who do not see or touch Jesus but are called to faith in him by means of verbal testimony.

In both his previous appearances in the gospel (11:16; 14:5) Thomas is pictured not as doubter or as unbeliever so much as a disciple who fails to understand the path Jesus travels to the cross. For him the way to the cross seemed only a road to destruction.

20:25 The other disciples act out the vocation for which they had just been commissioned. They preach to Thomas, in the attempt to lift his unbelief and so remove or destroy his sin (v. 23). They bring to him the Easter proclamation in summary form: "We have seen the Lord" (cf. v. 18). That is, the crucified is the victor who has overcome the world. The seed fallen into the ground has sprung up and is bearing fruit.

At that moment Thomas had the opportunity to be the first person in the history of the world to come to faith on the basis of the word, the Christian message, without any seeing. But he failed by demanding proofs and evidence in a manner previously condemned by Jesus (4:48).

Thomas voices the desire not simply to handle the body of Jesus but to see and touch the mark of the nails and spear in his hands and side. Thomas does not want just any visible and tangible proof. He does not ask to hear Jesus' voice or see his face or grasp his wrists or ankles or watch him as he eats. He fixes his request and the readers' attention on the crucifixion. He wants to see wounds on a resurrected body. He wants convincing that the glorified one is identical with the crucified.

20:26 On the Sunday following Easter, when all the disciples including Thomas were together, Jesus came just as before. The repetition of the mention of closed doors enhances the mysterious character of the coming and underlines the marvelous nature of his resurrected existence, but it does more than that. The account stresses the gracious condescension of the resurrected one who will not be hindered or put off. He came from above to destroy the unbelief of the doubter and to give him peace. He came to Thomas without scolding or censure and met his demands point for point.[27]

20:27 Luke in his climactic narrative of the appearance of Jesus before the gathered disciples (Luke 24:36-43) accented the "flesh and bones" of Jesus' "hands and feet," as he worked to dispel the illusion that Jesus was merely a spirit or phantom (Luke 24:40). John had other goals in view. Therefore Thomas does not ask to be convinced of the solidity and liveliness of the Lord. He can believe in a resurrection as well as Martha, since that much was part of ordinary piety (11:24). But can mortal wounds belong to the Son of God? Are not death and the Christ mutually exclusive realities? (12:34). Does not dying on a cross with nails through the hands and spear thrust through the ribs spell humiliation and disgrace? Is not any death a plunging down into the darkness and hopelessness of the grave? What has life to do with death? What has God to do with the crucified? Jesus had struggled with enemies both seen and unseen and had ended on a cross constructed by them. What other name but defeat can be attached to such an end?

For Luke the resurrection is largely the cancellation of the cross. John, like Paul, ponders the positive significance of the cross itself. John meditates upon the infinite fruitfulness of the passion.[28]

How it is fruitful and what its fruit may be is not stated in this passage, but the coincidence of victory with the death on the cross is John's overriding message. The living Jesus displays the wounds which exhibit the depth of his love for his own, his obedience to the Father, and his scorn for the blandishments of the evil one. They are badges of victory.

20:28 The doubter and unbeliever (v. 27) turned confessor at the sight of those wounds: "My Lord and my God!" Thomas declared not only what the Prologue says at its beginning, that "the Word was God" (1:1) but, in accord with what it says at its climax, he acknowledged the glory of the word made flesh (1:14); and, as the reader of the gospel knows, that flesh was given for the life of the world (6:52-59).

The words "Lord and God" fill Jewish devotional literature. In the Shema each day the pious declare, "Hear, O Israel, the Lord our God *(adonai elohenu)* is one Lord."

But another context also suggests itself. Near the end of the first century the Emperor Domitian (A.D. 81-96) styled himself "Lord and God" (dominus et deus). Like Nero before him, he sought divine honors before his death and dealt severely with "atheists," that is all who denied his deity. In confessing Jesus as Lord and God, is the author declaring that the crucified is worthy of the highest titles known to Jewish and Roman culture?[29]

John's gospel begins with lofty assertions concerning Jesus: Lamb of God, rabbi (which means teacher), Messiah (which means Christ), him of whom Moses and the prophets spoke, Son of God, King of Israel, and Son of Man. According to the Prologue he is the Word, and "the Word was God" (1:1; cf. Heb. 1:8-9; Titus 2:13). So the beginning and end of the gospel correspond.

The crucified Jesus is "Lord and God." He is God in his turning to the world. He is in the Father and the Father is in him (10:38). He who has seen and heard the Son with his wounds has seen and heard the Father (14:9).

Now, at the climax of the gospel, Thomas obeys the Father's will "that all may honor the Son even as they honor the Father" (5:23). This Sunday is for Thomas that climactic and eschatological day spoken of earlier by Jesus: "On that day you will know that I am in my Father, and you in me, and I in you" (14:20; cf. 16:23, 26).

20:29   Jesus commented on Thomas' confession, or rather on all it took to bring Thomas to the point of confessing; and he pronounced a blessing upon those who believe without benefit of the sights demanded by Thomas.[30] Blessed are those who come to faith without laying eyes (or hands) upon Jesus. Blessed are those who come to faith simply on the basis of the story concerning Jesus (cf. 1 Peter 1:8). Blessed are believers of the second, third, and following generations.[31]

20:30-31   Conclusion

The topic of the chapter is Christian faith—its basis, its beginning, its content. Once Jesus has been confessed in faith as Lord and God, the chapter and indeed the whole gospel can come to rest. In summation the author declares that Jesus performed far more signs than his book records. His selection however is sufficient. His book, substituting for the words and deeds Jesus spoke and performed in the presence of the first generation, is able to generate and then deepen faith in Jesus as Christ (7:26; 9:22; 10:24; 12:42) and Son of God (1:49) and so bestow life (1:4).

The conclusion emphasizes the word and life. Faithful reception of the word means many things: the receiving of forgiveness; the destruction of one's sin; being brought out of darkness into light and from hostility to friendship with God; coming to life.

John 21: The Editor's Conclusion

A reader arriving at John 21 fresh from the synoptic gospels hears familiar echoes: the call of the disciples at the lakeside (Mark 1:16-20), including the sons of Zebedee, nowhere previously mentioned in John; the miraculous catch of fish (Luke 5:1-11); a meal with the resurrected Jesus (Luke 24:13-35, 41-43; Acts 10:41); Peter's protestations of fidelity and readiness to follow Jesus all the way to prison or even to death (Luke 22:33) accompanied by Jesus' prophecy that Peter would only too quickly break his promise three times (Luke 22:34).

Other passages outside of John ring rather more faintly, but their sounds may be perceived: confusion about Jesus' identity at the Sea of

Galilee (Mark 6:45-52); Simon's confession to Jesus at Caesarea Philippi and Jesus' exclamation and bestowal of the name "Peter" upon Simon (Matthew 16:16-19); Peter's vision calling him to proclaim good news to Cornelius, and the subsequent events culminating in Peter's living and eating at the house of that Gentile centurion for a period of three days (Acts 10–11).

But in John 21 all these remembered sights and sounds are confused, occurring in new combinations and settings. Traditions are recycled, events are reported with fresh twists, and the whole is seen through a glass at once Johannine and yet not quite Johannine.[32]

The reader searches Chapter 21 in vain for central Johannine themes and motifs:

- the cross of Jesus as his exaltation
- the oneness of God's children springing from the dying of Jesus
- mutual indwelling of Father and Son with believers
- the Paraclete leading into all truth
- enmity between church and world
- the dualisms of light and dark, love and hate, truth and falsehood
- the unique sonship of Jesus
- present possession of eternal life
- Jesus as fulfiller of Jewish institutions or festivals.[33]

Furthermore, this final chapter in the gospel relates awkwardly to Chapter 20. It is not the climax of the preceding narrative. It is difficult if not impossible to take the chapter as a record of events occurring some days after the confession of Thomas. Why are they fishing as though there had been no empty tomb, no vision of angels, no appearances of the resurrected Jesus, no outpouring of the Spirit, no high commission (John 20)?

At first the chapter gives the impression of being more afterthought or appendix than climax. For all the foregoing reasons, many commentators operate with the assumption that Chapter 21 is the work of a later editor, who prepared the gospel for publication some time after the death of the evangelist. The work of evangelist and editor and their relationship to one another and to the Beloved Disciple are discussed below in the comments on verses 23 and 24.

Introducing an editor or redactor answers some but not all of the questions. Even if it is granted that Chapter 21 is a separate piece, written after the composition of the body of the gospel in a new situation by a person other than the evangelist, someone might well still raise the objection that the chapter, at least at first sight, seems to be impossible as a climax to the gospel. What kind of editor would deliberately have designed such a conclusion?

Even on the level of narrative it is difficult to take the chapter as a straightforward record reciting what actually happened one morning some days after Easter. The chapter bristles with difficulties.

In the first place, the Johannine tendency to symbolic writing nearly gets out of hand here and threatens to sweep realism clean out of the narrative: seven disciples, fishing, the right side of the boat, 153 large fish, the unsplit net, the meal of bread and fish, the third appearance or epiphany, sheep and lambs, being girded and led.

Also contributing to the difficulty of the passage as narrative is the fact that the events recited seem like fragments hastily gathered lest anything be lost, and then thrown together into the basket with too little care for how they fit together. Gaps remain and questions cannot be repressed.

Why does Jesus inquire whether they have food (21:5) and then ask them to bring some of their catch to him (21:10), when he already has fish and bread on the fire (21:12-13)? Or did he use the fish caught by the disciples? The narrative line is unclear. If the fish represent people caught by the church's mission, what is the meaning of their being broiled and eaten? Or are two originally independent narratives—one about Jesus' directing the fishing and another about his provision of a meal—awkwardly combined? After their previous encounters with him (John 20), why could they not recognize him at once (21:4)? What did Peter do when he reached Jesus after splashing through the water (21:1-7)?

Why does the writer announce after the meal that the preceding events constitute the third appearance of Jesus (21:14), as though he were rounding off the event and concluding it, when he continues the scene immediately? There is no intervening disappearance and reappearance of Jesus, so the conversations of 21:15-23 must be part of the third appearance. Without bothering to prepare the reader in any way, the writer suddenly pictures the disciples walking along the shore, or at least Peter with Jesus and the Beloved Disciple behind them, while the other five are out of sight and out of mind.

Nevertheless, the narrative is not without its unifying elements. As it stands, Chapter 21 is a unit, at least in the eyes of its writer (the editor of the gospel). It is composed of several pieces or fragments, but it is a unit nonetheless. Having tied a fishing to a feeding (verses 3-13), the writer has proceeded to attach the first part of Jesus' conversation with Peter (verses 15-18) to the preceding scenes by the introductory chronological note, "after breakfast" (21:15). Then he has bridged the gap between verses 15-18 and the paragraph on the fate of the Beloved Disciple (verses 20-23) by his repetition of the word "following" (21:19, 20, 22). Verses 1-2, 14, and 24 are the clamps securing the pieces, and verse 25 then concludes the entire book in its present form.

In the second place, and more importantly, the chapter possesses unity in the way every part of it holds up to the reader familiar symbols of the church and of various aspects of the church's existence: catching fish, providing bread, pasturing sheep, following the Lord, obeying his will, enduring death, bearing witness. The perspective is ecclesiastical.

Thirdly, the entire chapter is unified by the relationship between Jesus, Peter, and the Beloved Disciple.[34]

1.   *1-14:* The tradition contained accounts of Jesus and his dealings with Peter in the call at the lakeside, in the miraculous catch of fish, and in postresurrection meals. Those traditions were used in some parts of the ancient church as the basis of Peter's unique position and authority and became the boast of communities which he had founded or in which he had labored.

The new and provocative element in Chapter 21 is precisely the presence of the Beloved Disciple alongside Peter. His intrusion into these familiar scenes calls into question the centrality of Peter and asserts the Beloved Disciple's priority as believer and witness.

2.   *15-24:* Two episodes dependent upon the appearance at the lakeside follow next:

15-19: Peter is here called to be a provider of food, a nurturer, and a leader, as Jesus was in the preceding verses. This section is like a commentary on the preceding.

20-24: The Beloved Disciple follows Jesus and is pictured as a witness to Jesus here as also in the opening episode of the chapter. So once again we have a commentary on verses 1-14.

As usual when the Beloved Disciple and Peter appear together in the Fourth Gospel, the light shining on Peter in Chapter 21 is critical and that on the Beloved Disciple is laudatory.

A schematic outline of the chapter focusing on discipleship and on the relations between Peter and the Beloved Disciple shows how carefully crafted the chapter is, in spite of all the apparent roughness:

1. 21:1-14 Call to Discipleship and Initial Characterization of Discipleship
    - A   Peter takes the lead in fishing (v. 3)
    - B   Beloved Disciple is first to discover and testify to Jesus (v. 7)
    - A' Peter brings in the fish (v. 11)
    - B' The disciples know Jesus not in the breaking of the bread but on the basis of the Beloved Disciple's testimony (v. 12)
2. 21:15-24 Two Forms of Discipleship
    - A   Feed my sheep (Peter, vv. 15-17)
    - B   A martyr's death (Peter, vv. 18-19)
    - B' Long Life (Beloved Disciple, vv. 20-23)
    - A' Bearing Testimony and Writing (Beloved Disciple, v. 24)

So the concern of the editor in this odd chapter on fishing and feeding, on dying and witnessing, on Jesus, Peter, and the Beloved Disciple seems clearly ecclesiastical. The issues which particularly engage his attention come into sharper focus alongside a list of the churchly concerns of other New Testament writers:

1. Jews, Jewish-Christians, and the synagogue in relation to the church.
2. Lawlessness or lovelessness in the Christian community.
3. Endurance in persecution.
4. Encouragement in mission to the Gentiles.
5. Right confession of Jesus.
6. Church order or ecclesiastical offices.
7. Sacraments and worship life.
8. Correct understanding of the Old Testament.

The Easter traditions in Matthew speak to questions like those in 1, 2, 4, and 7. Mark addresses 3 and 4. Luke focuses on 4, 5, 6, 7, and 8. Paul deals with all of them in one place or another. Outside of Chapter 21, most of these topics appear somewhere in the gospel of John. Of these items, the one that is closest to the heart of the editor's concern in chapter 21 is number 6, but it will be better to rephrase it.

Both Peter and the Beloved Disciple seem to be represented as having died. The members of the Johannine church, guardians of a rich tradition, were especially hard hit by the death of their beloved teacher and leader. They suffered a sense of loss and perplexity.

Gathered around the Beloved Disciple, they had developed and preserved a special form and understanding of the traditions reaching back to Jesus, and in the company of that eyewitness they had felt close to the Word made flesh and confident in the truth of their special fund of knowledge and perception.

With the Beloved Disciple gone, doubts arose all along the line. How were they and others to have contact with Jesus? Were the communities that looked to Peter gloating over their discomfiture and hitting home with their barbs? Were some members of the Johannine community being attracted away to Christian communities that laid more stress on the sacraments as channels of communication with Jesus? Were they plunged into a gloom parallel to that which threatened to overcome the Twelve as they contemplated the departure of Jesus (John 13-17)? Did they think of themselves as forsaken, abandoned, or orphaned (14:18)?

Of all the familiar themes of the Fourth Gospel still sounding in Chapter 21, most prominent are the notes of rivalry between Peter and the Beloved Disciple, the concern about abandonment, and the word of testimony as Jacob's ladder stretching from heaven to earth.

John 21:1-14: The Net Was Not Torn

John 21:1-14   After this Jesus revealed himself again to the disciples by the Sea of Ti-be' ri-as; and he revealed himself in this way. [2]Simon Peter, Thomas called the Twin, Na-than'a-el of Cana in Galilee, the sons of Zeb'e-dee, and two others of his disciples were together. [3]Simon Peter said to them, "I am going fishing." They said to him, "We will go with you." They went out and got into the boat; but that night they caught nothing.

[4]Just as day was breaking, Jesus stood on the beach; yet the disciples did not know that it was Jesus. [5]Jesus said to them, "Children, have you any fish?" They answered him, "No." [6]He said to them, "Cast the net on the right side of the boat, and you will find some." So they cast it, and now they were not able to haul it in, for the quantity of fish. [7]That disciple whom Jesus loved said to Peter, "It is the Lord!" When Simon Peter heard that it was the Lord, he put on his clothes, for he was stripped for work, and sprang into the sea. [8]But the other disciples came in the boat, dragging the net full of fish, for they were not far from the land, but about a hundred yards[k] off.

[9]When they got out on land, they saw a charcoal fire there, with fish lying on it, and bread. [10]Jesus said to them, "Bring some of the fish that you have just caught." [11]So Simon Peter went aboard and hauled the net ashore, full of large fish, a hundred and fifty-three of them; and although there were so many, the net was not torn. [12]Jesus said to them, "Come and have breakfast." Now none of the disciples dared ask him, "Who are you?" They knew it was the Lord. [13]Jesus came and took the bread and gave it to them, and so with the fish. [14]This was now the third time that Jesus was revealed to the disciples after he was raised from the dead.

21:1   In Chapter 21 the writer seems at pains—strained and straining—to address the reader directly, continuing the editorial style of 20:30-31. His tone reveals his anxiety that the preceding 20 chapters would by themselves not suffice to meet the crisis arising in his community at the death of the Beloved Disciple. The "many other signs" of 20:30 gave the editor his opening, providing him with the license to continue.

A vague and undetermined time has elapsed since the events of Chapter 20. The writer's own time is full of false notions attendant upon the deaths of some of the chief actors of the preceding chapter.

He announces twice in the opening verse of the chapter that what he will describe is an appearance, an epiphany of the resurrected Jesus. His words here are echoed at the conclusion of the paragraph in verse 14, and both verses appear to be patterned on 2:11 (cf. also 1:31; 7:4).[35]

21:2   Consistent with all other New Testament narratives, the appearance involves "disciples" and not unbelievers. This one occurs not in Jerusalem (Chap. 20; Luke 24; Acts 1) but in Galilee (Mark 16:7; Matt. 28:7, 16) at the Sea of Tiberias (Sea of Galilee), where Jesus had fed the 5000 (6:1) and revealed himself suddenly to his disciples as the "I AM" (6:16-21).

The author mentions seven disciples, of whom "the sons of Zebedee" appear for the first time in this gospel. Two besides them are unnamed. Simon Peter and Nathanael have been present from the first, and the ensuing narrative resembles the one in which those two first joined Jesus and confessed him (1:35-51). Thomas was present in Chapter 20, and his name, with Peter's, links Chapters 20 and 21. The Beloved Disciple is not yet mentioned, and it is useless to attempt to identify him as one of the sons of Zebedee or as one of the two unnamed. The list of names has a synoptic flavor in naming Peter first.

The seven may be a symbol for the whole church in the time after Jesus' resurrection (cf. the seven churches of the Apocalypse, Rev. 2–3). The chapter in its entirety wrestles with questions confronting the post-Easter Christian community.

21:3   Peter announced that he was going fishing (cf. Gos.Pet. 60), and the others declared their intention of accompanying him (cf. 11:16). They climbed into a boat (6:17) and caught nothing (Luke 5:6). In the lack of success there sounds the same sad note as in the depletion of the supply of wine at Cana (2:3). Where is the promised accomplishing of greater works (14:12)? Where are answers to prayer (14:13) and the experience of the love of God (14:23)? Where is the gift of "life in his name" (20:31)? Where is he himself in these days of the church?

In the Greek world fishing was a standard metaphor for teaching, by which people are brought out of their old and comfortable environ-

ment into a new and unfamiliar one. In the Semitic East fishing was a
symbol of being caught and hauled before the bar, to stand in the presence of the great judge of the world. The latter notion may lurk behind
the portrait of Luke 5:1-11, the miraculous catch of fish, where Peter
falls before Jesus, confesses his sin, and pleads with Jesus to depart
and leave him unscathed. But the good news is that the judge of the
world has arrived and upsets human calculations and expectations by
forgiving sins. The Christian mission came to be thought of in terms
of catching people (cf. Matt. 13:47-48).[36]

21:4   Early in the morning, as day was breaking (20:1; Mark
16:2), Jesus stood unrecognized on the shore. How were their eyes kept
from knowing him (Luke 24:16; John 20:14)? Can he be known only in a
characteristic deed or gesture or in the giving of a name or in the obedience of discipleship? Or is this a piece of Johannine contrasting: in
the night without Jesus the disciples caught nothing (cf. 15:5); in the
morning Jesus' presence led the way to bountiful success.

21:5   Jesus called across the water asking about food (cf. Luke
24:41). He addressed the fishermen with a word (*paidia*, 1 John 2:13,
18) which can be translated "children" (RSV) but is used here like the
Spanish "muchachos" to mean not inferiors or juniors but comrades.
So the NEB is on the right track with "friends."

21:6   They readily confessed that they had labored all night
for nothing (Luke 5:5), and they showed no reluctance to follow his instructions. When they cast the net as Jesus directed, on the right side
(side of good fortune? cf. Mark 16:5), they enclosed a whole school of
fish (Luke 5:6). "Cast . . . and you will find" (cf. Matt. 7:7-8). They
could not—at least not yet—lift the net into the boat, so they dragged
it behind the vessel in the water to the shore.

21:7   Up to this point Peter has been pictured as leader, and
the Beloved Disciple has not even been mentioned; but in the moment
of success, the author says that the Beloved Disciple revealed to Peter
(cf. 13:24-26, alluded to once more in 21:20), "It is the Lord." Identical
wording is in verse 12. So the Beloved Disciple came quickly to faith
and confession (as in 20:8) and in a sense opens the door to Peter, as he
had done once previously at the court of the High Priest (18:16).

When Simon Peter heard that it was the Lord, he immediately
dressed—for he had been practically naked while working—and
sprang into the sea. Why does the author bother with trivia of dress?
It could simply be a matter of remembered facts, the kind of minute
detail loved by storytellers conjuring up the sense of place and time.
When fishermen stripped for work, they set aside the encumbrance of

their long outer robes and worked in the freedom of briefer undergarments. Their long robes would be a dangerous anchor if they ever became soaked while they were working. However, in order to greet Jesus properly (Luke 5:8), Peter had to be decently dressed, so he put on his robe and then tucked it up to keep from getting entangled as he swam or waded the hundred yards to shore.

But perhaps this action of Peter should be read as a parable. It echoes the symbolic act of Jesus in 13:4-5 and prepares for the saying of Jesus in 21:18. At the supper Jesus laid aside his garments, girded himself with a towel, and washed his disciples' feet. That signified that he voluntarily yielded up his life (cf. 10:18; 19:23; cf. 2 Cor. 5:2, 4) and dedicated himself to dying as to a servant's task; namely, the work of cleansing his disciples totally and initiating them perfectly. Furthermore, Peter's action in the boat is a perfect preparation for the following material which builds to Jesus' climactic announcement that Peter, when he became old, would be girded not by himself, but by others who would take him where he did not want to go.

21:8   The other six disciples came to shore in the boat, dragging the net full of fish behind them. In contrast to the story in Luke 5, John says that the fish were brought by one boat, not two, and it was not swamped or endangered in any way by the size of the catch (cf. Luke 5:7 and see below on v. 11).

21:9   As soon as they landed, they saw fish cooking on a charcoal fire and bread also there. The particular word for "fish" or "food" *(opsarion)* is used only in this chapter (21:9, 10, 13) and in John 6:9, 11 in the entire New Testament. The mention of the "charcoal fire" reminds the reader of the one in the court of the high priest (18:18) where Peter had denied Jesus, and this may be one more preparation for the following paragraph (21:15-19).

21:10   Why did Jesus invite them to bring some of their catch? Did he not have enough for all? Did he seek the cooperation and contribution of his disciples? As he had said, they will do works in some sense greater than his own (14:12). They will, if they abide in him, bear much fruit (15:5, 16). The fact that some believe because of Jesus' word and some because of the disciples' word is a theme of the great prayer (17:20-21).

21:11   Peter "drew" or "hauled" the net ashore, although all seven had not been able to haul it into the boat until Jesus called for it (21:6). In the word describing the act of drawing *(helkyō)* there echo the assertions of Jesus that no one can come to him unless the Father "draw" him (6:44) and that when he would be exalted upon the cross he would "draw" all people to himself (12:32).

Furthermore, in spite of the phenomenal size of the catch, "the net was not torn" (contrast Luke 5:6). The crowds were regularly torn or divided by Jesus' words and deeds (7:43; 9:16; 10:19) but his will is that people be drawn by his glorification into a oneness as tightly woven as the seamless robe bequeathed by his dying (19:23-24).

The unbroken net was "full of large fish, a hundred and fifty-three of them." The mention of the exact number, 153, could be the touch of the eyewitness: Fishermen count them and weigh them, and that is all there is to it. On the other hand, fishing is a metaphor, and the chapter appears to be full of figures and symbols. For example, the fish are all "large" so that not a single one needs to be thrown back as too small (cf. Matt. 13:48). Furthermore, as has long been noted, 153 is a triangular number as can best be seen in a diagram:

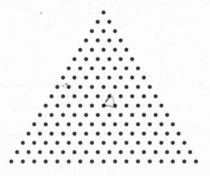

The figure is an equilateral triangle with 17 dots on each side, and the total number of dots is 153. Commentators play with 153, with 10, and 7, but the simplest interpretation is to say that the author declares that the catch is mysterious, full, and perfect.[37] Time and again the author of the gospel pondered the complex oneness of the Christian community on the basis of the work of Jesus and his disciples: the fragments of the five loaves were gathered lest anything be lost, and they filled 12 baskets full (6:12-13); the small number of sheep who heard his voice first and those others who would hear it later will be one flock under one Shepherd (10:16); by his dying Jesus began the gathering of the children of God into one (11:52); the grain of wheat fell into the ground and was buried but then sprang up as a head of grain with much fruit (12:24); he prayed that those who had heard and accepted the word already and those who would come to faith on the basis of the disciples' word might all be one (17:20-21). So here also all the fish were drawn to the shore by one boat, and the one net was not torn.

21:12   For the third time in this paragraph Jesus speaks in the imperative mood: "Cast" (v. 6), "fetch" (v. 10), "come have breakfast" (v. 12). Believers in the post-Easter generations are reminded that they eat their meals at the invitation of Jesus and in his presence.

21:13   The actions of Jesus here—he came, he took, he gave—correspond to his actions in the feeding of the 5000 (6:11; cf. Luke 24:30, 41-42; Acts 1:4; 10:41). He is the Bread of Life to all generations. They know him as Lord and experience his coming on the basis of his word of invitation and the word of testimony. For our author as for Paul (1 Cor. 11:26), the meal is a form of proclamation.

Verses 11-13 as a unit picture Jesus as providing the catch and feeding his people. He is Lord of the missionary outreach and the internal nurture of the community. Those of the second, third, and succeeding generations are not abandoned but have been caught and fed, not just by people who came to faith before them, but by the Lord himself. He willed their being caught and fed. He is present and working in and through those who know him and testify to him. If the meal is eucharistic, then it is so in the sense of a commentary on the Eucharist. The commentary says that the gift Jesus offers is not a medicine of immortality, but a revelation of the meaning of his person and a sharing of himself with the church in its tasks and mission.

21:14   The appearance at the lakeside is the "third" revelation of Jesus to his disciples after he was raised and is one of the "many other signs" of 20:30. If the appearance to the ten disciples on Easter night was the first (20:19-23) and the appearance to the eleven a week later was the second (20:26-29), then the appearance to Mary Magdalene (20:11-18) is not counted. Perhaps the writer means members of the Twelve—and that would exclude Mary Magdalene—when he speaks here of "disciples" (cf. 20:24). But not counting the appearance to Mary when it figures so prominently in the preceeding chapter is puzzling.

The verse is a kind of conclusion and comes early, interrupting the flow of the chapter. What follows is not counted as a fourth appearance and must be intended as a comment on the preceding.

John 21:15-25: We Know His Testimony Is True

John 21:15-25   [15]When they had finished breakfast, Jesus said to Simon Peter, "Simon, son of John, do you love me more than these?" He said to him, "Yes, Lord; you know that I love you." [16]He said to him, "Feed my lambs." A second time he said to him, "Simon, son of John, do you love me?" He said to him, "Yes, Lord; you know that I love you." He said to him, "Tend my sheep." [17]He said to him the third time, "Simon, son of John, do you love me?" Peter was grieved because he said to him the third time, "Do you love me?" And he said to him, "Lord, you know everything; you know that I love you." Jesus said to him, "Feed my sheep. [18]Truly, truly, I say to you, when you were young, you girded yourself and walked where you would; but when you are old, you will stretch out your hands, and another will gird you and carry you where you do not wish to go." [19](This he said to show by what death he was to glorify God.) And after this, he said to him, "Follow me."

[20]Peter turned and saw following them the disciple whom Jesus loved, who had lain close to his breast at the supper and had said, "Lord, who is it that is going to betray you?" [21]When Peter saw him, he said to Jesus, "Lord, what about this man?" [22]Jesus said to him, "If it is my will that he remain until I come, what is that to you? Follow me!" [23]The saying spread abroad among the brethren that the disciple was not to die; yet Jesus did not say to him that he was not to die, but, "If it is my will that he remain until I come, what is that to you?"

[24]This is the disciple who is bearing witness to these things, and who has written these things; and we know that his testimony is true.

[25]But there are also many other things which Jesus did; were every one of them to be written, I suppose that the world itself could not contain the books that would be written.

At first the second half of the chapter seems to follow loosely and strangely upon the foregoing. The scene has shifted. In verse 20, and not until then, it appears that the author pictures Jesus and Peter as walking together during their conversation. But where are they going? And in what direction? Are they hiking through the rock-strewn fields along the lake going towards Capernaum? Or climbing the hill away from the water? Or does the physical mirror the spiritual, so that the description of walking and following not only provides an appropriate setting for the discussion but evokes a concrete image of discipleship?

21:15-17   In spite of all shifts and discontinuities, the new paragraph opens by telling what happened "when they had finished breakfast." That note helps to connect the two halves of the chapter, as does the repetition of the names of Jesus and Simon Peter. But most of all, Jesus' feeding breakfast to the disciples has prepared for the ensuing dialogue on Peter's role as a feeder and nurturer.

Three times Peter heard the hard question of Jesus, "Do you love me?" Only in John is the bond uniting disciples to Jesus designated as love. When Jesus three times asked Peter, "Do you love me?" he was really asking him, "Will you be my disciple—whatever the cost— or not?"

And it will cost. Jesus alludes to the price both in the word "love" and also in his unfolding of love as shepherding (cf. 10:11, 17-18).

In this paragraph the author uses two different words for love. John delights in the use of synonyms, and by employing two different terms here, he not only avoids monotony but broadens the range of reference: for he has used both terms previously in the gospel (*agapan* in 13:33-35; *philein* in 16:27; both together in 11:3, 5, 36; 15:12-17). The words are most precisely defined by the Father's gift of the Son (3:16) and the Son's gift of his own life (15:13).

By asking whether Peter loved him "more than these" (namely, the other disciples), Jesus was alluding to the fact that Simon Peter alone of the disciples had boasted on the night of the arrest, "I will lay down my life for you" (13:37), a curious and ironic inversion of the actual state of affairs. Mark (14:29) records the more exclusive wording, "Even if all fall away, yet not I!"

And by putting his question to Peter three times, Jesus was plainly echoing the tragic fact of the collapse of Peter's discipleship in the threefold denial (John 13:38; 18:17, 25, 37).

Each time Peter professed his love for the Lord, Jesus followed up with the command, "Feed my sheep." As John has used synonyms for "love" so also for "feed" (vv. 15, 17) and "tend" (v. 16) and for "lambs" (v. 15) and "sheep" (vv. 16, 17). The words conjure up the full range of the shepherd's work: leading to pasture, protecting while grazing, recalling from straying, binding up injuries, providing shelter.

From the beginning "shepherd" has been a standing description of leadership and service in the Christian community (Acts 20:23; Ephesians 4:11; 1 Peter 5:24; 2:25). But in the Fourth Gospel, Jesus is most powerfully and movingly depicted as the Good Shepherd who laid down his life for the sheep. The whole business of feeding, leading, tending, and guarding flocks has been defined not in terms of a pastoral idyll but in pictures of mortal combat and the death of the Good Shepherd (Chap. 10).

Should Peter's grief (v. 17) at Jesus' repeated inquiry be interpreted psychologically, by imagining the shame he felt at the memory of his cowardly denials? Or is this not the same sorrow Jesus described in the Farewell Discourse, the sorrow and pain arising from the inevitable conflict between God and the world (16:6, 20-24)? As the cost of discipleship dawns on the follower, he is grieved; at the same time, responding positively to the summons to loving and to shepherding, he rests on the omnipotence of Jesus' own love and knowledge (cf. 1 John 3:19-20).

The dialog between Jesus and Peter at the lakeside resounds with echoes of Peter's position as spokesman or representative of all twelve disciples (6:68; 13:24), his confession of Jesus (6:68-69), and his declaration of undying loyalty (13:37); but the strongest tones are those of the three denials (18:17, 25, 27; cf. 13:38). Peter is here being shriven and forgiven, and Jesus himself is pictured as the inaugurator of the shepherding and pastoral mission of the church.

21:18-19   In the most solemn tones—"Truly, truly, I say to you"—Jesus, perhaps adapting a familiar proverb to fit Peter's case, announced that the free and impetuous spirit of Peter was being bound in two ways: 1) he was being harnessed in discipleship to Jesus, and 2) he would finally be tied and confined as a prisoner (cf. Acts 21:11-14), with his arms stretched out on the crossbeam, imitating Jesus (12:33; 18:32) and glorifying God. Here and in 13:36 ("You will follow me later") are the only two predictions in the New Testament of Peter's martyrdom (cf. 2 Peter 1:14).[38]

21:20-23   It is useless to ask where the other disciples were during the exchange between Jesus and Peter, how they were scattered in the backdrop of the scene, or why Peter turned around. The author wants to draw a twofold contrast between Peter and the Beloved Disciple: 1) Jesus does not need to wrestle with the Beloved Disciple in order to rehabilitate him and reestablish him in discipleship. 2) The shape and content of the discipleship of Peter differs from that of the Beloved Disciple.

The Beloved Disciple follows Jesus without a single word of bidding or summons. Immediacy and spontaneity mark his discipleship, whereas Peter was from the beginning dependent on his voice and the voices of others (1:40-41; 18:15-16; 20:6; 21:7; but 6:68-69).

The Beloved Disciple is described as the one who had been closest to Jesus in the place of honor at the last supper (13:25) and as the one upon whom Peter had to wait for information (13:24). If the author merely wanted to identify the Beloved Disciple, so that the reader could keep straight the cast of characters, he should have done so at his mention of him in verse 7. With the defining phrases of this verse the author is carving out for the Beloved Disciple a special role in early Christianity and heading for the climax of the book.

21:21   Peter saw him and asked about his destiny. If Peter's death has been foretold, what about the end of the Beloved Disciple?

It is precisely his end, his fate, his death that has confused the community.

21:22   Jesus declared, "If it is my will that he remain until I come, what is that to you?"

21:23   The saying of Jesus regarding the abiding of the Beloved Disciple spread abroad and was misunderstood. At first, it appears that the author's response to the misappropriation of the saying is weak and only negative. Jesus did utter the words ascribed to him; that is not denied. But he did not mean that the Beloved Disciple would never experience death.

It may seem odd that the misunderstood saying is then repeated. And yet in the Fourth Gospel repetitions are designed to compel the reader to look twice and to search for clues in words which at first seem quite transparent.

The author is playing with the word "remain" (*menō*). Does he mean "remain alive" (keep on living; cf. 1 Thess. 4:13-17; Mark 9:1), "remain in me and I him" (mutual indwelling, cf. John 14), or "remain witnessing" (continue through all time to bear testimony)?

The Beloved Disciple apparently outlived Peter, but the brethren would be mistaken to boast about that longevity and to see something special in length of years, just as the partisans of Peter would be wrong to boast of the spiritual superiority of martyrdom. Something outlives the Beloved Disciple—something of him abides—and it is not just the community but the Beloved Disciple's word of testimony. Testimony is the form of his remaining and following; it remains alive in his book, and the author underscores that fact three times in verse 24.

The Beloved Disciple will thus have his way of following Jesus "until I come." This "until I come" is an odd expression for John, who usually stresses the presence of salvation and is nearly silent about its futurity. The future reference is encountered more frequently in other writings associated with the Johannine circle (1 John 2:28; 3:2; Rev. 3:11; 22:7, 12, 20; but see also John 6:40, 44, 54).

Finally, there is more than rebuke in the phrase, "What is that to you?" (cf. 2:4). What is given to the disciples is not understanding of all mysteries, not solutions for all problems, not mastery of all questions, but the call to discipleship, and every disciple has his or her own destiny and an individual manner of following Jesus on his way.

The Beloved Disciple, like John the Baptist, was himself content to decrease that Jesus might increase (3:30). Modern readers would still like to know at least as much of the Beloved Disciple as is known of John the Baptist, but he remains a shadowy figure, identified by some today as John the Son of Zebedee, by others as Lazarus. Lazarus was loved by Jesus (11:3, 5), and early Christians might well imagine that Lazarus, raised from the tomb, would remain alive until the coming of Jesus. Still others have argued that the Beloved Disciple was an eyewitness but belonged not to the Galilean Twelve but to a larger, southern or Judean contingent of disciples. For yet others he is not a real but an invented figure: the ideal disciple, the model Christian, the inspired witness, the true believer, or a representation of Gentile-Christianity (and then his rival Peter—or perhaps Jesus' mother, John 19:26-27—represents Jewish-Christianity).

The Beloved Disciple appears in the gospel for the first time as the passion narrative opens. He lay in Jesus' bosom at the supper, closest to Jesus, as Judas was farthest from him (13:23, 25); he unhesitatingly followed Jesus into the court of the high priest, where he did not deny Jesus as Peter did (18:15 f.); and he stood, alone of all the male disciples, at the foot of the cross (19:26-27). The Beloved Disciple was an eyewitness of the passion of Jesus. He penetrated to the glory, saw the death of Jesus as the wellspring of life and spirit and cleansing (19:35), and, when he saw the grave cloths left behind within the tomb, he came to faith (20:8).

21:24   The final editor of the gospel (who added Chapter 21 and perhaps also the prologue, 1:1-18, and other material) describes the Beloved Disciple as the source of all the traditions about Jesus in the gospel. As far as the editor is concerned, the Beloved Disciple is also the one "who wrote these things." So in his view the Beloved Disciple and evangelist are one and the same. However, the picture that emerges in 19:35 is one that seems to distinguish between Beloved Disciple and evangelist. The evangelist had the Beloved Disciple as his inspiration and authority. Perhaps the phrase in 21:24 should be translated "who caused these things to be written" (cf. 19:22). Then the view of 21:24 would coincide with that of 19:35, and three people would be responsible for the production of the gospel: the Beloved Disciple (the great eyewitness and source of the Johannine tradition), the evangelist (who wrote on the basis of the Beloved Disciple's testimony), and the editor or redactor (who added materials and published the gospel).

As Jesus is the sufficient witness of the Father, so the testimony of the Beloved Disciple to Jesus abides, and it suffices. God may seem distant, aloof, careless. "No one has ever seen God" (1:18), but the gospel declares that Jesus, who is in the bosom of the Father, has made him known (1:18), so that he who has seen Jesus has seen the Father (14:9), for indeed Jesus and the Father are one (10:30).

When Jesus was crucified, he was not defeated nor did he cease to be the link with the Father. But the postpassion, post-Easter situation is complicated. The Beloved Disciple lay in the bosom of Jesus (as Jesus is in the bosom of the Father) and has borne witness to him. Death has removed the Beloved Disciple, but he bequeathed to the community his testimony. It has been committed to writing, and the community declares that he continues to bear witness to "these things," the words and deeds and signs which fill the gospel. He wrote or caused these things to be written, and "we know that his testimony is true."

So this passage, together with the prologue, pictures a series of links between God and contemporary Christians: God, Jesus (in the bosom of the Father), the Beloved Disciple (in the bosom of Jesus), the Fourth Gospel (abiding testimony). It is strange and noteworthy that no place is found for the Paraclete in this series.

21:25 The testimony of the Beloved Disciple is true and sufficient, even if not exhaustive. The final verse of the gospel as it now stands seems to many to be a lowly end to a glorious book, a mundane comment concluding the high and spiritual gospel. It is seen as an effort to glorify the deeds of Jesus with a hyperbole of quantity, whereas the gospel has insisted on the dimension of depth, spying the glory of Jesus in his lowliness, love, and cross. It sounds like a secular advertisement, and yet the writer desires to share his conviction that the spiritual treasures of Jesus are inexhaustibly great.[39]

Summary: Glorified Son of God

It is a fundamental Christian conviction that Jesus bridges the gap between the holy God and sinful humankind. He is the ladder (1:51) graciously provided by God himself. But when the physical, visible, tangible presence of Jesus was withdrawn, when time passed without his coming, when the entire first generation of Christians perished, and when finally the voice of the last surviving eyewitness was stilled by death, the question arose with terrible poignancy and sharpness: What and where is the link with life?[40]

Various strategies and answers were, and are, essayed by Christian communities struggling with that question. At least four distinct and different answers (not necessarily mutually exclusive of one another) were available as responses to the question of the bridge to life.

Apocalyptic

The apocalyptic answer is that life lies in the future. Jesus is temporarily absent or has, for the time being, withdrawn his presence

and abstains from intervening directly in the world and acting powerfully on behalf of his people. The present is a time of testing in which
the devil rages, and the community of believers must exercise pa-
tience. This present evil age will come to an end shortly and will be re-
placed by the glorious reign of the Son of God, who will destroy all the
enemies of God, subdue them beneath his feet, and exalt the belea-
guered people of God who have kept faith in dark times.

Such an apocalyptic view was held widely in the early church, but
an apocalyptic or futuristic eschatology is not John's response to the
crisis, even though a few traces of traditional apocalyptic can be discovered in the gospel.

Apocalyptic implies postponement. It is inadequate in John's view
because it allows the present to lie unfilled and empty (11:24). Jesus in
the Fourth Gospel continually presses for perception and reception of
new life, fullness of life, eternal life here and now (11:25-26). John
presses the view, not shared by all New Testament writers (cf. 2 Tim.
2:18), that for the believer in Jesus the resurrection has already
occurred; judgment belongs to the past; the believer has already
passed from death to life (3:18, 36; 5:24-25; 8:51; 1 John 3:14). Jesus is
present, not absent, and because he is present with all his powers and
gifts, apocalyptic will not do.[41]

Word and Memory

Rather than straining forward towards an apocalyptic tomorrow,
the answer to the question of abandonment can be sought in the opposite direction, throwing a bridge not to the future but to the past.

The words of Jesus and the deeds of Jesus were remembered and
transmitted. The communities in which the gospels were committed
to writing certainly did find sustenance, strength, and guidance in the
historical Jesus. He was honored as teacher and prophet, as wonder
worker and Messiah.

However, with a sure instinct John criticized the tactic of traveling backwards in time as betraying a low christology—too low in view
of the high status Jesus actually held as Son, and too low also to account for the present rich experience of Christians.

John asserts that confessing Jesus as prophet-teacher or Messiah
is but the barest beginning, a starting place only, and a dangerously
inadequate place to stop. Time and again in his gospel the discussion
of Jesus' identity begins with a consideration of his status as teacher
or wonder worker and moves to the higher ground of prophet and

Messiah, but only when the glorified (crucified and resurrected) Jesus is perceived as the Son (Son of God or Son of Man) does the author then let his case rest and move on to a fresh episode.[42]

Thus it is consistent with John's procedure everywhere in his gospel that Chapter 20 progresses from a low to a higher christology, from "Rabboni" or "Teacher" (20:16) to "My Lord and my God" (20:28).

Jesus belongs more to the present than to the past. He is not just the great founding teacher whose ancient words are treasured in the community, committed to memory, and transmitted to the next generation. Memory is strong and memory is dangerous, but the Christian community is not just a schoolhouse in the charge of pedagogues inculcating the memory of the dead founder's words and deeds.[43]

Of course John has very positive statements to make about the words of Jesus and Jesus as the Word. He obviously cherishes the speech of Jesus and has reported his words organized in stunning discourses. What John rejects is the notion that the words are lodged in the past, that they belong to Jesus' biography, that the church lives by the memory of a figure of the past.

In fact the effect of the discourses is to display the living Jesus as addressing the reader in the present. More will be said below about John's combining of Word and Spirit in the elaboration of his own positive answer to the question of distance.

The Ecclesiastical and Sacramental Answer

By the end of the first century the Christian movement was defining itself as an entity distinct from Judaism. Institutionalization proceeded at varying rates of speed and in varying fashions in different geographical areas, but widespread was the development of official leadership (with a distinction between ordained clergy and unordained laity), a body of authoritative traditions (with a distinction between genuine books and teachings on the one hand and those deemed misleading and false on the other), and a set of liturgical forms (hymns, creeds, times, places, and rituals, prominent among which were Baptism and the Lord's Supper).

Some claim to discern in the Gospel According to John strong ecclesiastical and sacramental currents. They regard the gospel as full of direct and indirect references to Baptism and the Eucharist and believe that the author of the gospel represented the conviction that the link to the departed Jesus is ecclesiastical and that it was established primarily in sacrament and cult.

The sacramental interpretation assumes that John has shaped the words and deeds of the historical Jesus to point forward to his saving death, and that the evangelist then goes on to teach that the full potency of that death is available to future generations in the church primarily through the sacraments. In fact, the sacraments are viewed as continuations of the signs Jesus performed when he enlightened the eyes of the blind man (Baptism) and fed the hungry multitude (Eucharist).[44]

Although it is not the case, as is often alleged, that the attitude of Jesus according to the Fourth Evangelist is antisacramental, it is equally wrong to describe the Jesus of the Fourth Gospel as cult-minded and ecclesiastical.

The gospel contains neither a command to baptize nor a charge to eat and drink in remembrance of Jesus, but there is also no direct criticism of baptismal or eucharistic practice. Just as Paul believed that it was all too possible to eat and drink unworthily (1 Cor. 11:29), and thus was glad he did not do much baptizing because of actual and potential misunderstandings of that practice (1 Cor. 1:14), so the author of the Fourth Gospel, while taking it for granted that Baptism and Eucharist are celebrated, desires above all that Christians who are touched by the water and who taste the bread and wine should come to faith in Jesus and so to life in his name. He is very far from promoting the sacraments, making them central, or insisting upon them. His attitude appears to be that the sacraments, like the miracles of Jesus, are at best signs.

The Spirit and Charismata

John is far closer to Luke than to Mark or Matthew in the number of references to the Holy Spirit and in the positive significance he assigns to the Spirit.[45] He speaks of the Spirit or Paraclete and his work far more directly and unambiguously than of the sacraments. However, the finely tuned description of the work of the Spirit in the Paraclete passages (14:15-17, 25-26; 15:26-27; 16:7-11, 12-15) makes one suspect that the evangelist is using the passages to combat at least two different kinds of abuses and misunderstandings of the Spirit and his work.

On the one hand, some Christians apparently found that the outpouring of the Spirit exorcized the sense of having been abandoned and filled them with a sense of belonging, of being caught up into the divine life, of being filled with the energy of God. Relief, release, joy, ecstasy—not frustration, forsakenness, abandonment—was the experience of Christians inspired by the Spirit.

That was all well and good as far as it went, but it hardly went far enough, or it tended to veer off into exotic, individualistic, and selfish byways. In the Paraclete passages Jesus declares that the Spirit is the Spirit of truth, and those who receive the Spirit will keep his commandment (the commandment he gives is that they love one another), do and tell the truth in a hostile world (14:15-17), and press God's lawsuit against the world (16:8-11).

Furthermore, the infusion of the Spirit led to an outpouring of fresh teachings in the community. Working like new wine, they threatened to burst apart the seams of the community.

The Johannine world was acquainted with spirits and inspired teachers. The First Epistle speaks of spirits which did and of others which did not confess that Jesus is of God. There is the spirit of antichrist and error on the one hand, and there is on the other hand the Spirit of God or the Spirit of truth (1 John 4:1-6).

The Paraclete passages do not pour cold water on the Spirit. They speak positively, even glowingly of the Spirit-Paraclete, but they function as a guarded, carefully worded job description for the Spirit. That description serves as a criterion for assessing inspired workings within the Johannine community.

The Paraclete passages state as clearly as possible that the Spirit is the Spirit of Jesus, binding the recipient to Jesus and Jesus to the recipient, so that the works and obedience of Jesus are replicated in the life of the disciple (14:15-17). The Paraclete teaches and speaks nothing new but makes Jesus present (14:26-27; 15:26-27). He leads into all the truth which, as the reader knows, is Jesus himself, the one who has ascended to the Father by cross and resurrection (14:6; 16:12-15).

Word and Spirit

John criticizes these four answers—apocalyptic, sacraments, word and memory, and the spirit—yet he affirms elements of each answer. He insists that apocalyptic hope has been realized and all that it promised for the distant future is now already available in Jesus.

John does not repeat words of Jesus commanding Baptism and Eucharist, nor does he send people to them as to great arching bridges across the chasm to life. Nevertheless water, bread, and wine can serve as potent signs.

To exalt word alone or the Spirit alone as the bridge would have been to tread a dangerous path, but the word and Spirit together form the basic elements in the evangelist's understanding of Jesus' approach to the community here and now.

Jesus is himself the Word, the unique exegete of the Father in whose bosom he reclines. Daily he springs forth into the darkness, summoning into life things that are not. His word is not just a teaching from yesterday to be memorized today and remembered tomorrow. His word is the voice of the Creator and the trumpet of the Judge daily calling forth from the dust and from the tomb into new life; therefore he is called by the old apocalyptic title "Son of Man." The believers live by fresh decisions, daily rendered, opening themselves to indwelling by the Word from above—from above and not merely out of the past.

The Paraclete passages are detachable from the surrounding material in the Farewell Discourse. They could be lifted out and the discourse would still flow smoothly, but then John would indeed be describing the Christian fellowship as primarily the community of the word. At some stage in his thinking and writing John added the Paraclete passages, and the result is a shift in accent.

He has not simply abandoned the notion of community of the word for a picture of the fellowship as community of the Spirit. John needed and wanted to say both simultaneously. Whatever problems he may have had with inspired teachers and with ecstatic excesses, he still recognized the strength and truth of the link forged by Jesus through the Spirit.

Jesus makes himself present to the believer through the Paraclete, manifests himself in the Spirit, and breathes upon the believer the pneumatic gift, closing the gap, bestowing life, and grafting the branch into the vine.

But if the word alone might become a merely historical report about the past, calling for the exercise of memory, the Spirit alone might become an unhistorical energy lifting people out of the body and out of the world.

A low christology in which Jesus is confessed as a great religious figure of the past, whose word is available for doctrinal and ethical instruction in the present, was rejected by John. Also rejected was a high christology in which Jesus is confessed as present like an angel, having laid aside his human past (with all its words and deeds and wounds), or in the form of Spirit, infusing his community with pure divine energy.

Word and Spirit both have their source and content, their potency and purpose in the glorified Jesus. They are more than his instruments. John dares to say that Jesus is the Word and the Paraclete is his alter ego.

The Word is quick and powerful, and the Spirit is a teacher. The glorified Jesus is the Word and he has the words of eternal life, the revelation that produces life (6:69). The Spirit does not destroy the past or ignore the past but takes the things of Jesus out of the past and makes the words of the past lively in the present (14:26; 15:26).

The task both of word and of Spirit is to reveal the exalted Son of God who still bears the wounds in his body and to make him present.

Wounds in Hands and Side

The Johannine Jesus glows with a strange austerity and a fascinating power because of his fierce concentration on the fundamentals of existence ("I am the bread of life, the light of the world, the resurrection and the life . . . "), his magisterial criticisms of the seductive power of political and religious forces, his prescience and sovereign control over all events and authorities, and the intensity of his direct address and appeal to his readers.

From some angles he seems less human than the Jesus of the synoptics, resembling not so much a rabbi from Galilee as a Greek god striding across the earth.[46] He is like a comet streaking across the night sky, glowing before it becomes visible and glowing after it disappears from view, changing not at all.

And yet finally the exalted character of the Johannine Jesus derives not from his power and prescience but rather from the author's insistence on seeing cross and glory together and simultaneously. By etymology and usage "glory" bears the connotations of weight, light, and victory. The cross is no defeat in John; at the cross Jesus threw his weight around and gained an impressive victory. John's Good Friday was not marked by any sudden darkness over all the earth. According to John, Jesus was crucified at high noon (19:14), and his crucifixion was his most brilliant and splendid hour, when he most clearly revealed his oneness with the Father.

John's own answer to the question of the distance from Jesus begins with his development of the most exalted teaching on Jesus in the New Testament. But that teaching is high, lifted up, and even otherworldly not because it involves an antiseptic avoidance of the contamination of common humanity but because it runs against the grain of ordinary, secular, down-to-earth considerations.

Features of John's portrait of Jesus make him look less than fully and really human. He does not become tired, hungry, or dirty, and he does not exhibit human weakness. When he asks the Samaritan woman for water (4:7), it is because he wishes to engage in conversation leading to the revelation that he is giver of a "spring of water welling up to eternal life" (4:15), and when on the cross he says, "I thirst," it is only "to fulfill the scripture" (19:28). Synoptic tradition knows of the drink offered to him and ascribes it to the soldiers' pity of a broken man or their mockery of a failure, but John portrays Jesus as a king summoning his servants to fetch a drink in fulfillment of what is written.

John's gospel lacks temptation narratives at the beginning and the agonies of Gethsemane at the end. John's Jesus is never confused, never unsure, never in the throes of doubt. When he prays he does not beg favors or seek clarity but issues proclamations and revelations to those standing by (11:41-42; 17:1-26). He is not limited in his knowledge and therefore compelled to face the future risking like a human being; he rather knows the end and reveals the end from the beginning. Nor is he pictured as sweating blood, racked with pain, and acquainted with grief, as in the synoptics. He is not only Pilate's prisoner but also his interrogator and judge (18:37; 19:11). The soldiers who robe and crown him testify ironically to the truth of his kingship (19:1-3). He does not stumble beneath the weight of the cross, requiring the assistance of a Simon, but he strides forth with strong step "bearing the cross by himself" (19:17). When he is crucified, he is not mocked or pitied, and no darkness descends. He reigns from the cross (19:19-22), holds court, speaks commandingly, disposes of cases (19:25-27), finishes his appointed task, and himself gives up his spirit (19:30).

But it is not John's intention to portray Jesus as passionless and nonhuman. John has rather contemplated the human life and human death of Jesus and in them he has beheld the glory. To his eye that life and death are luminous and glowing with the victory of God and the love of God. He wrote in order to reveal to others the majesty and the exaltation which he himself saw in the earthly and the crucified. John saw Jesus' ministry and death as from the beginning the incursion of God's light and life and love, and he wrote of him as glorious from the first moment. He knew no other Jesus than the one who lives mightily with the print of the nails in his hands.

The crucified and no other is one with the Father, one with the Creator of all things visible and invisible. He is the Word revealing the mind of God, the light shining from the heart of God, the life surging from the bosom of God, the love welling out of the depths of God. It is ultimately the crucified Jesus who says, "I and the Father are one" (10:30), and "He who has seen me has seen the Father" (14:9). He has come forth from God and returns via the cross to God. In him the community beholds the glory of God (1:14-18).

He is light and life, but since he came into the world of death and darkness, he was opposed and denied, even in the name of God (16:2).

The clash is heard from the beginning and it is clear that the invasion of light and infusion of life is costly (1:10-11). John does not say that success is achieved by the mere shining of the light and appearing of life. Their success among people is linked to a mysterious exchange of life and death, of light and darkness.

Jew, Samaritan (4:21), and Greek (12:20) will see the Father and meet the Father in the temple of the crucified and resurrected body of Jesus (2:19-22). His corpus, exalted on the cross, is the healing caduceus and effective emblem of regeneration (3:12-15). The water, wine, and spirit that really gladden the heart and slake thirst forever pour from a riven side (4:13-15; 7:37-39; 19:34). His flesh consumed in death is the life-giving food from heaven (6:50-51). The glory and truth of his word that he is the I AM and the light of the world streams forth from the stake high and lifted up (8:12, 28, 58).

In order that the sheep might have pasturage, protection, and abundant life, the Shepherd laid down his life (10:10-18). He gave life to dead Lazarus and by so doing called down upon himself the verdict of death, and yet his death is the source of life for the nation and for all the scattered children of God (11:45-53). That there might be a grand and fruitful harvest he became a seed buried in the earth (12:24). That people might become the children of light, the true light had not only to shine but also to expose himself to the darkness and to submit to efforts to snuff him out (12:35-36).

He permitted himself to be taken captive that his own, given to him by the Father, might go free and that not one of them might be lost (18:8-9). He came as the light of the world and was at high noon suspended upon the cross like a great lantern more brilliant than the sun; sought out by captors with lamps and torches in the night, and exalted there upon the cross, he draws all people to himself as the sun by its burning enlivens and draws plants upwards toward itself (12:32; 18:3).

Because light and life do not triumph automatically or easily but at great cost, and because the real life of the world and its enlightening shine forth from the real death of Jesus, the words life and light drawn from nature give way in the second part of the gospel to the word love, full of associations at once human, familial, and moral.[47]

Of course, love is there from the beginning, but it comes into its own in the second part and constitutes the dominant note of Jesus' final discourses of farewell in which he interprets the great events of his crucifixion and resurrection for his disciples. Indeed the chapters of the discourse open and close on the note of love (13:1; 17:26), a love grounded in the glory of the cross.

The cross is glorious:

because the cross enacts the boundless love of God and his determined outreach to his scattered children (3:16; 11:52; 17:23);

because it is Jesus' final concentrated act of love towards his own, given to him by the loving Father (13:1, 34; 15:6, 12-15);

because it is aglow with the joyous sacrifice of the Son for his own whom he names not servants but friends and brethren (15:13-15; 20:17);

because it is a concise and shattering vision of the mind of the Father bent on providing a way to himself (1:51; 14:1-10);

because it is not the devil's doing or humanity's doing but God's doing and therefore God's hour, and so also the hour of the glory of God and the glory of Jesus who loves God (14:31) instead of fearing death, and so that hour spells defeat for the powers of death and is the source of real life (17:1-2);

because his laying aside of the garments of life and girding himself for the work of dying is the one indispensable and totally sufficient service of cleansing and purification for humankind (13:3-10);

because it is not the end of Jesus, spelling defeat and his disappearance, but is his triumph and the vehicle of his everlasting presence, for it is his union with the Father (17:11, 13, 21).

To make the cross the mark of union with the Father was a radically new teaching. In the time of Jesus it was a cultural and biblical axiom that the word of God and human flesh are opposites:

"All flesh is grass
and all its glory like the flower of grass.
The grass withers, and the flower falls,
but the Word of the Lord abides for ever."

(1 Peter 1:24-25; Isaiah 40:6-9)

John however climaxes the opening hymn on the Word as light and life with the paradoxical statement: "The Word became flesh and dwelt among us" (1:14). The Son, the eternal Word, the Life, the Light, he who is one with the Father became vulnerable, so that he can be believed or rejected, confessed or killed. John fastened the eye of faith on the moment of Jesus' highest vulnerability, and saw in his lifting up onto the cross the glory of God and the victory of God. To know the sending God and to know Jesus, given in the flesh and sent to the cross, to see the glory at the cross, that is believing and that believing yields life in his name.

His acceptance of vulnerability signifies that his descent and ascent were the movements of love, and the community's acceptance of him as Lord and confession of him as Son is both a decision of faith and a commitment to love. Faith means having the loving Father and the loving Son come and make their home with the believer and in the believer (14:20, 23; 15:4-7; 17:21-23). Faith means ingesting as food and drink the Son of Man crucified and resurrected (6:51-59), not being offended but abiding with him when he ascends by the cross (6:60-71). It means being drawn to him (12:32), engrafted in him, and so living his life and loving his love (15:1-17). This for John is Easter faith.

epilog

The Gospels are Easter books. They all conclude exactly the same way—with Easter narratives. They differ from one another more in the recounting of the Easter events than in the telling of any other major narrative which they all have in common. But they all agree that Jesus' ministry and suffering were crowned with life and triumph on Easter. The Easter narrative may be exceedingly brief and enigmatic as in Mark, or it may have a sequel in ascension and Pentecost as in Luke, but it is always the climax of his earthly life and the great pivot or turning point in his relationship with his disciples and the world.

However, the Gospels are Easter books not only because they end as they do. They are Easter books from beginning to end, penned by people who in various ways—not in the same way—knew Jesus as raised from the dead, forever alive, and mighty.

So each gospel as a whole is a richly patterned icon, tracing the character and lines of him who was and is and is to come. His words and deeds recorded in the Gospels are the marks by which his face is still known and his voice still recognized as he moves in the present time in the midst of the faithful.

From their first pages to their last the evangelists have supplied the passports and papers of identification, not of one who once walked the earth only to disappear in dust and ashes, but of the one who today continues to meet the congregation and to confront the world.

The evangelists describe his presence and the contemporary encounter in divergent terms. They describe the living one variously as servant and leader in service, as teacher of all teachers and master of all church leaders, as Lord of all lords and rulers, sovereign over all lands and empires and nations and generations, as divine indwelling presence, and as sole revealer and ladder to God. They also declare that what he once was, he still is today.

The evangelists differ and they agree. They differ in their experience and in their individual portrayals of the resurrected Jesus, but they agree that he is present with and sovereign over his people and the world.

The writers of the Gospels are evangelists of Easter. If they had not themselves met and experienced him as the resurrected one they might have been historians of the life and times of Jesus, the teacher and wonderworker from Nazareth who was crucified under Pontius Pilate. But since the resurrected Jesus was for them the decisive and overwhelming reality, they composed gospels and not histories. In all the pages of their gospels, and not only in their final pages, they have shared what they knew and believed of the resurrected one.

They had an ear for the memories and traditions circulating in their communities. They sifted through them all and consciously or unconsciously they edited them, omitting a piece, including another, abbreviating, enlarging, and rewording. They pondered them in the light of their own experience and began to compose them on the gospel pattern.

How many drafts they wrote before the final one or for how many years they preached or taught their material in oral form before they ever committed it to writing we have no way of knowing. But finally they reissued the traditions of Jesus in fresh form, shaped and designed for maximum impact upon their respective audiences.

The traditions in their received form had to some extent lost their punch, as coins have a way of losing their purchasing power over the years. So they had to be overstruck with fresh insignia or even melted down and minted fresh in new weight and design.

This present book has displayed very little curiosity—some would say too little—about the chronologically earlier forms of the Easter tradition preceding the accounts written by the four canonical evangelists. It has studiously avoided the temptation to reconstruct an allegedly original story behind the canonical reports. It is with set purpose that this book has deliberately refrained from using the texts as springboards for leaping backwards in time into the first weeks of

April of the year 30 or 33 with the intention of establishing what really happened in Jesus' last days as opposed to what the texts allege to have happened.

Now there is no denying that the question about the connection between the biblical text and the history of Jesus is of utmost significance. The connection has proved elusive, and scholars have articulated it in numerous and differing ways, but the fact remains that investigation of that connection is not only legitimate but is vitally important. The business of proposing reconstructions of the prehistory of the Gospels and hypothesizing about sources will and should continue.

Nevertheless our attention has in this present work been focused deliberately and as steadily as possible on the words as they stand recorded in the Gospels.

This study has proceeded on the assumption that each evangelist was first of all a teacher or preacher rather than a historian, that his literary deposit has an integrity of its own, and that it is still supremely worth while tuning in to the message each composed for his community of believers or for his uncommitted but curious neighbors. Our Easter Gospels are certainly not the only way to proclaim the resurrection, but these documents have through most of their long life rightly enjoyed a privileged status among us. Each gospel is a remarkable application of the tradition about Jesus to a fresh situation and audience.

By attending to the Gospels we hear how ancient masters made use of the tradition of the resurrection of Jesus and how they put him to work in the context of their culture and church. They have yet many things to teach us.

appendix

OTHER ANCIENT ENDINGS OF MARK

1. The Short Ending

A few ancient witnesses continue Mark's narrative beyond verse 8 with the following:

> But they reported briefly to Peter and those with him all that they had been told. And after this, Jesus himself sent out by means of them, from east to west, the sacred and imperishable proclamation of eternal salvation. (RSV)[1]

This ending of two simple sentences originated in Egypt or Rome perhaps as early as the 2nd century.[2] It was designed to conclude the gospel on an unambiguously positive note, freeing the women from any suspicion of disobedience. The writer clearly understands the women's silence (16:8) as temporary and their subsequent report as full and complete.

Commentary

The first sentence says they reported to the disciples "briefly" or "promptly" (*syntomōs* may mean either). If the latter, then Matthew's "quickly" (*tachy*, 28:8) is a parallel.

The Christian community is described as "those around Peter," a view more suited to Matthew (cf. 16:18-19) or Acts (Chap. 1-5) than Mark, in the sense that those other writers emphasize the leading role of Peter in the church in a way that Mark does not. However, Mark does recall that Simon was the first to be called as disciple (1:16-18), names Simon first in the list of disciples (3:16), pictures Simon as spokesman (8:29-33; 10:28-30; 11:21; 14:54-72), acknowledges him as one of the inner circle of three (5:37; 9:2-13; 14:32-42; cf. 13:3), singles out his vows of loyalty to Jesus (14:29-31) and speaks of "Simon and those who were with him" (1:36; cf. "the disciples and especially Peter," 16:7: cf. "those around Peter" Ign. Smyrn. 3:2).

Is the author of the shorter ending deliberately exploiting the pious Christian memory of Peter's stature and the fact that Jesus appeared first of all to him (1 Cor. 15:5; cf. Luke 24:34)? Was there some particular reason in the author's situation for the accent on Peter? Were there those who claimed Paul as the great missionary and remembered Peter's denials or Peter's reluctance to engage in the mission to the Gentiles (Gal. 2:11-14)? The naming of Peter in the shorter ending seems purely conventional, not the premeditated tactic of an author addressing some burning contemporary issue.

The women reported to the disciples, and then "after this" at an unspecified later time and place Jesus himself appeared to them. The words of Jesus are not quoted directly. The author reports in summary fashion that Jesus inaugurated the mission. He himself sent out (*exapesteilen,* Luke 24:49; Acts 13:26; 22:21) the proclamation (*kerygma,* Romans 16:25 parallel to "gospel"; 1 Cor. 1:21 and 2:4 parallel to "logos"; 15:14). Jesus initiated a worldwide movement of the apostolic gospel "from east to west" or more literally "from the rising of the sun to its setting." That same description of the scope of apostolic laboring appears elsewhere (1 Clem. 5:6-7; Ign. Rom. 2:2; cf. Rom. 15:3-24) in contexts that picture the movement from Jerusalem westward to Rome or Spain, and there are those who think the description betrays a western or Roman perspective.

But it may simply be a piece of conscious or unconscious imitation of biblical rhetoric. The phrase occurs as an expression of geographical universality together with another phrase, "from now to eternity," expressing temporal universality in Psalm 112:3 LXX (cf. Is. 59:19; Zech. 8:7; Mal. 1:11; Matt. 8:11).

The disciples are merely the agents of the spread of the kerygma or gospel sent out by Jesus. Nothing is said of the reactions of the disciples to the appearance of Jesus, as the author focuses not at all on the biographies of the bearers but only on the character of the word entrusted to them. That proclamation is "sacred and imperishable" *(hieron kai aphtharton).* It is holy as the Scriptures of old were holy (2

Tim. 3:15; 1 Clem. 43:1; 45:2; 53:1; cf. *hagios* used of the law of God in Rom. 7:12 and of the commandment of Christ in 2 Peter 2:21), and it is imperishable or incorruptible. Corruptible describes everything in the world as weak, fallen, and passing away, while God alone is imperishable, incorruptible, or immortal (1 Tim. 1:17; Rom. 1:23). Christians are ransomed not by corruptible things such as gold or silver (1 Peter 1:18) but by the blood of Christ, and are born anew not of perishable or corruptible seed but by means of the incorruptible word (1 Peter 1:23), the word of God that is living and abiding.

In the book of Revelation the angel has "an eternal gospel" to proclaim (*euanggelion aionion,* Rev. 14:6) and Ignatius, who calls the eucharist "the medicine of immortality," contrasts the Old Testament word with the gospel: the former is anticipatory and prophetic but the latter is "the perfection of incorruption" (*apartisma aphtharsias,* Ign. Phil. 9:2).

The kerygma announces the good news of "eternal salvation." Elsewhere in Mark's gospel receiving salvation is a synonym for entering the kingdom of God (Mark 10:26) and an antonym of losing one's life (8:35). Everywhere in the New Testament salvation is a comprehensive term for the life of the new world in which God's gracious reign is full and unobstructed. The Johannine equivalent is "eternal life" (The noun "salvation" occurs only in John 4:22).

Conclusions on the Short Ending

The short ending consists of two simple, colorless sentences. The first is the briefest possible summary of the events immediately following the discovery of the empty tomb, and the second echoes the appearances of Jesus and the missionary charge.

The women of verse 8 are the subject of the action in the first sentence. The only persons actually named in the passage are Peter and Jesus. In neither sentence is there any reference to time, place, or circumstances. Nothing is said about Jerusalem, Emmaus, Galilee, an upper room, a village, the same night or a week later, fishing, a meal, touching, fear, doubt, or any conversation.

The fact that the author does not put the mission charge into direct speech or offer some paraphrase of the contents of the Christian message shows that he is not trying to drum up enthusiasm for the church's outreach or combat a misunderstanding about mission. He was simply attempting to round off Mark's gospel, using materials available already in Matthew and Luke.

The shorter ending became known alongside the longer ending in many communities, and the problem of two different endings was solved by conflation. The shorter ending became the prelude to the longer ending in all but one of the witnesses containing it. Codex Bobiensis (OL ms k) alone has the short ending as the conclusion to Mark without continuing with the longer ending. And of course there are many manuscripts with the longer ending but without the shorter ending.

2. The Longer Ending

Mark 16:9-20   [9]Now when he rose early on the first day of the week, he appeared first to Mary Magdalene, from whom he had cast out seven demons. [10]She went and told those who had been with him, as they mourned and wept. [11]But when they heard that he was alive and had been seen by her, they would not believe it.

[12]After this he appeared in another form to two of them, as they were walking into the country. [13]And they went back and told the rest, but they did not believe them.

[14]Afterward he appeared to the eleven themselves as they sat at table; and he upbraided them for their unbelief and hardness of heart, because they had not believed those who saw him after he had risen. [15]And he said to them, "Go into all the world and preach the gospel to the whole creation. [16]He who believes and is baptized will be saved; but he who does not believe will be condemned: [17]And these signs will accompany those who believe: in my name they will cast out demons; they will speak in new tongues; [18]they will pick up serpents, and if they drink any deadly thing, it will not hurt them; they will lay their hands on the sick, and they will recover."

[19]So then the Lord Jesus, after he had spoken to them, was taken up into heaven, and sat down at the right hand of God. [20]And they went forth and preached everywhere, while the Lord worked with them and confirmed the message by the signs that attended it. Amen.

The longer ending (Mark 16:9-20) is hallowed by tradition. It was known from the middle of the second century, perhaps to Justin Martyr, and certainly to his pupil Tatian and to Irenaeus. Most extant ancient Greek manuscripts include it as part of Mark's gospel.[3]

The longer ending was present in the manuscripts used by Erasmus to construct the first edition of his Greek New Testament (1516). He retained it in his later editions and it was translated as part of Mark's gospel by the King James Version (1611) and all other translations based on the Textus Receptus (3rd edition of Stephanus of 1550, 2nd edition of Elzevir of 1633).

The longer ending has had its passionate defenders. John Burgon in 1871 published a 334 page volume under the title *The Last Twelve Verses of the Gospel according to St. Mark*. It bore the subtitle "Vindicated against Recent Critical Objectors and Established."

As far as Burgon was concerned, any person arguing that verses 9-20 were inauthentic and that the gospel originally ended at 16:8 fell under the condemnation of Rev. 22:18-19, which he printed together with Mark 13:31 and Matt. 5:18-19 on the back of the title page.[4]

Today the vast majority of modern scholars of all persuasions, the most conservative as well as the most critical, agree that all the ancient endings beyond 16:8 are later non-Markan additions to the text.

However some scholars do defend the authenticity of all or part of the longer ending. William R. Farmer has published a monograph with a title nearly identical to that of Burgon's book of a century ago: *The Last Twelve Verses of Mark*.[5] Farmer reexamines the external evidence of the manuscripts and versions and the internal evidence of individual words in the longer ending and concludes that the question of the authenticity of verses 9-20 should not be regarded as fully and finally settled. He wants readers to consider the possibility that the longer ending represents older traditions and is not merely the product of the second century.

Eta Linnemann contends that 16:15-20 but not 16:9-14 formed part of the original ending of Mark. She believes that something similar to Matthew 28:16-17 originally followed Mark 16:8 and preceded Mark 16:15.[6]

Nevertheless, in spite of all the ingenuity of Farmer and Linnemann, most do and should continue to regard 16:8 as the last piece from Mark's own pen and as the conclusion he designed for his work.[7]

The RSV and other modern translations customarily print verses 9-20 and one or both of the other, shorter ancient endings in smaller type at the end of Mark and separate those endings from verse 8 by some blank space or print them as part of the footnotes.

As a Unit

The longer ending betrays signs of having been cut from a more extensive document, now lost, before it was added to Mark's gospel. For example, verse 9 does not mention Jesus by name but simply plunges in and says "he" rose and appeared, as though the immediately preceding had been narrating events in which Jesus had been called by name and of which he was the chief subject. Furthermore the longer ending makes no effort to continue the flow of thought begun in 16:1-8, since it does not talk at all of movement to Galilee and an appearance there. It has its own focus.

Whatever its origin, what is its character? It looks at first like a digest of various appearances of the resurrected Jesus culminating in the mission command and concluding with his ascension and session. It ticks off a number of easily identifiable appearances of Jesus:

I.   Appearances (16:9-14)
        1.   "First" to Mary Magdalene (16:9; Luke 24:10; John 20:1-2, 11-18)
              Reaction to her report: they would not believe (16:10-11)
        2.   "After this" to two of them (16:12; Luke 24:13-35)
              Reaction to their report: they did not believe (16:13)
        3.   "Afterwards" a third and climactic appearance to the eleven at a meal (16:14a; Luke 24:36-42)
              Jesus scolds them for their unbelief and hardness of heart because they had not believed (16:14b)
II.   Commissioning (16:15-18)
        1.   Missionary Command (16:15; Luke 24:47-48; Acts 1:8)
        2.   Promise (16:16)
              Positively: the baptized believers will be saved.
              Negatively: the unbeliever will be condemned.
        3.   Five signs accompanying and supporting the believers (16:17-18)
III.   Conclusion: "So then . . . after he had spoken" (16:19-20)
        1.   Ascension and Session of the invisible Lord (16:19; Luke 24:50-53; Acts 1:9-11)
        2.   Visible signs confirming the message (16:20; Acts 14:3)

Commentary

The following comments on the longer ending cite many passages in Luke-Acts which seem parallel in wording or outlook. The similarities probably indicate not direct use of Luke-Acts by the composer of the longer ending but rather a common dependence upon a fund of words and ideas current in the Gentile Christian church of the early second century. The comments also offer many examples of parallels in the Apostolic Fathers, Justin Martyr, and Irenaeus.[8]

16:9   The use of the active "when he rose" *(anastas)* instead of a passive or other form indicating that God did the raising and Jesus was the object of the Father's action, is typical of the second century (1 Clem. 24:1; Ign. Magn. 11:1; Ign. Phil. 8:2; 9:2; Ign. Smyrn. 1:2; 3:1, 3; Just. Apol. 21:1; 50:12; Polyc. 9:2).

Jesus appeared (*ephanē*, Luke 9:8; cf. 24:11; Just. Dial. 67:7; Trypho 138:1) to Mary Magdalene, the only woman named in the resurrection accounts of all four Gospels (cf. John 20:1-2, 11-18). Elsewhere Luke alone describes Mary Magdalene as one from whom seven demons had been exorcised (8:2). The longer ending uses that description of Mary, not really to identify her, but because from beginning to end it is intent upon reminding readers of the power of Jesus.

16:10   Mary Magdalene reported (*apaggellō*, 16:10 and 13; cf. Luke 24:9) to the others who "mourned and wept" (Luke 6:25; 23:28D; James 4:9; Gos. Pet. 7:27; 14:58-59), normal behavior of the friends of the deceased at a funeral.

16:11   She said to them, "He is alive" (*zaō*, Luke 24:5, "Why do you seek the living—*ton zōnta*—among the dead?" cf. Luke 24:23; Acts 1:3; 25:19; Rev. 1:18; 2:8). And she reported that he had let himself be seen by her (*etheathē*). They responded with disbelief (*apisteō*, in 16:11 and 14 and never elsewhere in Mark, but see Luke 24:11, 41; Acts 28:24).

16:12   "After this" (*meta de tauta*, only here in Mark but frequently in Luke, John, and Revelation) Jesus appeared (*ephanerōthē*, 16:14; John 21:1, 14) in another form (Luke 9:29; 24:16, 35) to two of them (exactly as Luke 24:13) as they were walking (Luke 24:17) to the country (cf. Mark 15:21; cf. "going to a village," Luke 24:13). This is obviously intended as a digest of the Emmaus encounter of Luke 24:13-35.

16:13   The two reported to "the others" (Luke 24:9-10; Acts 2:37), presumably back in Jerusalem, and those others did not believe them. That this response contradicts Luke's conclusion to the Emmaus pericope (Luke 24:34) underscores the fact that the longer ending is designed to deal with the problem of unbelief. It is the author's focus and overriding concern throughout the passage.

16:14   "Afterward" (*hysteron*) he appeared to the eleven (Matt. 28:16; Luke 24:9, 33; Acts 1:26; 2:14) at a meal (Luke 24:30-31, 36-42; Acts 1:4; 10:41; John 21:9-13; Ign. Smyrn. 3:3).

If the composer of the longer ending had known John's gospel and its account of doubting Thomas, there is no doubting he would have employed it. When Jesus appeared to the eleven in Luke 24, they found his being alive too good to be true and "disbelieved for joy." But there is no such excusing of the eleven or softening of their disbelief here, although such an excusing was introduced in the Freer Logion (see page 214).

Jesus reproached them (*oneidizō*, used at Mark 15:32 of the reviling of Jesus by his enemies) for their "unbelief and hardness of heart" (see Luke 24:25, "slow of heart to believe"). For unbelief as skeptical response to the Christian message see Rom. 11:20, 23; 1 Tim. 1:13.

16:15   The rebuke ended and so presumably did their unbelief. Then Jesus commanded outward movement "into all the world" (Mark 14:9; Matt. 26:13; Rom. 1:8; Acts 2:47; 1 Clem. 5:7; 7:4; 59:2) and universal proclamation of the gospel.

"Gospel" is a Markan word and preaching the gospel is a prime Markan concern; and yet these words in the longer ending are signs of common Gentile Christian focus of the late first and early second century. (On "preach the gospel" see 1 Thess. 2:9; Gal. 2:2; Col. 1:23; Barn. 5:9; Hermas Sim. 9, 25, 2; cf. 2 Tim. 4:2; Rom. 10:8; Matt. 4:23; 9:35; 24:14; 26:13 and the variant reading at Acts 1:2).

"To every creature" here means "among all people" (Col. 1:23). The desire of the author might seem to be to assert emphatically that the mission and proclamation of the church rest upon the direct utterance and will of Jesus. But surely in the Christian church of the second century there existed no widespread denial of that fact. Why then the fresh formulation of the great commission? What is new is not the wording but the setting or context and use of the commissioning. The same Jesus who rebuked the eleven has sent out the word which confronts the Christian of the second century and calls for belief.

16:16   Both believing and not believing are described by verbs in the aorist tense, indicating definite acts or moments of confession. Whoever comes to faith or confesses faith and then expresses that faith in the act of Baptism (Acts 2:38; 8:36; 16:31, 33) will be saved.

16:17   Here the seriousness of the response to the word about Jesus and the decisive character of the relationship with that word is stated again but in a negative form: Whoever makes a response of unbelief and comes to a decision against Jesus, will be condemned.

Eschatological sanctions are brought to bear upon the readers in order to impress upon them the momentous consequences of faith and unfaith (cf. John 3:18).

16:18   An explosion of signs and wonders as in the days of the Exodus under Moses (Exodus 7:3; Acts 7:36) was expected for the last times immediately before the dissolution of the present world order and the appearance of full salvation and the new creation (Joel 2:28-32; Acts 2:17-21). Jesus performed signs, and signs were a regular feature of the life and worship of the first Christians (Acts 2:43; 4:30; 5:12; 1 Cor. 12-14).

The initial turning to faith is frequently described as an occasion marked by an outburst of charismatic activity (1 Thess. 1:5; 1 Cor. 2:4; 2 Cor. 12:12; Romans 15:19; Acts 14:3; 19:11). But early Christians differed markedly in their evaluation of the relative importance of signs. Among New Testament writers Luke seems to be least critical of charismatic activity and the performance of signs. For him they are encouragement for faith and they undergird faith. He looks back on the ministry of Jesus and the earliest days of the church as a time of mighty signs and wonders. Signs of healing performed by the preacher or the sign of charismatic speech uttered by the new believer were taken by him as proof that God himself vouched for the preacher, guaranteed the truth of his proclamation, and approved of his activity (Acts 2:22; 6:8; 15:12).

Luke is fascinated by signs and features them in his narratives, while Paul tries to turn attention from them to the wonder of the weakness of the gospel (1 Cor. 2:1-5; 2 Cor. 11–12).

Luke's gospel lacks the warning that demonic activity can also produce signs and wonders and so has no parallel to Mark 13:22 (Matthew 24:24; cf. 2 Thess. 2:9; Rev. 13:13). In its view of signs as in other respects the outlook of the longer ending is decidely Lukan. And yet the positive and uncritical attitude toward signs is more than Lukan. It characterizes a broad stream in early Christianity, and is represented also in the letter to the Hebrews (see 2:3-4 and the list of signs in Chap. 11). However, in Hebrews the major accent rests on the sacrifice of Jesus and the joy of the cross as encouragement to patient endurance and obedience in spite of suffering.

16:17b-18   Five signs will accompany proclamation and coming to faith: exorcism, charismatic speech, touching snakes and drinking poison without ill effects, and healing the sick. All are remarkable, but most surprising are the handling of snakes and drinking of poison.

These two promises have stimulated bizarre responses. In 1909 in rural Tennessee, George W. Hensley interpreted this passage as a literal promise to believers, searched out a rattlesnake, and handled it as a test of his own faith in that word of promise. He then began to make propaganda for his interpretation, and he has had a following ever since, primarily in the backwoods and mountain regions of the southeastern United States.

In services marked by speaking in tongues and contagious emotion, the followers of Hensley (who died of a snakebite in 1955) prove their faith both by handling copperheads and rattlesnakes and by drinking a "salvation cocktail" of strychnine and water. Only volunteers, and then only those who are regarded as having been especially anointed, are permitted to handle the snakes or drink the poison concoction.[9]

Luke reports that when the seventy returned from their mission of preaching, healing, and exorcism, Jesus told them that he had given them "authority to tread upon serpents and scorpions and over all the power of the enemy" (Luke 10:19; Psalm 91:13; cf. Test. Levi 18:12; Test. Simeon 6:6), and Luke tells later how Paul was unharmed by the bite of a poisonous snake (Acts 28:8).

The promise in Mark 16 is related to the Old Testament expectation that in the last times the Creator would act again to renew his world, banishing everything evil and harmful, binding Satan, and restoring peace throughout the universe not only among people but also between human beings and the animals and insects:

The wolf shall dwell with the lamb,
and the leopard shall lie down with the kid,
and the calf and the lion and the fatling together,
and a little child shall lead them.
The sucking child shall play over the hole of the asp,
and the weaned child shall put his hand in the adder's den.
They shall not hurt or destroy in all my holy mountain;
for the earth shall be full of the knowledge of the Lord,
as the waters cover the sea (Isaiah 11:6, 8-9; cf. 65:25).

The author of the longer ending sees the knowledge of the Lord filling the earth, the way the waters cover the sea, as the gospel is proclaimed everywhere by the church. And as the gospel is preached and believed, signs of the new creation spring up on all sides.

Ancient rabbis said that the passengers on board Noah's ark (symbol of the restored creation rising out of the watery chaos) could walk unharmed on snakes and scorpions.[10]

The promise about drinking any fatal potion *(ti thanasimon)* is odd and obscure. According to Eusebius *(EH* III 39:9) Papias recorded the tradition that Justus Barsabbas (Acts 1:23) survived drinking poison, and the ancient apocryphal Acts of John describe the son of Zebedee as drinking poison without ill effect when the same draught had killed unbelievers.[11]

The ordinary Greek word for poison *(pharmakon)* is not used here. The cognate noun *(pharmakos)* can be translated either poisoner or magician, and the verb *(pharmakeuō)* can mean either practice magic or mix poison. The poisoner (or magician) is excluded along with murderers and adulterers from the new creation in the book of Revelation (Rev. 21:8; 22:15; cf. Didache 2:2).

In the Testament of Joseph (Chap. 6) Potiphar's wife attempted to lead Joseph astray and break down his resistance to her advances by lacing his food with "deadly enchantments." He ate and drank, but only in order to show that "the wickedness of the ungodly has no power over them that worship God with chastity." Deceitful teaching and alluring notions or heresies are called a deadly poison *(thanasimon pharmakon)* in Ignatius (Ign. Trall. 6:1-2). Elsewhere Ignatius calls the Eucharist the potion or drug of immortality (*pharmakon athanasias*, Ign. Eph. 20:2).

Perhaps the reference to poison means that evil people may do their worst—or fallen nature may gather its most deadly potions—without really being able to harm the people of God or halt the progress of the gospel on its triumphant way toward the kingdom of God.

The other three signs—exorcisms, healings, and speaking in tongues—are met more frequently in the New Testament. All three are attested especially in Luke-Acts.

That the tongues are "new" *(kainais)*[12] means that, like all the other wonders in the series, they signify the inbreaking of God's final dominion.

"New" is a word that expresses a basic conviction of early Christians about the work of God in their midst and in their time through the death and resurrection of Jesus. There is a new creation already present (2 Cor. 5:17; Gal. 6:15; cf. Eph. 4:24), and a new covenant (1 Cor. 11:25; Heb. 8:8-12; Jer. 31:31-34; Heb. 9:15; 12:24), and Christians look forward to a new heaven and a new earth (2 Peter 3:13; Rev. 21:1; Isaiah 43:18; 65:17; 66:22) and the descent of the New Jerusalem (Rev. 21:2) from the presence of God who makes all things new (Rev. 21:5).[13]

16:19   In verse 19 the proper name "Jesus" is lacking in some ancient manuscripts. If it is original, it is the only place in the passage where Jesus is actually named. Calling him "the Lord" *(kyrios)* is quite in keeping with the total thrust of the passage and its focus on Jesus' sovereign power, and it is a favorite Lukan way of referring to Jesus. Also Lukan are the "so then" *(men oun,* Luke 3:18; Acts 1:6) and "after he had spoken to them" *(meta to lalēsai autois,* Acts 1:9).

The entrance upon lordship is expressed pictorially in language derived from the narrative of Elijah's ascension (2 Kings 2:11). Some of the same language occurs in Luke (9:51; Acts 1:2, 11, 22; cf. 1 Tim. 3:16; Gos. Pet. 5:19). More importantly, the same temporal scheme of a series of separate events—death, resurrection, appearances, ascension, session—appears elsewhere in the New Testament only in the writings of Luke (Luke 24:1-53; Acts 1:3-11; 2:29-35; 5:30-31).

Sitting at God's right hand is a standard New Testament expression of the majesty of Jesus, picturing him in the way the Old Testament describes the king of Israel (Psalm 110:1; Matt. 22:44; Mark 12:36; Luke 20:42; Acts 2:34; Heb. 1:13; 1 Clem. 36:5; Barn. 12:10; cf. Matt. 26:64; Mark 14:62; Luke 22:69).

16:20   For their part the first disciples, their unbelief dispelled by the scolding and visible appearance of the resurrected Jesus, went forth and heralded the news everywhere (*pantachou*, Luke 9:6; Acts 17:30; 24:3; 28:22; 1 Cor. 4:17; 1 Clem. 41:2; cf. Mark 1:28, where the word may carry the slightly different sense of "in every direction," *BAGD*).

The Lord himself by means of signs bore witness to the truth of the word they proclaimed (Acts 14:3; Heb. 2:4).

Concluding Reflections on the Longer Ending

The author of the longer ending is agitated by the problem of unbelief in the Christian community, and he pulls out all the stops to ridicule and condemn that unbelief.

The vocabulary of belief and unbelief dominates the passage: "they disbelieved" (v. 11), "they did not believe" (v. 13), "unbelief and hardness of heart" (v. 14), "they did not believe" (v. 14), "whoever has come to faith and has been baptized will be saved, but whoever has disbelieved will be condemned" (v. 16), "signs will accompany believers" (v. 17).

The passage encourages belief not so much by proclaiming the good news of the grace of God in Jesus as by scolding, by the issuance of threats, and by appeals to the power of Jesus.

For the author, the resurrection of Jesus is the greatest of all the signs and wonders. In fact, it is what makes all the others possible. The signs occur in support of the church's proclamation. That message, if it is anywhere explicitly enunciated in the longer ending, is that "He lives" (v. 11), and the reader is told that he lives powerfully—resurrected, ascended, and seated at the right hand of God. And that powerful one can be counted on to bring salvation for believers.

As the passage opens (16:9) it identifies Jesus as the resurrected one who appeared in the power of God *(ephanē)*, and it describes Mary Magdalene as the one from whom Jesus had cast out seven demons. Seven is a number signifying the completeness of the demonic possession, and so the beginning of the passage depicts Jesus as the all-powerful victor over evil. At the close of the passage (16:19) Jesus is portrayed as having been taken up into heaven and as having assumed his seat of power and privilege. Then the passage closes (16:17-20) with Jesus' promise that five powerful signs will accompany the believers.

It is entirely in keeping with the tone of the whole passage that the only name or title attached to Jesus in the longer ending is not his given name Jesus (see comment on v. 19) nor the title Christ (used in the Freer Logion) but only Lord *(kyrios)*.

The events of Easter and the days leading up to the ascension are recalled in order to provoke faith and to rebuke unbelief. Christians contemporary with the author are warned of the danger of a faith that has gone slack. The wonders of the present and the past, including the worldwide proclamation of the gospel itself, are evidences of divine favor arguing for belief.

The author of the longer ending was nothing if not a serious soul in dead earnest about faith. His view of faith is different from Mark's, however. He does not proclaim the good news of Jesus, confident that the gospel will exercise its mysterious spiritual power. He thinks of faith as a kind of emotion, a human production, that can be cranked up by exhortations and threats such as he has uttered.

Why did the author of the longer ending retell the tradition of the resurrection of Jesus? The outline indicates that the longer ending is really something different from a synopsis of the various post-resurrection appearances of Jesus. The compiler's contemporaries did not need to be told what happened in the days following Easter. Presumably they knew as well as the author did how the gospels of Mark and Luke (and perhaps Matthew and John, but that is not likely) ended.

The commissioning seems to hold center stage, and yet it would be misleading to say that the longer ending was designed to whip up enthusiasm for missions. The wording of the appearances, the recital of the commissioning, and the statement on Jesus' ascension and session are all in the service of the author's rebuke of unbelief.[14]

The longer ending is an elaborate set of parallels between the experience and reactions of the earliest disciples and the author's contemporaries. The Jesus who appeared to the disciples has been at work among the author's generation not visibly and palpably but through the church's proclamation. Unfortunately, the author's contemporaries were responding to Jesus as badly as the first disciples had.

The longer ending sounds very much like a commentary on Luke's resurrection material by a Christian who was discouraged and perhaps disgusted by the evidences of unbelief in his community. His words are critical and threatening. Indeed they tend toward the negative and joyless.

3. The Freer Logion

One Greek manuscript, the Washington Codex from the late fourth or fifth century, discovered in Egypt in 1906, preserves an expansion of the longer ending known previously only in a Latin version of Jerome.[15]

It is inserted immediately after verse 14 and may be translated as follows:

1.	And they defended themselves by saying,
2.	"This age of lawlessness and unbelief is subject to Satan, who
3.	-by means of spirits does not allow the unclean to comprehend the true power of God (or, the truth, the power of God), or -by means of unclean spirits does not allow the true power of God to be comprehended, or -does not allow the true power of God to master the unclean things of the spirits.
4.	Therefore," they said to Christ, "Reveal your righteousness now."
5.	And Christ replied to them, "The limit of the years of Satan's authority has been reached,
6.	but other terrible things are drawing near,
7.	even for those people for whom I, since they were sinners, was delivered into death,
8.	that they might turn to the truth and no longer sin, that they might inherit the spiritual and incorruptible glory of the righteousness (kept) in heaven."

Line 1: Jesus' disciples speak up in defense of themselves, and the passage is clearly an apology. Its second word is in Greek *"apelogounto"* and it is shaped in response to the rebuke in 16:14. That rebuke is aimed not only at the eleven but at the contemporaries of the author of the longer ending, so the defense also excuses their lack of faith or weakness in faith (cf. Luke 18:8).

Line 2: They describe the present as an age of lawlessness and unbelief, subject to Satan. The periodization of history into distinct aeons and the pessimistic estimate of this present age as one of almost unrelieved darkness (Gal. 1:4) under the lordship of Satan (John 14:30; Eph. 2:2) reflect an apocalyptic view, common among early Christians. The present means lawlessness, unbelief, and evil, while the future is full of righteousness (twice in the passage). Lawlessness will be especially virulent in the last days (2 Thess. 2:3; cf. 2:7; Matt. 24:12; Did. 16:4).

Line 3: The exact reading and rendering of the clause are disputed. Four possible translations are offered, beginning with the most satisfactory.

Satan is not alone but is lord or leader of a multitude of unclean spirits (see Mark 3:22-26). He has hindered the disciples, living in an unclean world, from comprehending the truth of God and the power of God exhibited in Jesus (2 Cor. 4:3-4). The letter of Barnabas characterizes Satan as the ruler of this present time of lawlessness but Jesus as Lord from eternity to eternity (18:2; cf. 15:7).

The phrase about not comprehending the power of God is reminiscent of the Prologue to John's gospel. There the darkness has not comprehended or mastered the light, either in the sense of not accepting and understanding it or in the sense of not having overpowered it.

Line 4: The disciples beseech Jesus to terminate the rule of evil by revealing his righteousness (cf. Acts 1:6-8). As the opposite of lawlessness, righteousness means salvation, since it entails rescue from the defilement and dominion of evil. Righteousness can therefore mean about the same as God's ultimate victory (cf. John 16:8; 1 Tim. 3:16). Paul announces the theme of Romans in terms of the revelation of the righteousness of God (1:17) and simultaneously the revelation of the wrath of God from heaven against all ungodliness and wickedness (1:17-18; cf. 1 Peter 1:3-9). Christians look for new heavens and a new earth in which righteousness is perfectly at home (2 Peter 3:13).

Line 5: Christ's response to the disciples' plea recognizes that Satan has had considerable authority (*exousia*, Luke 22:53; Acts 26:18; cf. 1 John 5:19), but not as much as the devil claimed for himself in Luke's temptation narrative (Luke 4:6-8); furthermore, the time of his reign has been fulfilled (cf. Mark 1:15, *peplērōtai*). His authority has now finally ended (Luke 10:18; John 12:31; 16:11; 1 John 2:8; Rev.

12:7-12). That means that another, namely God or his Christ, has seized power in the world. Matthew describes the resurrected Jesus as having all authority both in heaven and upon the earth (*pasa exousia,* Matt. 28:18). A new age is about to dawn.

Line 6: But before it appears in all its glory, certain fearful things *(deina)* must yet occur. Elsewhere New Testament writers speak of the new age like a child ready to be born, and the terrors of afflictions of the present moment are compared with labor pains (John 16:21; 1 Thess. 5:3).

Line 7: They will overtake even those for whom Jesus was given up into death. These are presumably Christians, the people who identify themselves as the objects of Christ's love.

Line 8: Present horrors are no indication that God has lost his grip or that evil is triumphant. They are a prelude, a testing, or a tempering (1 Peter 1:6-7), a set of signs to awaken Christians to the urgency of repentance, watchfulness, and faith (Mark 13). The delay of the final victory of God allows humankind time to repent, turn to the truth, and abandon sin (2 Peter 3:9). The death of Jesus is expected to bear fruit before the last day.

And beyond the dark terrors is the bright dawn of the new age, not an earthly kingdom but a spiritual and heavenly inheritance, unfading, undefiled, and imperishable (1 Peter 1:4).

Conclusions Regarding the Freer Logion

The Freer Logion probably originated in the second or third century at the hand of a scribe interested primarily in softening the harsh condemnation of the disciples in 16:14. It also introduces a positive note into an otherwise negative passage. The saying of Jesus in response to the disciples is a word of encouragement to people disheartened and on the verge of unbelief. Christ's answer is that the time remaining before the full revelation of his glory is brief. The composer of the passage may also have thought he was providing a bridge over the awkward gap between verse 14 with its criticism of the disciples and verse 15 with the mission command.[16]

notes

Introduction

1. In his book *Jesus—God and Man* (Philadelphia: Westminster, 1968), p. 149, Wolfhart Pannenberg quotes with approval these words of Paul Althaus from *Die christliche Wahrheit*, p. 443.

2. Ernst Käsemann, *The Testament of Jesus* (Philadelphia: Fortress, 1968), p. 1.

Mark

1. Reviews of recent research on the gospel of Mark can be found in Werner Georg Kümmel, *Introduction to the New Testament* (Nashville: Abingdon, 1975), pp. 80-101; Robin S. Barbour, "Recent Study of the Gospel according to St. Mark," *ExpT* 79 (1967/8): 324-329; Joachim Rohde, *Rediscovering the Teaching of the Evangelists* (Philadelphia: Westminister, 1968), pp. 113-152; Ralph Martin, *Mark, Evangelist and Theologian* (Grand Rapids: Zondervan, 1973); Howard Clark Kee, "Mark's Gospel in Recent Research," *Int* 32 (1978): 353-368; Jack Dean Kingsbury, "The Gospel of Mark in Current Research," *Religious Studies Review* 5 (1979): 101-107. Of course commentaries also usually review research up to the time of their publication.

2. From the beginning of his ministry Jesus aroused opposition by his unorthodox pronouncements and behavior (2:7, 16, 24; 3:5), and early on his enemies plotted his death (3:6). Scribes accused him of being in league with Beelzebub (3:22), and members of his own family feared he was beside himself (3:21; cf. John 8:48; 10:20,33). His forerunner was beheaded (6:27-28), and John's death was a grim foreshadowing of Jesus' own. Jesus three times prophesied his own passion (8:31; 9:31; 10:33-34), and the passion narrative, whether it is regarded as beginning with the entry

into Jerusalem in Chapter 11 or with the priests' plot in Chapter 14, takes up a disproportionate amount of space in Mark's gospel.

3. Martin, *Mark*, offers an extensive review of the whole question of Mark's historical situation and purpose in writing. Martin thinks that Mark wrote in the mid-60's in Rome to encourage a community perplexed by persecution (pp. 51-83) but insists that theological considerations (pp. 84-139) must be given greater weight than the historical setting in elucidating Mark's story of Jesus. Mark does address the question of his community's suffering, but speaks especially to false christologies and then encourages his readers to face the tasks of missionary service with confidence (pp. 140-226). The false christologies arose, Martin thinks, among Paulinist Gentile Christians who carried to an extreme certain features of the apostle's teaching and who were led to deny Jesus' true humanity and to repose their confidence in a heavenly redeemer, remote from earth and history (p. 214).

4. The theory, so briefly summarized here, is identified with Theodore J. Weeden, *Mark: Traditions in Conflict* (Philadelphia: Fortress, 1971), and parts of it are represented in different ways by John Dominic Crossan "Empty Tomb and Absent Lord," in *The Passion in Mark*, ed. Werner H. Kelber (Philadelphia: Fortress, 1976), pp. 135-152, and by Werner H. Kelber *The Kingdom in Mark* (Philadelphia: Fortress, 1974) and *Mark's Story of Jesus* (Philadelphia: Fortress, 1978). See below, additional note on The Silence of The Women, pp. 98-99, and footnote 62.

5. Howard Clark Kee, "Mark's Gospel," p. 366. See also his book, *Community of the New Age* (Philadelphia: Westminster, 1977). James M. Robinson, *The Problem of History in Mark* (London: SCM, 1956) also interpreted Mark as an apocalyptic document.

6. According to Eusebius (*EH* III.v.3) writing early in the fourth century and then Epiphanius (Against Heresies xxix.7; cf. xxx.2.2) writing a short time later. S. G. F. Brandon, *The Fall of Jerusalem and the Christian Church* (London: S.P.C.K., 1957), pp. 169-173, raises serious questions about the tradition. Sidney Sowers, "The Circumstances and Recollection of the Pella Flight," *ThZ* 26 (1970): 305-320, collects evidence and argument in favor of the tradition. John J. Gunther, "The Fate of the Jerusalem Church: The Flight to Pella," *ThZ* 29 (1973): 81-94, thinks the naming of Pella as a major refuge is credible.

7. Willi Marxsen both in his *Introduction to the New Testament* (London: Blackwell, 1968), p. 143, and in his *Mark the Evangelist* (Nashville: Abingdon, 1969), pp. 107, 114-116.

8. For other objections to the views of Marxsen see Rohde, *Rediscovering*, pp. 113-140, and Martin, *Mark*, pp. 70-75.

9. C. E. B. Cranfield, *The Gospel according to St. Mark* (Cambridge: The University Press, 1959), citing W. M. Ramsay. Also Vincent Taylor, *The Gospel according to St. Mark* (London: Macmillan, 1952), p. 43. On the latinisms see Taylor and also C. F. D. Moule, *An Idiom Book of New Testament Greek* (Cambridge: The University Press, 1953), p. 192.

10. See Robinson, *Problem of History*, pp. 63-66, Martin, *Mark*, pp. 219-225, and Norman Perrin, *The New Testament: An Introduction* (New York: Harcourt Brace, Jovanovich, 1974), pp. 143-167.

11. Other places have been suggested: the Decapolis (S. Schulz); Tyre, Sidon, or the Decapolis (J. Schreiber); Syria (J. V. Bartlet, W. G. Kümmel); Asia Minor or Greece (H. Koester). Cautious but favoring Rome as the place of authorship are Taylor, Cranfield, Brandon, and Martin in works previously cited, and also W. D. Davies, *Invitation to the New Testament* (Garden City: Doubleday, 1966), pp. 207-208.

Brandon thinks the gospel was written in Rome but not on the background of Nero's persecution. Instead he pictures the Christian community lining the streets of Rome watching the triumphal procession of Vespasian and Titus, returning successful from the Jewish War, displaying the identity symbols of Jewish religion plundered from the temple in Jerusalem: the seven-branched candelabra and the golden trumpets. Brandon speculates that Jesus had actually been a zealot bent on liberating his people from the Roman yoke and that Mark's gospel is designed to transform Jesus into an unJewish and nonpolitical Christ. See his book, *Jesus and the Zealots* (New York: Charles Scribner's Sons, 1967), pp. 227-281. See also Walter Wink, "Jesus and Revolution: Reflections on S. G. F. Brandon's ' Jesus and the Zealots'," *USQR* 25 (1969): 37-59.

The gospel is, of course, anonymous and bears no postmark proving beyond question that Rome is the place of origin, but early tradition inside the New Testament connects Mark with Paul (Philemon 24; Col. 4:10; 2 Tim. 4:11) and Peter (1 Peter 5:13; Acts 12:25; 13:5, 13) and connects Paul and Peter with Rome (2 Tim. 1:17; Acts 28; 1 Peter 5:13).

Beyond the New Testament 1 Clement 5 speaks of the martyrdom of Peter and Paul, apparently at Rome. Papias, according to Eusebius (*EH* III.xxxix.15) calls Mark the interpreter of Peter in producing the gospel, and Justin Martyr (ca. A.D. 150 in *Dialogue with Trypho* 106,3) indicates that the phrase Boanerges, "sons of thunder," found only in Mark 3:17, is in a book which he calls the memoirs of Peter. The Anti-Marcionite Prologue says that Mark after the death of Peter wrote the gospel "in the regions of Italy" but the date of the prologue, once regarded as around A.D. 160-180, has become a matter of debate. Irenaeus had lived at Rome, and he states that Peter and Paul founded the church there and that Mark wrote his gospel after their deaths, transmitting the things Peter had preached (*Against Heresies* III.i.2). Clement of Alexandria, at the beginning of the third century, testifies that Mark wrote the gospel at the request of Peter's Roman followers (Eus. *EH* VI.xiv.6-7; II.xv.1-2; Clement, *Adumbr. in 1 Peter* v.13).

Paul J. Achtemeier, *Mark* (Philadelphia: Fortress, 1975), pp. 111-117, subjects to critical review the tradition connecting the gospel to John Mark and Mark to Peter and both of them to Rome, and he comments on other theories of authorship, date, and place of origin, concluding that the author of the gospel has successfully maintained his anonymity and the uncertainty of the place of writing. For a most careful review of the ancient traditions regarding authorship see Everett R. Kalin, "Early Traditions About Mark's Gospel," *Currents* 2 (1975): 332-341.

12. Tacitus, *The Annals of Imperial Rome*, XV, translated by Michael Grant (Middlesex: Penguin Books, 1971), p. 365. See also Suetonius, *Nero* 16.2. It is not likely that after Nero's persecution Christianity was formally outlawed, forbidden by a decree of emperor or senate. No trace of such legal action exists. But the affair surely put the church on the wrong side of the state and constituted a menacing precedent. See W. H. C. Frend, *Martyrdom and Persecution in the Early Church* (Garden City: Anchor Books, 1967), pp. 126-132.

13. Some comparisons are illuminating. See Fabian von Schlabrendorff, *The Secret War Against Hitler* (New York: Putnam, 1965), especially Chapters 14-23. An even more chilling account of the terrors of persecution is offered by Hans Helmut Kirst in his novelized report, *Soldiers' Revolt* (New York: Harper & Row, 1966). Both books describe the horrors unleashed in the aftermath of the abortive July 1944 attempt on Hitler's life.

14. Ernst Käsemann in *Jesus Means Freedom* (Philadelphia: Fortress, 1969), pp. 55-58, writes that Mark's gospel is a product of early Christian enthusiasm and that it portrays Jesus as the great cosmic victor over the devil and death. His views are not unlike those of Robinson, *Problem of History*, except that Robinson speaks not of enthusiasm but of Jesus as locked in cosmic apocalyptic combat with Satan. Ernest Best, *The Temptation and the Passion* (Cambridge: The University Press, 1965), has attempted to show that Mark focuses not just on demons and supernatural powers but on sin.

15. The story is well told by Bo Reicke, *The New Testament Era* (Philadelphia: Fortress, 1968), pp. 240-270.

16. See Robert H. Smith, "Darkness at Noon: Mark's Passion Narrative," *CTM* 44 (1973): 325-338.

17. The outlining of Mark's gospel offered here is a common enough one. It rests on various kinds of data scattered in the gospel, and it makes excellent sense. For a discussion of a number of schemes and for cautions about all of them, see Achtemeier, *Mark*, pp. 31-40.

18. See Bruce Metzger, *A Textual Commentary on the Greek New Testament* (London and New York: United Bible Societies, 1971), p. 73.

19. Philip Vielhauer, "Erwägungen zur Christologie des Markusevangeliums," in *Zeit und Geschichte*, hrsg. Erich Dinkler (Tübingen: J. C. B. Mohr, 1964), pp. 155-169, develops the suggestion following Eduard Norden and using the observations of Joachim Jeremias and others on enthronement patterns in the New Testament. See Rohde, *Rediscovering*, pp. 147-148, for discussion of Vielhauer's views.

20. Achtemeier in his book on *Mark* and especially in his article, "Mark as Interpreter of the Jesus Traditions," *Int* 32 (1978): 339-352, has empha-

sized the centrality of the cross in Mark's gospel. Martin, *Mark*, has also described in great detail how Mark relates all the traditions about Jesus to the cross.

21. Burnett Hillman Streeter, *The Four Gospels* (London: Macmillan, 1930), p. 336.

22. Stephen Neill, *Jesus Through Many Eyes* (Philadelphia: Fortress, 1976), pp. 76-79. Eduard Schweizer, *The Good News According to Mark* (Richmond: John Knox, 1970), also expresses the thought that the original, longer ending has been accidentally lost.

23. In this judgment Neill is following H. B. Swete, *The Gospel According to St. Mark* (London: Macmillan, 1898).

24. G. W. Trompf, "The First Resurrection Appearance and the Ending of Mark's Gospel," *NTS* 18 (1972): 308-330.

25. Streeter, *Four Gospels*, pp. 351ff. Austin Farrer, *The Glass of Vision* (Westminster: Dacre, 1948), pp. 136-149, not only accepted the pericope (Mark 16:1-8) as it stands but defended it as having "poetical inevitability," but later in his *St. Matthew and St. Mark* (Westminster: Dacre, 1954), pp. 144 he suggested as a tolerable alternative one further sentence: "But Jesus sent forth his disciples to preach the gospel among all nations."

26. An ancient nickname for Mark, attested in the writings of Hippolytus of Rome (ca. A.D. 200), is "stump-fingered" *(kolobodaktylos)*, a word originally applied to a man who cut off a thumb to escape military service. Wordsworth and White thought Hippolytus found the term applied to Mark in Marcion who had used it to discredit the gospel of the man who had deserted Paul on the first missionary journey and indirectly to support his preference for Luke. Streeter thought that "stump-fingered" or "short-thumbed" might well apply both to Mark and to his gospel. The author was a shirker and his gospel is a broken and incomplete piece. The Muratorian Canon (second century or fourth century?) uses the Latin transliteration "colobodaktylos" and explains it simply as meaning that Mark has short fingers. Other ancients claimed that Mark cut off his thumb to signal a radical break with his Levitical past (cf. Col. 4:10; Acts 4:36; Lev. 21:16-21).

    See Streeter, *Four Gospels*, p. 337; Walter Grundmann, *Das Evangelium nach Markus* (Berlin: Evangelische Verlagsanstalt, 1977), p. 21; J. L. North, "Markos ho kolobodaktylos: Hippolytus *Elenchus* vii. 30," *JTS* 28 (1977): 498-507.

27. Besides the commentaries see BAGD on *gar* and see P. W. van der Horst, "Can a Book End with GAR? A Note on Mark 16:8," *JTS* 22 (1972): 121-124, with its excellent bibliography and fresh example from the end of the 32nd treatise of the Enneads of Plotinus. Frederick W. Danker, "Menander and the New Testament," *NTS* 10 (1964), notes that the *Dyscolos* of Menander ends with *gar*. William L. Lane, *The Gospel according to Mark* (Grand Rapids: Eerdmans, 1974), says that Musonius ends his Discourse xii, *Peri Aphrodision*, with *gar*.

28. Bruce Metzger, *The Text of the New Testament*, 2nd ed. (New York and Oxford: Oxford University Press, 1968), p. 228.

29. Robert H. Lightfoot, *Locality and Doctrine in the Gospels* (New York: Harper, 1937), pp. 9-19, and *The Gospel Message of St. Mark* (Oxford: The University Press, 1950), pp. 80-97, 106-116. Following the lead of Lightfoot is Günter Stemberger, "Galilee—Land of Salvation?" in W. D. Davies, *The Gospel and the Land* (Berkeley: University of California Press, 1974), pp. 409-439. John's gospel confronts the notion of the privileged first generation at 20:29 and in the whole of the pericope on Thomas.

30. Frank Kermode, *The Genesis of Secrecy* (Cambridge: Harvard University Press, 1979), p. 64, discusses the way modern readers are "programmed to prefer fulfillment to disappointment, the closed to the open."

31. Matthew and Luke parallel one another closely as long as they have Mark as the middle member between them. So they tell basically the same story all through the passion narrative and up to the discovery of the empty tomb and the appearance of the angel to the women. They recite all that material, with variations to be sure, along remarkably similar lines. However, as soon as Mark breaks off (at 16:8), Matthew and Luke begin immediately to diverge, and they do so dramatically and unmistakably. They are no longer under the control exercised by the Markan tradition. The fact that the divergence begins exactly when Mark 16:8 ends, shows that both Matthew and Luke, working independently of one another and in quite different geographical regions, knew the gospel of Mark only in its short form.

32. Taylor, *Mark*, pp. 651-653.

33. M. Rosh Hashanah 1:8; M. Shebuoth 4:1; Josephus *Ant.* 4:219. See Joachim Jeremias, *Jerusalem in the Time of Jesus* (London: SCM, 1969), pp. 374f.

34. See the separate note on "Silence and the Women" in the text following the commentary on 16:8.

35. Semachoth 8, according to Paul Billerbeck, *Kommentar zum neuen Testament aus Talmud und Midrasch* (München: C. H. Beck, 1924), 1:1048, and also Gen. Rabba 100 (64a), according to August Strobel, "Discipleship in the Light of the Easter Event," in *The Beginnings of the Church in the New Testament* (Minneapolis: Augsburg, 1970), note 32, pp. 80-81.

36. Joachim Jeremias, *The Eucharistic Words of Jesus* (New York: Charles Scribner's Sons, 1966), p. 17. On the reckoning of time in the ancient world see Taylor, *Mark*, pp. 604-605, and James A. Kleist, *The Gospel of Saint Mark* (Milwaukee: Bruce, 1936).

    On doubling see Frans Neirynck, *Duality in Mark* (Leuven: Leuven University, 1972).

37. Gabriel Hebert connects the passage with the promised advent of the Sun of Righteousness (Mal. 4:2 LXX) and sees a kind of Johannine strug-

gle between the powers of light and darkness. See his "The Resurrection Narrative in St. Mark's Gospel," *SJT* 15 (1962): 66-73.

Grundmann, *Evangelium nach Markus*, p. 445, also perceives the possibility of a symbolic interpretation and comments that perhaps Mark means to say that "the sun has risen upon the dark night of the grave."

See also Amos 8:9; cf. 5:18,20; Joel 2:2,10,31; 3:15; Wisdom 17:20—18:4. Vergil, *Georgics* I.463-9; The sun hid its shining face in dusky gloom as Caesar sank from sight. Philo, *On Providence* 2.50, regards eclipses (cf. Luke 23:45) as announcements of the deaths of kings. So also the risen sun announces the beginning of the reign of Jesus.

38. For discussion of the addition see Metzger, *Textual Commentary*, pp. 121 ff.

39. Some ancient authorities, including codices D and Theta, minuscule ms 565, the Sinaitic Syriac, and others, actually have the clause "for it was very great" at the end of verse 3. Taylor, *Mark*, p. 606, notes other delayed explanatory clauses in Mark at 5:8; 6:52; 16:8.

40. Grundmann, *Evangelium nach Markus*, suggests a symbolic interpretation when he comments on this verse that "the might of the resurrection shatters completely the stubborn power of death and the finality of the grave."

41. The Greek word for young man is *neaniskos*, and a related word, *neanias*, is used of a heavenly messenger in 2 Macc. 3:26,33 and in Josephus *Ant.* The Greek word *angelos* itself does double duty, since it retains its original meaning of human messenger and at the same time also serves as designation for the angels of heaven, since those heavenly beings are often sent on missions with messages from God. Angels are usually depicted as men in Scripture (e.g., Dan. 10:5,16,18), and it is not surprising that they should be pictured as young or strong. In Luke "two men" replace the "young man" of Mark's gospel as heavenly envoys, while Matthew talks of "an angel of the Lord" and John of "two angels ." The white garb further identifies the young man as an angel (cf. Mark 9:3; Acts 1:10; 10:30; Rev. 7:9,13-14; Dan. 7:9).

42. For other possible Markan allusions to the prophet Amos compare Mark 14:47 and Amos 3:12; Mark 11:12-14 and Amos 4:9; Mark 15:33 and Amos 8:9; cf. 4:13, 5:8,18,20; Mark 14:61; 15:5 and Amos 5:13; Mark 15:38 and Amos 9:1.

43. The old notion that the author is discreetly painting himself into the picture in 14:51-52 has nothing to commend it, and the parallelism of the passages weighs against it.

It has been noticed that Joseph fled, leaving his clothes behind, was taken to prison, and later was exalted. Herman C. Waetjen, "The Ending of Mark and the Gospel's Shift in Eschatology," *ASTI* 4 (1965): 120, points to the background in the story of Joseph, but then the young man (and Joseph) are turned into Christ figures. John Knox, "A Note on Mark 14:51-52," in *The Joy of Study*, ed. S. Johnson (New York: Macmillan,

1951), pp. 27-30, and Albert Vanhoye, "La fuite du jeune homme (Mc 14,51-52)," *Biblica* 52 (1971): 401-406, suggest that the young man leaving the cloth and escaping prefigures Jesus who left behind the gravecloths and escaped in resurrection. Robin Scroggs and Kent I. Goff, "Baptism in Mark: Dying and Rising with Christ," *JBL* 92 (1973): 531-548, suggest that the young man represents first Jesus and then also the Christian in their dying and rising. John Crossan, "Empty Tomb and Absent Lord," pp. 147-148, thinks along similar lines and develops the notion that the "young man" in both cases represents the Christian community reborn in the resurrected Christ. Frans Neirynck, " La fuite du jeune homme en Mc 14:51-52," *EphThLov* 55 (1979): 43-66, and Harry Fleddermann, "The Flight of a Naked Young Man (Mark 14:51-52)," *CBQ* 41 (1979): 412-418, argue that the young man represents the disciples in their failure in contrast to Jesus who stands and accepts death. Frank Kermode, *Genesis of Secrecy*, pp. 55-63, finds in the young man fleeing away from Gethsemane an image of desertion, as Peter is of denial and Judas of betrayal, and the desertion is all the more poignant in that the typical deserter is one who by Baptism or other rite of initiation has been reborn.

44. Further discussion of *nazarēnos* and the related *nazōraios* together with bibliography in articles by H. H. Schaeder in *TDNT* 4:874-879 and by Oscar Cullmann in *IDB* 3:523-524.

45. Martin Hengel, *Crucifixion* (Philadelphia: Fortress, 1977).

46. The translation, "Look at the place" (RSV), is not strictly accurate. "The place" *(ho topos)* is a nominative and not the direct object of "look" *(ide)*. So it is "Look! Here is the place. . . ." or "Behold! This is the place. . . ."

E. L. Bode, *The First Easter Morning* (Rome: Biblical Institute, 1970), strongly and rightly opposes the notion favored by Gottfried Schille, Wolfgang Nauck, Jacob Kremer, and especially Ludger Schenke that 16:6 reflects a primitive Christian weekly or annual pilgrimage to the tomb of Jesus. Bas van Iersel, "The Resurrection of Jesus—Information or Interpretation?," in *Immortality and Resurrection*, ed. Pierre Benoit and Roland Murphy (Herder and Herder, 1970), pp. 54-67, tries to support Schenke's views with references to Joachim Jeremias, *Heiligengraeber in Jesu Umwelt* (Gottingen: Vandenhoeck und Ruprecht, 1958), and to the ancient (4th century) accounts of the Burgundian Pilgrim and Egeria. It is true that peoples of all cultures visit tombs, that the passage stresses time and place, and that pilgrims' diaries are full of the phrase, "This is the place where. . . .," but that hardly proves that Mark's account has been shaped by liturgical processions to the tomb.

Among others, Hans Grass, *Ostergeschehen und Osterberichte* (Göttingen: Vandenhoeck und Ruprecht, 1962), p. 180, has said that Jesus must have been laid by his enemies into a common grave reserved for criminals. However in Jerusalem in 1970 the bones of a crucified man were discovered in a first century tomb. The discovery shows that the executed were permitted to be claimed by their families and given decent burial. V. Tzaferis, "Jewish Tombs at and near Giv 'at ha-Mivtar, Jerusalem" *IEJ* 20 (1970); 18-32

47. Contra Theodore Weeden, *Traditions.* See Jack Dean Kingsbury, "The Gospel in Four Editions," *Int* 33 (1979): 366.

48. Numerous interpreters have followed Ernst Lohmeyer, *Galiläa und Jerusalem* (Göttingen: Vandenhoeck und Ruprecht, 1936), and *Das Evangelium des Markus*, 15th ed. (Göttingen: Vandenhoeck und Ruprecht, 1959) in interpreting "Galilee" not literally and geographically but as "the land of eschatological expectation." Lohmeyer's views have been developed particularly by Willi Marxsen, *Mark the Evangelist*, who believes that the ending of Mark looks forward to the parousia.

   Robert H. Lightfoot, *History and Interpretation in the Gospels* (London: Hodder and Stoughton, 1935) as well as in *Locality and Doctrine* and in *Gospel Message of St. Mark* began with the views of Lohmeyer and interpreted Galilee as standing for renewed service and ministry. C. F. Evans, "I Will Go Before You Into Galilee," *JTS* 5 (1954): 3-18, in the tradition of Lightfoot, takes Galilee to mean the Christian mission in the whole world under the leadership of the resurrected and exalted Jesus. For a history of the interpretation of "Galilee" with critique, see Günter Stemberger, "Galilee—Land of Salvation?" (Note 29). Stemberger finally stands very close to the views of Lightfoot. The body of the present work reflects the views of Lightfoot and Stemberger in highly compressed form.

49. See Lohmeyer's works cited in the previous note, and see also Hans Conzelmann, *An Outline of the Theology of the New Testament* (New York: Harper & Row, 1969), and Norman Perrin, *The Resurrection according to Matthew, Mark and Luke* (Philadelphia: Fortress, 1977).

   Robert H. Stein, "A Short Note on Mark 14:28 and 16:7," *NTS* 20 (1974): 445-452, reviews the question and asserts that seeing Jesus in Galilee cannot mean the parousia and must mean appearances, since the retention of a promise of parousia would be nonsense when Peter was already dead. Willi Marxsen is usually taken as an advocate of the view that the promised seeing has to do with the parousia, but he modifies it existentialistically. In *Mark the Evangelist*, pp. 92-94, he says that "where Jesus worked, there is Galilee," and Jesus continues to work in the proclamation, and wherever the proclamation is heard, the "secret epiphany" occurs and the parousia is anticipated in hiddenness.

50. On the pericopes dealing with seeing and discipleship refer to Earl S. Johnson, Jr., "Mark 8:22-26: The Blind Man from Bethsaida," *NTS* 25 (1979): 370-383, and "Mark 10:46-52: Blind Bartimaeus," *CBQ* 40 (1978): 191-204. See also Vernon Robbins, "The Healing of Blind Bartimaeus (10:46-52) in the Marcan Theology," *JBL* 92 (1973): 224-243, and Paul J. Achtemeier, " 'And He Followed Him': Miracles and Discipleship in Mark 10:46-52," *Semeia* 11 (1978): 115-145.

   Some think that Mark throughout his gospel polemicizes against the disciples and/or Jesus' family. See, for example, Weeden, *Traditions in Conflict*, and Werner Kelber, *The Kingdom in Mark* (Philadelphia:

Fortress, 1974). J. D. Crossan, "Mark and the Relatives of Jesus," *NovT* 15 (1973): 81-113, includes Jesus' family together with the disciples as constituting a core of Jerusalem opposition to Mark and his community. See also J. Lambrecht, "The Relatives of Jesus in Mark," *NovT* 16 (1974): 241-258.

For a review of scholarship on disciples in Mark see Ernest Best, "The Role of the Disciples in Mark," *NTS* 23 (1977): 377-401. See also his "Mark 3:20,21,31-35," *NTS* 22 (1975/6): 309-319, and "Discipleship in Mark (Mark 8:27—10:52)," *SJT* 23 (1970): 323-337. See now Ernest Best, *Following Jesus: Discipleship in the Gospel of Mark* (Sheffield: JSOT Press, 1981).

Best's views of the historical setting and purpose of Mark's gospel, of the themes of blindness and sight, and of the passion and resurrection narrative are quite similar to those offered in this present work.

51. Evans, "I Will Go Before You," says that the seeing would be like that recorded in Matthew 28:16-20, and he asks what the disciples there saw. They saw that Jesus had all authority and that he was present with them in universal mission to the close of the age. Ernest Best, *The Temptation and the Passion*, pp. 173-177, agrees.

52. See Table 3, "Mark's Vocabulary of Fear, Astonishment, etc.," in Bode, *First Easter Morning*, p. 38.

53. Suggested to me some years ago by a former student, the Rev. John Strelan.

54. See Frans Neirynck, *Duality in Mark*.

55. So C. F. D. Moule, "St. Mark 16:8 Once More," *NTS* 2 (1955/6): 58-59. Frederick W. Danker, "Postscript to the Markan Secrecy Motif," *CTM* 38 (1967): 26, has written on completely other grounds of "the silence of the women in their encounter with all others except the disciples." See the additional note below on "Silence and the Women."

56. Julius Wellhausen, *Das Evangelium Marci* (Berlin: Georg R. Reimer, 1903), p. 136; Wilhelm Bousset, *Kyrios Christos* (Nashville: Abingdon, 1970), p. 106; Rudolf Bultmann, *The History of the Synoptic Tradition* (Oxford: Blackwell, 1963), pp. 284-287.

57. Julius Schniewind, *Das Evangelium nach Markus* (Göttingen: Vandenhoeck und Ruprecht, 1952), p. 205. See also Ulrich Wilckens, "The Tradition History of the Resurrection of Jesus," in *The Significance of the Message of the Resurrection for Faith in Jesus Christ*, ed. C. F. D. Moule (London: SCM, 1968), p. 71, and his book, *Resurrection* (Atlanta: John Knox, 1978), pp. 34-35.

In addition see Albert Descamp, "La Structure des Récits Evangéliques de la Résurrection," *Biblica* 40 (1959): 728-741.

58. Hans Freiherr von Campenhausen, "The Events of Easter and the Empty Tomb," in *Tradition and Life in the Church* (Philadelphia: Fortress, 1968), pp. 69-77.

59. Hans Grass, *Ostergeschehen,* p. 22. Compare Wilckens, *Resurrection,* p. 35.

60. Martin Hengel, "Maria Magdalena und die Frauen als Zeugen," in *Abraham Unser Vater,* hrsg. O. Betz et al. (Leiden: Brill, 1963), pp. 243-256.

61. Theodore Weeden, *Traditions in Conflict.*

62. John Crossan, "Empty Tomb and Absent Lord." Kelber, *Kingdom in Mark* and *Mark's Story of Jesus* thinks of a Galilean setting for the gospel and a date of composition after A.D. 70. He argues that Mark represents a Galilean community with a theology of the cross set in opposition to the twelve disciples as members of a Jerusalem community with a theology of power. For a reaction see Robert Smith, "Thy Kingdom Come: Some Recent Work on Mark's Gospel," *Currents* 8 (1981): 371-376, and see Best, *Following Jesus: Discipleship in the Gospel of Mark.*

63. See Harald Riensenfeld, *Jésus Transfiguré* (Copenhagen: Ejnar Munksgaard, 1947); Arthur Michael Ramsey, *The Glory of God and the Transfiguration of Christ* (London: Longmans, Green & Co., 1949); and Heinrich Baltensweiler, *Die Verklärung Jesu* (Zurich: Zwingli Verlag, 1959).

64. The various relationships between these two parables and between the parables and their encompassing contexts are treated by Paul Ricoeur, "The Bible and the Imagination" in *The Bible As a Document of the University,* ed. Hans Dieter Betz (Chico, CA: Scholars Press, 1981), pp. 49-75.

65. Dan O. Via, Jr., *Kerygma and Comedy in the New Testament* (Philadelphia: Fortress, 1975); Norman R. Petersen, *Literary Criticism for New Testament Critics* (Philadelphia: Fortress, 1978); and Robert C. Tannehill, "The Gospel of Mark as Narrative Christology," *Semeia* 12 (1979): 57-95.

66. John Macquarrie in the first chapter of his *Christian Hope* (New York: Seabury, 1978), investigates the structure of hope and shows how it differs from optimism.

67. Lohmeyer, *Das Evangelium des Markus,* pp. 357-358. August Strobel, "Discipleship," p. 68, notes that "the beginning of the tradition is marked by the overwhelming recognition of the deeply eschatological significance of the event."

68. Robert C. Tannehill, "The Disciples in Mark: The Function of a Narrative Role," *JR* 57 (1977): 386-405, provides a general and theoretical framework for a fruitful approach to Mark's portraits of the disciples and of the healings of blind men. He thinks Mark composed his gospel in such a way as to take advantage of the initial tendency of the Christian readers to identify with the disciples, those characters who at least at the start react positively to Jesus. Would there not also be the tendency to identify with Jesus, the baptized, the Son, called to service?

   In his essay, "The Gospel of Mark as Narrative Christology," Tannehill says that it is simply nonsense to interpret the "seeing" promised in 16:7 in terms of the parousia. He refers to chapter 13 and also to 14:28 as well as to 16:7 as anticipating a shift from failure to faithfulness. See further the bibliography on disciples and on the accounts of the healing of blind men in footnote 37 above.

69. Petersen has written of the open-ended character of Mark's final verses both in *Literary Criticism* and in his article, "When Is the End Not the End?" *Int* 34 (1980): 151-166. He has suggested that the postcrucifixion events narrated or hinted at in Mark 13 undercut the finality of the disciples' actions before Easter and demand an ironic reading of Mark 16:8. The irony compels the readers to work at the business of closure within the framework not of the text but of their own lives, to close the narrative with the faith that the things of God do indeed override things human.

On the open-ended character of the final paragraph see also Stemberger, "Galilee—Land of Salvation?" p. 437, and Robert H. Smith, "New and Old in Mark 16:1-8," *CTM* 43 (1972): 518-527.

Matthew

1. J. C. Fenton, *The Gospel of Saint Matthew* (Baltimore: Penguin Books, 1963), pp. 368 f.

2. Josephus *War* 2:165; *Ant* 18:16; M. Berakoth 9:5; Sanhedrin 10:1.

3. On excommunication from the synagogue see J. L. Martyn, *History and Theology in the Fourth Gospel*, second ed. (Nashville: Abingdon, 1979), pp. 37-62. See also Wolfgang Schrage, "aposynagōgos" in *TDNT* 7:848-852.

4. So in various ways Burnett Hillman Streeter, *The Four Gospels* (London: Macmillan, 1930); Ernst von Dobschutz, "Matthaeus als Rabbi und Katechet," *ZNW* 27 (1928): 338-348; G. D. Kilpatrick, *The Origins of the Gospel according to St. Matthew* (Oxford: Clarendon Press, 1946); Krister Stendahl, *The School of St. Matthew*, rev. ed. (Philadelphia: Fortress, 1968); E. P. Blair, *Jesus in the Gospel of Matthew* (New York: Abingdon, 1960); C. F. D. Moule, *The Birth of the New Testament* (New York: Harper and Row, 1962); William G. Thompson, *Matthew's Advice to a Divided Community* (Rome: Biblical Institute, 1970); David Hill, *The Gospel of Matthew* (London: Oliphants, 1972); Werner Georg Kummel, *Introduction to the New Testament* (Nashville: Abingdon, 1975); Peter F. Ellis, *Matthew: His Mind and His Message* (Collegeville: Liturgical Press, 1974); O. Lamar Cope, *Matthew: A Scribe Trained for The Kingdom of Heaven* (Washington: Catholic Biblical Association, 1976); Herman C. Waetjen, *The Origin and Destiny of Humanness* (Corte Madera: Omega, 1976); Schuyler Brown, "The Matthean Community and the Gentile Mission," *NovT* 22 (1980): 193-221.

5. So Kenneth W. Clark, "The Gentile Bias in Matthew," *JBL* 77 (1947): 165-172; Poul Nepper-Christensen, *Das Matthaeusevangelium: ein Judenchristliches Evangelium?* (Aarhus: Universitetsforlaget, 1958); Georg Strecker, *Der Weg der Gerechtigkeit* (Göttingen: Vandenhoeck und Ruprecht, 1971); Wolfgang Trilling, *Das wahre Israel* (München:

Kosel Verlag, 1964); Sjef van Tilborg, *The Jewish Leaders in Matthew* (Leiden: Brill, 1972). The shifts in perspective in studies of Matthew are well chronicled by John P. Meier, *Law and History in Matthew's Gospel* (Rome: Biblical Institute, 1976), and one may consult also his more popular work, *The Vision of Matthew* (New York: Paulist Press, 1979).

6. Ernst Käsemann, "The Beginnings of Christian Theology," in *New Testament Questions of Today* (Philadelphia: Fortress, 1969), an essay which first appeared in *ZThK* 57 (1960): 66-81; Gerhard Barth, "Matthew's Understanding of the Law," in *Tradition and Interpretation in Matthew*, ed. Günther Bornkamm, Gerhard Barth, and Heinz Joachim Held (Philadelphia: Westminster, 1963), pp. 58-164; Reinhart Hummel, *Die Auseinandersetzung zwischen Kirche und Judentum im Matthaeusevangelium* (München: Chr. Kaiser Verlag, 1963); Günther Bornkamm, "The Risen Lord and the Earthly Jesus: Matthew 28:16-20," in *The Future of Our Religious Past*, ed. James M. Robinson (London: SCM, 1971), pp. 203-229; Charles Carlston, "The Things that Defile (Mark 7:14) and the Law in Matthew and Mark," *NTS* 15 (1968/9): 75-96; Eduard Schweizer, " Observance of the Law and Charismatic Activity in Matthew," *NTS* 16 (1969/70): 213-230, and also his essay, "The Gospel of Matthew," in *Jesus and Man's Hope*, ed. D. Hadidian, et al. (Pittsburgh: Pittsburgh Theological Seminary, 1971), 2:339-341, and his "Matthean Church," *NTS* 20 (1973/4): 216, and his commentary, *The Good News according to Matthew* (Atlanta: John Knox, 1975); J. Massingberde Ford, *Baptism of the Spirit* (Techny, Illinois: Divine Word, 1971); Walter Grundmann, *Das Evangelium nach Matthaeus*, 3. Aufl. (Berlin: Evangelische Verlagsanstalt, 1972); Lloyd Gaston, "The Messiah of Israel as Teacher of the Gentiles," *Int* 29 (1975): 24-40; James P. Martin, "The Church in Matthew," *Int* 29 (1975): 41-56; R. G. Hammerton-Kelly, "Matthew, Gospel of," *IDB* 5:580-583.

7. Van Tilborg, *Jewish Leaders*, and Paul S. Minear, "False Prophecy and Hypocrisy in the Gospel of Matthew," *Neues Testament und Kirche: Festschrist fur Rudolf Schnackenburg*, ed. Joachim Gnilka (Freiburg: Herder, 1974), pp. 76-93.

8. See David Hill, "False Prophets and Charismatics: Structure and Interpretation in Matthew 7:15-23," *Biblica* 57 (1976): 327-348.

9. See especially Ford, *Baptism of the Spirit*, for comments on the beatitudes and on prayer in Matthew.

10. For a recent study of Matthew 23 which comes to the same conclusion see David E. Garland, *The Intention of Matthew 23* (Leiden: Brill, 1979).

11. Perhaps a parallel slur underlies the narrative at 1:18, but there too the author in his response has a larger, positive message to deliver and not merely an apology. Rudolf Bultmann, *History of the Synoptic Tradition* (London: Blackwell, 1963), pp. 274 and 286, refers to 27:62-66 and 28:11-15 as an apologetic legend and refers to the Gospel of Peter as a parallel. Van Tilborg, *Jewish Leaders*, sees the positive thrust and not just the apologetic.

12. Luke 11:29-32 understands Jesus' preaching as the sign of Jonah. Justin Martyr interpreted Jesus' resurrection as the sign. See Dialogue 107:1-2.

13. See C. H. Giblin, "Structural and Thematic Correlations in the Burial-Resurrection Narrative," *NTS* 21 (1974/5): 406-420.

14. Kilpatrick, *Origins*, pp. 47, 131-132, says that "earthquake" is one of Matthew's favorite words. On earthquakes as an element in theophanies and as eschatological sign see Günther Bornkamm, *"seiō, seismos,"* in *TDNT* 7:196-200, and Jorg Jeremias, "Theophany, Old Testament," in *IDB* 5:896-898. Parallels with 27:51b-53 and their meanings have been worked out by Donald Senior, "The Death of Jesus and the Resurrection of the Holy Ones," *CBQ* 38 (1976): 312-329.

15. Wolfgang Trilling, *Christusverkündigung in der synoptischen Evangelien* (München: Kosel Verlag, 1969), pp. 218f.
    The Gospel of Peter outdoes Matthew in insisting on divine rather than human agency in the emptying of the tomb: the stone rolled aside all on its own power; two figures descended from heaven, entered the tomb, and emerged supporting a third; the heads of the two touched heaven, and the head of the third reached beyond heaven; the cross, travelling unassisted, followed them out of the tomb. The supernatural character of Easter is thus underscored and emphasized.

16. Even as it is, there are those who think that Matthew's gospel as a whole portrays Peter as "the supreme rabbi" of the church. See Streeter, *Four Gospels*, p. 515, who characterizes Peter thus, on the basis of 16:17-19 especially. On the omission of Peter's name in Chapter 28 see *Peter in the New Testament*, ed. Raymond E. Brown, Karl P. Donfried, and John Reumann (Minneapolis and New York: Augsburg and Paulist Press, 1973), pp. 76f. Several theories are advanced for the omission: he is included in the eleven (28:16), or elements of resurrection appearances to him have been retrojected into accounts dealing with the earlier days of Jesus' ministry, or Matthew had available to him no narrative of an appearance to Peter. The view that Peter was chief rabbi of the church has been developed by Hummel, *Auseinandersetzung*, pp. 59-64. Jack Dean Kingsbury, "The Figure of Peter in Matthew's Gospel as a Theological Problem," *JBL* 98 (1979): 67-83, adopts a mediating stance between that which sees Peter as supreme rabbi and that which regards him as typical of all later Christians.

17. See Justin Martyr, *Dialogue with Trypho* 17 and 108, and Tertullian, *On Spectacles* 33.

18. So in differing ways Otto Michel, "Der Abschluss des Matthaeusevangeliums," *EvTh* 10 (1950-1): 16-16; Joachim Jeremias, *Jesus' Promise to the Nations* (London: SCM, 1958); Karl Heinrich Rengstorf, "Old and New Testament Traces of the Judean Royal Ritual," *NovT* 5 (1962): 229-244; Gerhard Barth, "Matthew's Understanding of the Law"; Ferdinand Hahn, *Mission in the New Testament* (London: SCM, 1965); Johannes Blauw, *The Missionary Nature of the Church* (London: Lutterworth, 1962), and many others.

Jack Dean Kingsbury, "The Composition and Christology of Matt. 28: 16-20," *JBL* 93 (1974): 573-584, regards verses 16-20 as a Matthean creation designed to exalt Jesus as Son of God.

19. Church order according to Heinrich Julius Holtzmann, *Lehrbuch der neutestamentlichen Theologie* (Freiburg: J. C. B. Mohr, 1897); cult legend and I-saying according to Rudolf Bultmann, *Synoptic Tradition;* mythical revelation speech according to Martin Dibelius, *From Tradition to Gospel* (New York: Scribner's, 1965); farewell discourse according to Krister Stendahl, "Matthew," in *Peake's Commentary on the Bible,* ed. H. H. Rowley and Matthew Black (London: Nelson, 1962), following Johannes Munck; shema according to Ernst Lohmeyer, "Mir Ist Gegeben Alle Gewalt," in *In Memoriam Ernst Lohmeyer,* ed. W. Schmauck (Stuttgart: Evangelisches Verlagswerk, 1951); concise narrative according to C. H. Dodd, "The Appearances of the Risen Christ," in *Studies in the Gospels,* ed. D. E. Nineham (Oxford: Blackwell, 1967), pp. 9-35; foundation myth according to Norman Perrin, *The Resurrection according to Matthew, Mark and Luke* (Philadelphia: Fortress, 1977); Hebrew Bible commission according to Benjamin J. Hubbard, *The Matthean Redaction of a Primitive Apostolic Commissioning* (Missoula: Scholars Press, 1974); a manifesto, legacy or testament, or a divine address according to Trilling, *Wahre Israel;* official or royal decree according to Bruce J. Malina, "The Literary Structure and Form of Matt. 28:16-20." *NTS* 17 (1970): 87-103.

20. See Johannes Lindblom, *Prophecy in Ancient Israel* (Oxford: Blackwell, 1962), pp. 103f.; Claus Westermann, *Basic Forms of Prophetic Speech* (Philadelphia: Westminster, 1967), pp. 98ff.; Raymond A. Bowman, "The Book of Ezra," in *The Interpreter's Bible* (Nashville: Abingdon, 1954), 3:571f., on messenger formula, forms of prophetic speech, and the form of official Persian royal decrees.

21. For an overview of issues and attempted solutions see John P. Meier, "Two Disputed Questions in Matt. 28:16-20," *JBL* 96 (1977): 407-424.

22. Already as an infant Jesus had avoided Judea and preferred Galilee (Matt. 2:22-23).

23. See 15:29 where the Markan parallel (7:31) has no mountain.

24. I. Ellis, "But Some Doubted," *NTS* 14 (1967/8): 574-580.

25. Luke 10:21-22 has a parallel in Matt. 11:25-27. The immediately preceding words in Luke 10:17-20, not paralleled in that earlier context, may have influenced the formulation of Matt. 28:18-20. Close connections obviously exist between Matt. 11:25-30 and 28:18-20. The passages abound in Matthean rhetoric and motifs. But it has not been noticed that Luke 10:17-20 contains material which parallels some of the great assertions of Matt. 28:18-20, especially the claim to authority.

26. Eduard Schweizer, "*huios*," *TDNT* 8:379-380. Jack Dean Kingsbury, *Matthew: Structure, Christology, Kingdom* (Philadelphia: Fortress, 1975) and his Proclamation commentary *Matthew* (Philadelphia: Fortress, 1977), pp. 30-57, and "The Composition and Christology of Mat-

thew 28:16-20," *JBL* 93 (1974), distinguish sharply between Son of Man and Son of God.

27. See Werner Foerster, *"exousia,"* in *TDNT* 2:566-571. W. D. Davies, *The Setting of the Sermon on the Mount* (Cambridge: The University Press, 1964), p. 198, cites David Daube, *The New Testament and Rabbinic Judaism* (London: University of London, Athlone Press, 1956), pp. 206-223.

28. On the vocabulary of the passage see among many others Günther Baumbach, "Die Mission im Matthaeus-Evangelium," *TLZ* 92 (1967): 889-893.

29. *Good News for Modern Man, Today's English Version* (TEV) (New York: American Bible Society, 1966), by construing " all peoples" more closely with "go" than with "make disciples," is even more misleading than the RSV. TEV reads, "Go then to all peoples everywhere and make them my disciples." The word *poreuomai* (go) functions as an auxiliary here and frequently in Matthew and is an example of a participle used pleonastically in order to enliven the narrative. See also 2:8; 9:13; 11:4; 18:12; 21:6; 22:15; 25:16; 27:66; 28:7. It is used absolutely in 2:9; 8:9, and 22:9. The last passage especially should be consulted. *Egeirō* is used pleonastically in 2:13,14,20. Other verbs are used in this fashion in 3:15 and 5:2. See *BDF* 419:2.

30. Davies, *Setting*, p. 295, interpreting "nations" in a geographical sense, says it is striking that Matthew has Jesus requiring the disciples to leave the land of Israel precisely at the same time when Judaism was emphasizing the necessity of remaining on the land in order to retain a claim on it.

31. J. D. M. Derrett, *Jesus' Audience* (New York: Seabury, 1973), pp. 53f., suggests that by accepting gifts from the gentile Magi in the beginning, Jesus acknowledged a relationship with them and accepted an obligation toward them. It appears that Jesus' response is the extension of the offer of discipleship to the Gentiles.

32. So Trilling, Strecker, cited previously, and Anton Vogtle, "Das christologische und ekklesiologische Anliegen von Mt. 28:18-20," in *Studia Evangelica*, ed. F. L. Cross (Berlin: Akademie Verlag, 1964), 2:266-294. See also Joachim Lange, *Das Erscheinen des Auferstandenen im Evangelium nach Matthaeus* (Wurzburg: Echter Verlag, 1973).

33. Acts 2:38; 8:16; 10:48; 19:5; cf. 1 Cor. 1:13,15; Didache 7:1,3; Justin, *First Apology* 60.

34. See Eduard Schweizer, *The Good News according to Matthew* (Atlanta: John Knox, 1975), pp. 532-536.

35. Georg Strecker, "The Concept of History in Matthew," *JAAR* 35 (1967): 219-230, connects the baptismal saying in 28:19 with righteousness. See also Hans Bietenhard, "onoma," in *TDNT* 5:242-280, and L. Hartmann, "Into the Name of Jesus," *NTS* 20 (1974): 432-440.

    Above all see Gerhard Krodel, "The Functions of the Spirit in the Old Testament, the Synoptic Tradition, and the Book of Acts," in *The Holy*

Spirit in the Life of the Church, ed. Paul Opsahl (Minneapolis: Augsburg, 1978), pp. 27-28.

Krister Stendahl, "Quis et Unde? An Analysis of Mt 1-2," in *Judentum, Urchristentum, Kirche,* ed. W. Eltester (Berlin: Topelmann, 1960), pp. 94-105, says Baptism in Matthew means inclusion into the eschatological community not on the basis of physical descent but by means of an act of God, as Jesus himself was inserted miraculously into the genealogy of Israel by means of his spiritual generation and virginal conception.

Note that Matthew 20:22-23 parallels Mark 10:38-39, but in Matthew there is no mention of Baptism. Did Matthew's community want the baptism of the Spirit without the cup of suffering which inevitably comes when Baptism is understood as the beginning of a life of discipleship? Also see the Gospel of the Hebrews on Matt. 3:15.

36. Deut. 1:3; 12:11, 14; cf. 4:2; 6:1; 7:11; Exodus 7:2; 29:35; 2 Kings 21:8; 2 Chron. 33:8; Jer. 1:7.

37. The phrase "all that I have commanded you" echoes the I-form of Jesus' teaching in the Sermon on the Mount in the so-called Antitheses (5:21-48), as noted by Hans Grass, *Ostergeschehen und Osterberichte* (Göttingen: Vandenhoeck und Ruprecht, 1962), p. 291. See Bornkamm, "Risen Lord," p. 225, note 65, for some similarities and differences between Matthew and John on the form of Jesus' assertions.

38. Matthew usually does not bother to translate Hebrew or Aramaic words, but in two instances he does offer a translation: the name Emmanuel (1:23) and the Cry of Dereliction (27:46).

39. Daube, *New Testament and Rabbinic Judaism,* pp. 27-32.

40. Trilling, *Wahre Israel,* p. 42, thinks "with you" conveys a sense of dynamic movement as compared with the more static conception of "in your midst" (18:20). See Gen. 26:24; Exodus 3:12; Deut. 20:1, 4; 31:6; Joshua 1:5, 9; Judges 6:12, 16; 2 Sam. 7:3; Isaiah 41:10; 43:2, 5; Luke 1:28; Acts 18:10; cf. Deut. 1:42.

41. C. F. D. Moule, *Idiom Book of New Testament Greek* (Cambridge: University Press, 1953), p. 34, suggests that *pasas tas hēmeras* may be an accusative of respect to be translated "the whole of every day."

42. This is a paraphrase of Trilling's comments on the final verse.

Luke
1. Some ancient MSS of the New Testament mention Nero by name at 2 Tim. 4:22.

2. Above all see A. N. Sherwin-White, *Roman Society and Roman Law in the New Testament* (Oxford: The Clarendon Press, 1963).

3. On these classifications and characterizations compare Leonhard Goppelt, *Apostolic and Post-Apostolic Times* (London: A. and C. Black, 1970), pp. 123-134, 223-225.

Missionary success brought its own peculiar problems. Luke is forced to inveigh against what today would be called secularism. Christians were indeed settling down in the world for the long haul—all too comfortably.

One very great problem in the west was the relaxation of the tension between being pilgrims on the way through the world and their everyday life in society. Luke himself seems to fall victim to the relaxation he abhors. He seems proud of the affluent and influential converts and loves to recount their story in Acts.

4. Hans Conzelmann, *The Theology of St. Luke* (New York: Harper & Row, 1960), p. 42.

5. See Adolf von Harnack, *The Acts of the Apostles* (London: Williams and Norgate, 1909), pp. 61 ff., and Henry J. Cadbury, *The Making of Luke-Acts* (New York: Macmillan, 1927; reprinted by S.P.C.K. in 1958), pp. 241-249.

6. The report of Philip's preaching to the Ethiopian, encountered on the road to Gaza (Acts 8:25-40), is an exception, but the Ethiopians were exotics. Ethiopia was a geographical and cultural extremity, and the narrative graphically exhibits the boundlessness of the gospel.

7. For reviews of research on Luke-Acts from a variety of viewpoints see C. K. Barrett, *Luke the Historian in Recent Study* (London: Epworth, 1961); Joachim Rohde, *Rediscovering the Teaching of the Evangelists* (Philadelphia: Westminster, 1968); W. C. Van Unnik, "Luke-Acts, a Storm Center in Contemporary Scholarship," in *Studies in Luke-Acts*, ed. Leander Keck and J. Louis Martyn (Nashville: Abingdon, 1966), pp. 60-83; I. H. Marshall, "Recent Study of the Gospel according to St. Luke," *ExpT* 80 (1968/9): 4-8, and "Recent Study of the Acts of the Apostles," *ExpT* 80 (1968/9): 292-296, and *Luke: Historian and Theologian* (Grand Rapids: Zondervan, 1971); Jerome Kodell, "The Theology of Luke in Recent Study," *BTB* 1 (1971): 115-144; W. Ward Gasque, *A History of the Criticism of the Acts of the Apostles* (Grand Rapids: Wm. B. Eerdmans, 1975); C. H. Talbert, "Shifting Sands: The Recent Study of the Gospel of Luke," *Int* 30 (1976): 381-395, and "An Introduction to Acts," *RE* 71 (1974): 437-449; Werner Georg Kümmel, *Introduction to the New Testament* (Nashville: Abingdon, 1975), pp. 122-188, and "Current Theological Accusations against Luke," *ANQ* 16 (1975): 131-145; W. C. Robinson, Jr., "Acts of the Apostles" and "Luke, Gospel of," in *IDB* 5:358-360.

8. Overviews of suggestions regarding Luke's purpose are offered by Gerhard Schneider, "Der Zweck des lukanischen Doppelwerks," *BZ* 21 (1977): 45-66; Charles H. Talbert, *Luke and the Gnostics* (Nashville: Abingdon, 1966), especially Chap. 7, and "The Redaction Critical Quest for Luke the Theologian," in *Jesus and Man's Hope*, ed. D. Hadidian,et al. (Pittsburgh: Pittsburgh Theological Seminary, 1971), 1:171-222; Schuyler Brown, "The Role of the Prologues in Determining the Purpose of Luke-Acts," in *Perspectives on Luke-Acts*, ed. Charles H. Talbert

(Danville, Va.: Association of Baptist Professors of Religion, 1978), pp. 99-111.

Much has been written suggesting that Luke had not (or not only) a historical purpose but instead (or also) an apologetic or kerygmatic purpose. See for example Robert Morgenthaler, *Die lukanische Geschichtsschreibung als Zeugniz* (Zurich: Zwingli-Verlag, 1949); Eduard Lohse, "Lukas als Theologe der Heilsgeschichte," *EvTh* 14 (1954): 256-275; D. J. Sneen, "An Exegesis of Luke 1:1-4 with Special Regard to Luke's Purpose as an Historian," *ExpT* 83 (1971/2): 40-43; Paul S. Minear, "Dear Theo: The Kerygmatic Intention and Claim of the Book of Acts," *Int* 27 (1973): 131-150; W. C. Van Unnik, " The 'Book of Acts' the Confirmation of the Gospel," *NovT* 4 (1960): 26-59.

Ward Gasque in his *History of Criticism of Acts* is one who has defended not only the historical reliability of Luke-Acts but also the intention of Luke to offer historical information. See also Martin Hengel, *Acts and the History of Earliest Christianity* (Philadelphia: Fortress, 1980).

A. J. Mattill, Jr. has authored numerous articles investigating ways in which the purpose of Luke-Acts has been perceived in the past. He himself thinks that Luke wrote to defend Paul against misrepresentations by Jewish-Christians. See "The Jesus-Paul Parallels and the Purpose of Luke-Acts," *NTS* 17 (1975): 15-46, and "The Purpose of Acts: Schneckenburger Reconsidered," in *Apostolic History and the Gospel*, ed. W. Ward Gasque and Ralph P. Martin (Grand Rapids: Eerdmans, 1970), pp. 108-122.

Talbert has argued in *Luke and the Gnostics* and elsewhere that the focus of Luke's work is not primarily salvation history (Cullmann), salvation (Marshall, Van Unnik) or ecclesiology (Jervell) but orthodoxy. He thinks that Luke is anti-gnostic. In *Literary Patterns, Theological Themes and the Genre of Luke-Acts* (Missoula: Scholars Press, 1974), Talbert identifies the issue of the threat of discontinuity and Luke's intention of bridging the generation gap. That concern for historical continuity and the right channel of authentic tradition, so apparent in Luke, Talbert takes to be a mark of an anti-gnostic spirit.

Especially Henry J. Cadbury and Burton Scott Easton but also many others see that one of Luke's chief purposes was to defend Christianity against Roman suspicions of lawlessness and rebellion. See Cadbury, *The Making of Luke-Acts* (1927), "Acts of the Apostles," in *IDB* 1:28-42, and "The Purpose Expressed in Luke's Preface," *Expositor* 21 (1921): 431-434. See also Easton, *Early Christianity: The Purpose of Acts and Other Papers*, ed. F. C. Grant (Greenwich: Seabury, 1954). Easton's essay on purpose was originally published in 1936.

Eckhard Plümacher, *Lukas als hellenistischer Schriftsteller* (Göttingen: Vandenhoeck und Ruprecht, 1972), sees the political apologetic but also thinks that Luke wrote to commend Christianity as a movement in tune with the Hellenistic ideals of *paideia*.

Richard Cassidy, *Jesus, Politics and Society* (Maryknoll: Orbis Books, 1978), plays down the political apologetic and wants to see Luke as portraying Jesus as a definite but nonviolent threat to the Jewish and the Greco-Roman social and political order. The case for a political apologetic is far stronger than he allows.

9. See Robert J. Karris, "Missionary Communities: A New Paradigm for the Study of Luke-Acts," *CBQ* 41 (1979): 80-97, and his article, "Windows and Mirrors: Literary Criticism and Luke's Sitz im Leben," in *Seminar Papers,* ed. Paul J. Achtemeier (Missoula: Scholars Press, 1979), pp. 47-58. Benjamin J. Hubbard, "Luke, Josephus and Rome: A Comparative Approach to the Lukan Sitz im Leben," also in the *Seminar Papers,* pp. 59-68, declares that on one front Luke's community had to contend with the power of the state. Nils Dahl, "The Purpose of Luke-Acts," in *Jesus in the Memory of the Early Church* (Minneapolis: Augsburg, 1976), pp. 87-98, notes that the question of purpose is intertwined with that of social and religious setting but concludes that unfortunately "we do not know exactly when and where, under what circumstances and in which milieu the work was written."

10. Books organizing their comments on Luke's theology around the notion of the lordship of Jesus include Helmut Flender, *St. Luke, Theologian of Redemptive History* (Philadelphia: Fortress, 1967), and Eric Franklin, *Christ the Lord* (Philadelphia: Westminster, 1975). See also Robert H. Smith, "The Theology of Acts," *CTM* 42 (1971): 527-535.

11. An exception is W. F. Albright, "Luke's Ethnic Background," in Johannes Munck, *The Acts of the Apostles* (Garden City: Doubleday, 1967), pp. 264-267.

12. Is it frequently stated that one of Luke's policies was to transfer the blame for Jesus' crucifixion and for Paul's arrests from the Romans to the Jews. Luke does often picture zealous Jews stirring up trouble against Jesus (Luke 23:2, 5, 18, 23) or against Christian figures (Acts 13:45; 14:2, 19; 17:5), but he is far from picturing all Jews as alike—opponents of the Christian movement—or all Romans as alike—invariably friends. Luke is well aware of Jewish friendship and of Roman enmity. Especially in Acts the Jewish crowds and the Pharisees are disposed to be friendly (Acts 2:47; 4:4; 5:12-16, 34; 23:6-10). Opposition stems especially from aristocratic Sadducees (4:1; 5:17; 9:1; 23:6-10) and from other high ranking Jewish and Roman officials (12:1; 24:26; 25:9). Luke saw fulfillment of prophecy in the joint opposition of Herod and Pilate to Jesus (4:25-28).

When the portrait of the Christian community offered by Luke is compared with that offered by Paul in his epistles, it becomes clear that one of the chief differences between them is that Luke describes disturbances involving the Christians as the result of external opposition—Jewish or Roman—while Paul speaks very candidly about internal dissension. It does not seem that Luke is trying so much to shift blame from Romans to Jews as it seems that he is attempting to clear the Christian community of the suspicion that it is inherently contentious and trouble-making.

13. See Horst Moehring, "The Census in Luke as an Apologetic Device," in *Studies in New Testament and Early Christian Literature,* ed. David

Aune (Leiden: Brill, 1972), pp. 144-160, and Robert Smith, "Caesar's Decree (Luke 2:1-2): Puzzle or Key?" *Currents* 7 (1980): 343-351.

J. Massyngberde Ford, "Zealotism and the Lukan Infancy Narratives" *NovT* 18 (1976): 280 ff., also interprets the text against a political background. She thinks Luke's main purpose in writing his gospel was to offer consolation to disappointed Jewish and Christian Zealots.

14. See Talbert and Barrett in works cited above and also Gunther Klein, *Die zwölf Apostel* (Göttingen: Vandenhoeck und Ruprecht, 1961). On Klein see Rohde, *Rediscovering*, pp. 219-229.

15. On the sermon see in addition to the commentaries Barrett, pp. 62-64; G. W. H. Lampe, " 'Grievous Wolves' (Acts 20:29)," in *Christ and the Spirit*, ed. Barnabas Lindars and Stephen Smalley (Cambridge: The University Press, 1973), pp. 253-268; and Hans Joachim Michel, *Die Abschiedsrede des Paulus an die Kirche, Apg 20, 17-38* (München: Kosel Verlag, 1973).

16. Henry J. Cadbury has written extensively on the preface of Luke's work: *The Making of Luke-Acts*, pp. 344-347, 358f.; "The Purpose Expressed in Luke's Preface," *Expositor* 21 (1921): 431-434; "The Knowledge Claimed in Luke's Preface," *Expositor* 22 (1922): 401-420; "Commentary on the Preface of Luke" *The Beginnings of Christianity*, ed. F. J. Foakes Jackson and Kirsopp Lake (London: Macmillan, 1920-32), 2:489-510; "We and I Passages in Luke-Acts," *NTS* 3 (1956/7): 128-132.

A fine survey of work on the preface (and on other questions relating to the authorship and editing of Luke-Acts) has been offered by Jacques Dupont, *The Sources of Acts* (London: Darton, Longman and Todd, 1964), pp. 101-112. See further W. C. Van Unnik, "Once More St. Luke's Prologue," *Neotestamentica* 7 (1973): 7-26, and I. I. DuPlessis, "Once More: The Purpose of Luke's Prologue," *NovT* 16 (1974): 259-271.

17. Cadbury, "We and I Passages," and also Ernst Haenchen, "We in Acts and the Itinerary," *JTC* 1 (1965): 65-99.

18. On cycles and patterns in Luke-Acts see M. D. Goulder, *Type and History in Acts* (London: S.P.C.K., 1964), and Talbert, *Literary Patterns*. Donald Miesner investigates chiastic patterns in Luke-Acts in *Chiasm and the Composition and Message of Paul's Missionary Sermons* (Unpublished Th.D. Dissertation; Christ Seminary-Seminex and Lutheran School of Theology at Chicago, 1974), and "The Missionary Journeys Narrative: Patterns and Implications," in *Perspectives on Luke-Acts*, ed. Charles H. Talbert (Danville: Association of Baptist Professors of Religion, 1978), pp. 199-214.

19. Extensive individual treatments of Luke 24 are offered by Paul Schubert, "The Structure and Significance of Luke 24," in *Neutestamentliche Studien für Rudolf Bultmann*, hrsg. W. Eltester (Berlin: A Toepelmann, 1954), pp. 165-186, and by Richard J. Dillon, *From Eyewitnesses to Ministers of the Word* (Rome: Biblical Institute, 1978). The subtitle indicates Dillon's focus: "Tradition and Composition in Luke 24."

20. See James Kleist, *The Gospel of St. Mark* (Milwaukee: Bruce, 1936), p. 259, for a discussion of expressions of time. See *BAGD* on *bathys*, *orthros, prōi.*

21. The following verses in Chapter 24 contain what Westcott and Hort
     called "Western Non-Interpolations": 3, 6, 12, 36, 40, 51, 52. See B. F.
     Westcott and F. J. A. Hort, *The New Testament in the Original Greek*,
     vol. 2: *Introduction and Appendix* (Cambridge and London: Macmillan,
     1896). See also Bruce M. Metzger, *A Textual Commentary on the Greek
     New Testament* (London and New York: United Bible Societies, 1971),
     pp. 183-193; C. F. Evans, *Resurrection and the New Testament* (London:
     SCM, 1970), pp. 96-98; and Ernst Haenchen, *The Acts of the Apostles*
     (Philadelphia: Westminster, 1971), pp. 56-60.

22. Luke 7:13; 10:1, 41; 22:61. See also Acts 1:21; 4:33; 7:59; 8:16; 11:17, 20;
     15:11, 26; 16:31; 19:5, 13, 17; 20:21, 24, 35; 21:13; 28:31.

23. See J. K. Elliott, "Does Lk 2:41-52 Anticipate the Resurrection?" *ExpT* 83
     (1971): 87-89.

24. *epestēsen* is used here and at 2:9 and Acts 12:7 of an angelophany, at
     Acts 23:11 of an epiphany of Jesus, and at Luke 21:34 (cf. 1 Thess. 5:3) of
     the sudden appearance of the last day, but Luke has other words to de-
     scribe the crossing of the boundary between the invisible and the visible
     worlds. He uses *ōphthē* (. . . *hestōs ek dexiōn*, of Gabriel at Luke 1:11,
     ophthentes (*en doxē*, of Moses and Elijah at the transfiguration at 9:30),
     ephanē (of Elijah at 9:8, cf. Mark 16:9) and *emphanē* (. . . *genesthai* of
     the resurrected Jesus at Acts 10:40) among other terms.

25. See Morgenthaler on doubling and on pairs of persons, traditions and
     phrases in Luke-Acts. Philip Seidensticker, *Die Auferstehung Jesu in
     der Botschaft der Evangelisten* (Stuttgart: Katholisches Biblelwerk,
     1967), p. 94, cites Philo who said legal witnesses could not be youths (age
     21-28) but must be mature men (over 28).
        On "two" see also Num. 35:30; Matt. 18:16; 2 Cor. 13:1; 1 Tim. 5:19;
     Heb. 10:28.

26. Paul Billerbeck, *Kommentar zum Neuen Testament aus Talmud und
     Midrasch* (München: C. H. Beck, 1924), 2:269. Alfred Plummer, *The
     Gospel according to St. Luke* (Edinburgh: T. and T. Clark, 1922), calls at-
     tention to the parallel rebuke in 2:49 (see note 17 above) and also suggests
     the influence of Isaiah 8:19.

27. "To Live" is used emphatically in 10:28; 15:32; 20:38; 24:23; Acts 1:3; 25:19.
     Xavier Leon-Dufour, *Resurrection and the Message of Easter* (New
     York: Holt, Rinehart and Winston, 1974), pp. 219-222, expresses the be-
     lief that Luke, aware of the unintelligibility of the notion of resurrection
     for the Greek imagination (cf. Acts 17:31), chose to convey the essential
     Christian message by focusing not on the act of God on Easter (God
     makes alive) but on the result of that act (Jesus lives). He continues to
     use the language of resurrection but alongside it he employs the equally
     biblical notion of life.

28. John Jansen, *The Resurrection of Jesus Christ in New Testament Theol-
     ogy* (Philadelphia: Westminster, 1980), p. 42, suggests that this verse
     could be cited as a disavowal of the sort of cultic interest in the tomb
     which some find in Mark 16:6.

29. Cf. Luke 2:49; 4:43; 9:22; 13:33; 17:25; 19:5; 22:37; 24:7, 26, 44; Acts 3:21; 17:3. "It is a Divine decree, a law of the Divine nature, that the Son of Man *must* suffer," says Plummer, p. 247. See Walter Grundmann, *"dei,"* in *TDNT*, 2:21-25, and Erich Fascher, "Theologische Beobachtungen zu *dei,"* in *Neutestamentliche Studien für R. Bultmann,* hrsg. W. Eltester (Berlin: A. Toepelmann, 1954), pp. 228-254.

30. *lēros* is "idle talk, nonsense, humbug" according to *BAGD.* Plummer says Hobart thought of "the wild talk of the sick in delirium." Cf. 4 Macc. 5:11.

31. A majority of the editorial committee of the United Bible Societies project think Luke and John drew from a common tradition. See Metzger, *Textual Commentary*, p. 184.

32. Gregory is cited by J. Duncan M. Derrett, "The Manger at Bethlehem," in *Studia Evangelica,* ed. F. L. Cross (Berlin: Akademie Verlag, 1973), 6:92. Derrett calls the manger "the counterpart" of the tomb, notes several parallels, and focuses especially on Jewish ideas of purity. He believes the rock-cut manger carries implications of cleanness, and thinks that Jesus is presented as taking the place of the Red Heifer, an idea which seems quite unlikely for Luke. Some of the same ideas are to be found in his article, "The Manger, Ritual Law, and Soteriology," *Theology* 74 (1971): 566-571.

33. Of the extensive bibliography on the Emmaus story the following may be noted: C. H. Dodd, "The Appearances of the Risen Christ," in *Studies in the Gospels,* ed. Dennis E. Nineham (Oxford: Blackwell, 1955), pp. 9-35; J. A. Grassi, "Emmaus Revisited," *CBQ* 26 (1964): 463-467; Arnold A. T. Ehrhardt, "The Disciples of Emmaus," *NTS* 10 (1964): 182-201; Jacques Dupont, "The Meal at Emmaus," in *The Eucharist in the New Testament,* ed. J. Delorme (Baltimore and Dublin: Helicon, 1964), pp. 105-121; Hans Dieter Betz, "The Origin and Nature of Christian Faith according to the Emmaus Legend," *Int* 23 (1969): 32-46; and Joachim Wanke, *Die Emmauserzahlung* (Leipzig: St. Benno-Verlag, 1973).

34. Emmaus was probably at the site of Motzah (cf. Josh. 18:26), a bit over four miles from Jerusalem just to the south of the present main road to Tel Aviv. Josephus calls the place Ammaous and says that Vespasian settled 800 veterans there (*War* 7:217). Its Arabic name, Qaloniyeh, preserves the memory of its Roman background (Colonia). The village is about 30 stadia from the city, and so the round trip would have been about 60 stadia (3.5 miles each way, as a stade = 607 feet).

   Three sites besides Qaloniyeh-Motzah vie for the honor of identification as Emmaus: 1) El-Qubeibeh, 7 miles north and west of Jerusalem on the road passing Nebi Samwil. In 1099 the crusaders found near there an old fort named Castellum Emmaus. In 1878 the Franciscans built a church of St. Cleophas on the site. 2) Abu Gosh, 9 miles west of the city just north of the main road to Tel Aviv at the foot of the mount identified with Kiriath-jearim where the ark stood before David took it to Jerusalem, boasts a beautiful crusader church built over the remains of a Roman fort. 3) Amwas, 20 miles west of Jerusalem, is the wrong distance but has preserved the right name and has the support of early pilgrims and fathers. This is the Emmaus or Ammaus where Judas Maccabeus defeated the Syrian Georgias (1 Macc. 3:40, 57; 4:1-15). Some manuscripts of the gospel read 160 instead of 60 stades and so make the text conform to the site, but the distance is impossibly far for a round trip in one afternoon or evening. This spot became the Hellenistic town known as Nicopolis. See K. W. Clark, "Emmaus," in *IDB* 2:97-98; Billerbeck, 2:269-271; R. M. Mackowski, "Where is Biblical Emmaus?" *Science et Esprit* 32 (1980): 93-103.

35.   Cleopas (short form of Kleopatros, a Greek name) could be the Clopas (an Aramaic name) mentioned in John 19:25. John there says that among the women at the cross was a certain Mary the mother of Clopas. According to Hegesippus, Simeon the son of Clopas was chosen to succeed James the brother of Jesus as leader of the Jerusalem church. Hegesippus further identified Clopas as the brother of Joseph and thus uncle of Jesus and James (see Eusebius EH 3.11.1 and 4.22.4).

    Origen (early 3rd c.) concluded that the unnamed companion of Cleopas/Clopas was his son Simeon. In 24:34 Origen interpreted the "who said" to refer to the report of the Emmaus disciples, who announced to the Jerusalem brethren that the Lord had appeared "to Simeon" (and to Cleopas). On Cleopas/Clopas see Hennecke-Schneemelcher, 1:425-427. Sometimes Nathanael or Luke was identified with the unnamed companion of Cleopas. See Hennecke-Schneemelcher, 2:65, 70.

36.   Ernst Haenchen, *The Acts of the Apostles*, p. 585, commenting on the many lamps in the room at Troas where the worshipers assembled and Eutychus fell from the window (Acts 20:7-12), takes up a suggestion of Ewald that Luke in more than one place combats the suspicion that immorality was practiced by Christians during their gatherings (cf. Acts 2:46-47).

37.   See note 7 above.

38   Bar Cochba (A.D. 132-135) inscribed his coins "Year One of the Redemption of Israel" and "Year Two of the Freedom of Israel" and in the third Year "For the Freedom of Jerusalem." See Ya'akov Meshorer, *Jewish Coins of the Second Temple Period* (Tel Aviv: Am Hassefer and Massada, 1967), pp. 94-96. Henry Cadbury, *Making*, p. 278, judged Luke as having either "accurate information or accurate imagination" concerning the nationalistic hopes of the Jews. "More than any other New Testament writer Luke brings to our sight the current Messianic hope of Judaism."

39.   E. L. Bode, *The First Easter Morning* (Rome: Biblical Institute Press, 1970), pp. 119-126, comments on the third day as the day of deliverance in biblical and Jewish tradition.

40.   See Betz on the Emmaus account as the story of the genesis of faith.

41.   For example Jakob Kremer, *Die Osterevangelien* (Stuttgart: Katholisches Bibelwerk, 1977), p. 135, writes, "What exposition of Scripture could not do—it has of course a preparatory function—does happen

in the meal." Similar sentiments are expressed by Leon-Dufour, Grassi, Dupont, and many others. Dillon, pp. 154-155, writes that "the 'breaking of bread' is the sacramental action which renders the teaching Lord present to his congregation disclosing to her the mystery of his person and laying upon her the burden of his own mission and destiny. As risen Lord, present in word and sacrament, he shows himself the goal and meaning of all the scriptures, and he imparts to his followers that ministry of the word."

42. See for example Reginald H. Fuller, *The Formation of the Resurrection Narratives* (New York: Macmillan, 1971), and Leon-Dufour, *Resurrection.*

43. Note the "with us" and "with them" of verses 29 and 30, and "in their midst" in verse 36. Compare Matt. 18:20; 28:20; Rev. 3:20. But the most important cross reference is Luke 17:21.

44. Paul Minear, "Some Glimpses of Luke's Sacramental Theology," *Worship* 44 (1970): 322-331.

45. It is frequently defined as a recognition story. See for example Dodd's article on "Appearances of the Risen Christ."

46. Some see an allusion to a special appearance to Peter in Galilee in Mark 16:7 and imagine that a trace of such an appearance to Peter is imbedded in John 21:1-13. Further comments are offered in the commentary and notes on John 21. It seems pointless to pursue the question of whether or not Luke 5:1-11 is a displaced resurrection account. Goulder, *Type and History*, notes several parallels between the accounts of the resurrection of Jesus and the release of Peter from prison. See also C. F. D. Moule, *The Birth of the New Testament* (New York: Harper and Row, 1962), p. 25, for comment on the parallels between those passages. On appearances to Peter see *Peter in the New Testament*, ed. Raymond E. Brown, Karl P. Donfried, and John Reumann (Minneapolis and New York: Augsburg and Paulist Press, 1973), p. 126.

47. Minear, p. 330, asks, "How can Jesus save transgressors except by eating with them?" Frederick W. Danker, *Jesus and the New Age* (St. Louis: Clayton Publishing House, 1972), p. 237, writes that "companionship with sinners was Jesus' method of actualizing forgiveness."

48. Cf. 2 Tim. 2:18 and see Talbert, *Luke and the Gnostics*, and Barrett, *Luke the Historian.*

49. See also Acts 17:27; Heb. 12:18; Gen. 27:12; Judges 16:26. See Eduard Norden, *Agnostos Theos* (Stuttgart: Teubner, 1912), pp. 14-18.

50. On the disgrace of broken bones see David Daube, *The New Testament and Rabbinic Judaism* (London: University of London Athlone Press, 1956), pp. 308-310. Cf. the crurifragium in John 19:31-37 and commentaries on that passage.

51. See Wilhelm Michaelis, *"meli,"* in *TDNT* 4:552-554, and "honey" in *OCD* and *IDB.*

52. On farewells see Raymond E. Brown, *The Gospel according to John* (Garden City: Doubleday, 1970), 2:597-601, for a discussion with bibliography.

53. George Foote Moore, *Judaism in the First Centuries of the Christian Era* (Cambridge: Harvard, 1927), 2:382, refers to a discussion between Sadducees and Rabban Gamaliel. They asked him for evidence of the resurrection (cf. Luke 20:27-40) and Gamaliel replied that it is "in the Law and in the Prophets and in the Writings" and proceeded to offer specific passages. Moore says that reference was frequently made to all three parts of the canon for the sake of complete demonstration.

54. John Martin Creed, *The Gospel according to St. Luke* (London: Macmillan, 1930), p. 301, notes that the phrase "beginning from Jerusalem" in the original Greek "stands outside the construction and almost has the force of an adverb." See also C. F. D. Moule, *Idiom Book*, pp. 181-182.

55. The gift of a savior (Acts 13:23) and the resurrection of Jesus (13:32-33; 26:6-8) are called promises or the fulfillment of promises of God. As Acts 23:21 shows, the language indicates the implementation of an announced plan, and so the word belongs to Luke's vocabulary of the purpose and providence of God.

56. The words "blessed" *(eulogētos)* and "bless" *(eulogeō)* occur especially at the beginning and end of the gospel: 1:42, 64, 68; 2:28, 34; 24:30, 50, 51, 53). But see also 6:28; 9:16; 13:35; 19:38. P. A. Van Stempvoort, "The Interpretation of the Ascension in Luke and Acts," *NTS* 5 (1959): 30-42, refers to the close parallels in Sirach 50:20-22. Grundmann in his commentary cites the description of John Hyrcanus in Josephus, *Ant* 13.10.7. Josephus there says Hyrcanus was counted by God as worthy of three of the greatest privileges: "the rule of the nation, the office of high priest, and the gift of prophecy." Ralph Marcus, editor of the Loeb edition of Josephus' works (7:378), says that the description means that Hyrcanus is portrayed as possessing the attributes of the ideal ruler, according to Stoic and Philonic standards.

57. *chara* in 1:14; 2:10; 10:7, 10; Acts 8:8; 13:52. *chairō* in 6:23; 15:5.

58. Hans Conzelmann, *The Theology of St. Luke* (New York: Harper and Row, 1960), pp. 209-213. See also Eduard Lohse, *"Sion,"* in *TDNT* 7: 331-336, and Flender, pp. 107-117.

59. C. H. Dodd, *The Apostolic Preaching and Its Developments* (New York and London: Harper and Brothers, 1936), proposed that the resurrection was one part of the kerygma preached in the earliest congregations. See also Eduard Schweizer, "Concerning the Speeches in Acts," in *Studies in Luke-Acts*, pp. 208-216.

60. Ethelbert Stauffer, *New Testament Theology* (New York: Macmillan, 1955), pp. 339-342, spoke of Petrine and Joseph formulas, connected them with the old theology of providence, and regarded the formulations in Acts as primitive rather than Lukan.

61. On the divine "must" *(dei)* and Luke's notion of necessity, see note 21. Luke is without peer in the New Testament as a theologian of the word of God. Word or *logos* appears in Luke 1:2, 4; 4:22; 5:1; 8:11, 12-13, 15, 21; 11:28; Acts 4:29, 31; 6:2, 4, 7; 8:4, 14, 25; 10:36; 11:1, 19; 12:24; 13:5, 7, 26, 44, 46; 14:3, 25; 15:35-36; 16:6, 32; 17:11, 13; 18:5, 11; 19:10; 20:32; word or *rhema* is used in Luke 1:38; 2:29; 7:1; 9:45; 18:34; 22:61; Acts 2:14; 5:20; 10:22; 11:14, 16. Luke speaks of the will or *thelema* of God in Luke 22:42; Acts 13:22; 21:14; 22:14, of the plan or *boulē* of God in Luke 7:30; Acts 2:23; 4:28; 5:38-39; 13:36; 20:27. Many times Luke uses nouns and verbs compounded with *pro-* (fore-): *proeipon*, Acts 1:16; *prognosis*, 2:23; *prokatangelo*, 3:18, 24; 7:52; *prokerysso*, 3:20; 13:24; *proorao* or *prooida*, 2:31; *proorizo*, 4:28.

62. J. M. Creed, p. lxxii.

63. Among the many who have probed the positive aspects of Luke's presentation of Jesus' death may be mentioned the following: Richard Zehnle, "The Salvific Character of Jesus' Death in Lucan Soteriology," *ThS* 30 (1969): 420-444; A. George, "Le Sens de la mort de Jesus pour Luc," *RB* 80 (1973): 186-217; Edward Schroeder, "Luke's Gospel through a Systematician's Lens," *Currents* 3 (1976): 337-346; Robert Smith, "Paradise Today: Luke's Passion Narrative," *Currents* 3 (1976): 323-336; Hans Rudi Weber, *The Cross* (Grand Rapids: Eerdmans, 1979), pp. 117-124.

64. Psalm 16:8-11 in Acts 2:25-28 and 13:35; Psalm 110:1 in 2:34-35; Deut. 18:15-19 in 3:22-23; Is. 53:7-8 in 8:32-33; Psalm 2:7 in 13:33; Is. 55:3 in 13:34; Amos 9:11-12 in 15:16-17.

65. Morton S. Enslin, "The Ascension Story," *JBL* 47 (1928): 60-73; Van Stempvoort, cited above; Gerhard Lohfink, *Die Himmelfahrt Jesu* (München: Kosel Verlag, 1971); Armin Schmidt, *Entrückung-Aufnahme-Himmelfahrt* (Stuttgart: Katholisches Bibelwerk, 1973). On the ascension as radical change of status see Charles H. Talbert, "The Concept of Immortals in Mediterranean Antiquity," *JBL* 94 (1975): 419-436.

66. On *analambanō* see 2 Kings 2:10-11; 1 Macc. 2:58; Philo, *Life of Moses* 2.291; Sirach 48:9; 49:14; 1 Tim. 3:16; cf. Mark 16:19.

67. Eduard Lohse, *"pentekostē," in TDNT* 6:44-53, says the new understanding of Pentecost as celebration of the giving of the law at Sinai and as renewal of the covenant occurred only after A.D. 70 and the destruction of the temple and of Jerusalem. See however Georg Kretchmar, "Himmelfahrt und Pfingsten," *ZKG* 66 (1954/5): 209-253. Kretchmar's views have been adopted by Bent Noack, "The Day of Pentecost in Jubilees, Qumran and Acts," *ASTI* 1 (1962): 73-95. See Jubilees 6:17-21; 15:1-24; 1QH 7:6-20; 14:13; 1QpHab 2:5-6; 7:4-7; 9:6; 1QS2; 1QS 4:16, 21.

68. Bruce M. Metzger, "Ancient Astrological Geography and Acts 2:9-11," in *Apostolic History and the Gospel,* ed. Ward Gasque and Ralph P. Martin, pp. 123-134, discusses and rejects alleged astrological connections of the list of nations.

69. See Ernst Haenchen's commentary, pp. 193 and 585.

John

1. Reviews of research and investigation into the background or situation of the Fourth Gospel are offered in Werner Georg Kümmel, *Introduction to the New Testament* (Nashville: Abingdon, 1975), pp. 188-247, 434-452; Robert Kysar, *The Fourth Evangelist and His Gospel* (Minneapolis: Augsburg, 1975), and "Community and Gospel, Vectors in Fourth Gospel Criticism," *Int* 31 (1977): 355-366; Wayne Meeks, "Am I a Jew?" in *Christianity, Judaism and Other Greco-Roman Cults*, ed. J. Neusner (Leiden: Brill, 1975), 1:163-186; Rudolf Schnackenburg, *The Gospel according to St. John* (New York: Seabury, 1980), 1:119-152, and "Zur johanneischen Forschung," *BZ* 18 (1974): 272-278; James M. Robinson, "The Johannine Trajectory," in *Trajectories through Early Christianity* (Philadelphia: Fortress, 1971), pp. 232-268; Raymond E. Brown, *The Gospel according to John* (Garden City: Doubleday, 1966), 1:xxi-xxiii, lii-lxxix; C. K. Barrett, *The Gospel of John and Judaism* (Philadelphia: Fortress, 1975), and *The Gospel according to St. John*, 2nd ed. (Philadelphia: Westminster, 1978), pp. 27-66, cited below as *Commentary;* D. Moody Smith, "Johannine Christianity: Some Reflections on its Character and Delineation," *NTS* 21 (1975): 222-248.

   Older work, from the middle of the nineteenth to the middle of the twentieth century, is surveyed by Edwyn Clement Hoskyns, *The Fourth Gospel*, ed. Francis Noel Davey (London: Faber and Faber, 1947), pp. 21-47.

2. J. Louis Martyn, *History and Theology in the Fourth Gospel*, rev. ed. (Nashville: Abingdon, 1979). See also his essay, "Source Criticism and Religionsgeschichte in the Fourth Gospel," in *Jesus and Man's Hope*, ed. D. Y. Hadidian and others (Pittsburgh: Pittsburgh Theological Seminary, 1970), 1:247-273, and *The Gospel of John in Christian History* (New York: Paulist Press, 1978). See also Raymond E. Brown, *The Community of the Beloved Disciple* (New York: Paulist Press, 1979).

   Brown, stressing the role of the Beloved Disciple and the impact of the influx of Samaritans and Gentiles into the Johannine community, locates the high christology early. Martyn nearly ignores the Beloved Disciple, locates the Johannine community on the trajectory of Jewish Christianity, and thinks of the high christology as a product of Christian reaction to expulsion from the synagogue. Martyn's reactions to Brown are to be found especially in the footnotes to his essay, "Glimpses into the History of the Johannine Community," in *The Gospel of John in Christian History*. Brown comments on the views of Martyn and others in Appendix 7 of his *The Community of the Beloved Disciple*. Kysar in *The Fourth Evangelist*, pp. 149-156, reviews Martyn's position favorably and something very much like it is assumed as an assured result of Johannine criticism in many recent works on the Fourth Gospel, such as R. Alan Culpepper, *The Johannine School* (Missoula: Scholars Press, 1975), and Norman Perrin, *The New Testament: An Introduction* (New York: Harcourt, Brace, Jovanovich, 1974).

3. Martyn assumes the essential correctness of the reconstruction of the signs gospel by Robert Fortna, *The Gospel of Signs* (Cambridge: The

University Press, 1969). Fortna has written extensively on the signs gospel and is at work on the theology of the source and its redaction. For bibliography and comment on the hypothesis of a signs source see Martyn, *History and Theology*, pp. 164-168. By speaking of a signs *gospel*, Fortna indicates his conviction that the source document included a passion and resurrection narrative.

4. Oscar Cullman in his book, *The Johannine Circle* (Philadelphia: Westminster, 1975), and in other publications, has for a long time theorized about the connections of Jesus with nonconformist Jewish movements and the relations between the early church and the Samaritans. See also James D. Purvis, "The Fourth Gospel and the Samaritans," *NovT* 17 (1975): 161-198.

5. A fuller sketch of developments in Judaism after A.D. 70 is given above in the introduction to the chapter on Matthew. Many scholars think especially of Matthew and John as reflecting the situation in Palestine after the destruction of Jerusalem and the temple.

6. On the relationship of the epistles to the gospel see especially the discussion of J. L. Houlden, *The Johannine Epistles* (New York: Harper and Row, 1973), pp. 1-20, 37-38; Barrett, *Commentary*, pp. 59-62, 123-134; Brown, *Community*, especially pp. 93-167.

7. Benjamin W. Bacon, *The Gospel of the Hellenists* (New York: Holt, 1933); Ernest C. Colwell, *The Greek of the Fourth Gospel* (Chicago: University of Chicago, 1931); C. H. Dodd, *The Interpretation of the Fourth Gospel* (Cambridge: The University Press, 1953); Amos Niven Wilder, *New Testament Faith for Today* (New York: Harper, 1955); Rudolf Bultmann, *The Gospel of John* (Philadelphia: Westminster, 1971); Howard Clark Kee, *Jesus in History*, 2nd ed. (New York: Harcourt, Brace, Jovanovich, 1977), and *Christian Origins in Sociological Perspective* (Philadelphia: Westminster, 1980); Ernst Kasemann, *The Testament of Jesus* (Philadelphia: Fortress, 1968).

8. J. C. Fenton, *The Gospel According to John* (Oxford: The Clarendon Press, 1970), p. 22.

9. Ernest C. Colwell, *New or Old? The Christian Struggle with Change and Tradition* (Philadelphia: Westminster, 1970).

10. Raymond E. Brown, *The Gospel According to John* I: LXXX1; Elaine H. Pagels, *The Johannine Gospel in Gnostic Exegesis* (Nashville: Abingdon, 1973).

11. Kee in the works cited above theorizes that the author was appealing particularly to persons marked by the kind of mystic piety which characterized the followers of Isis.

12. Eduard Schweizer, *Jesus* (London: SCM Press, 1971), pp. 160f.

13. Paul S. Minear, "The Audience of the Fourth Evangelist," *Int* 31 (1977): 339-354, and "The Beloved Disciple in the Fourth Gospel," *NovT* 19 (1977): 105-123.

14. In form the discourse belongs to a clearly defined genre of final utter-
     ances on the eve of departure. The patriarch or father gathers his chil-
     dren to his deathbed or to a final meal, announces his death or departure,
     offers comfort and encouragement along with final instructions, orders
     the ongoing life of his hearers or successors, cautions them about
     squabbling or disunity among themselves, reads the future with its
     dangers, speaks blessings, utters a prayer. The best known biblical fare-
     wells are those of Jacob (Gen. 47-49), Joshua (Josh. 22-24), David (1
     Chron. 28-29), and Paul (Acts 20:17-38; 2 Tim.).

     Luke 22 in many ways appears to anticipate John 13-17. On the form
     of farewell discourses in the biblical tradition see Ethelbert Stauffer,
     New Testament Theology (New York: Macmillan, 1955), pp. 344-347, and
     Brown, *Gospel according to John*, 2:597-604.

15. Barrett, *Gospel of John and Judaism*, and Leonhard Goppelt, *Apostolic
     and Post-Apostolic Times* (London: A. and C. Black, 1970), pp. 123-151.

16. W. D. Davies, *Invitation to the New Testament* (Garden City:
     Doubleday, 1966), pp. 389-439.

17. Barnabas Lindars, *The Gospel of John* (London: Oliphants, 1972), p. 595,
     writes, "All that remains to be done now is to explain more clearly the
     nature of the act of faith by which the life in Christ may be appropri-
     ated." Brown, *Gospel according to John*, 2: 1046, suggests, but very
     guardedly, that John intended to offer "four slightly different examples
     of faith in the risen Jesus."

18. Barrett, *Commentary*, pp. 562-575, describes John's attitude toward the
     traditional Easter narratives as one of "critical acceptance."

19. The symposium of scholars who produced *Peter in the New Testament*,
     ed. Raymond E. Brown, Karl P. Donfried, and John Reumann
     (Minneapolis and New York: Augsburg and Paulist Press, 1973), pp.
     138-139, shrink from speaking of the Beloved Disciple and Peter as rivals
     and say "both figures play a prominent role in the Johannine tradition.
     . . . This community has placed its apostolic figure (the Beloved Disciple)
     on a pedestal by showing him to be of competitive importance with Si-
     mon Peter."

20. Countering rumors of grave-robbing was no part of the author's purpose
     in his description of neatly folded cloths. They are rather a sign. S. H.
     Hooke, *The Resurrection of Christ* (London: Darton, Longman and
     Todd, 1967), p. 79, is closer to the truth with his comment that the cloths
     were left lying "like a chrysalis out of which the risen body of the Lord
     had emerged."

21. Brown, *Gospel according to John*, 2:989, mentions this interpretation in
     passing and seems to reject it.

22. Brown, *Gospel according to John*, 1:cxxxviii-cxliv, portrays Jesus as ful-
     filling Jewish institutions and festivals. The author displays a most re-
     markable interest in these matters. More than in any other gospel Jesus
     is pictured as acting and speaking in Jerusalem and in the temple on the

occasion of feasts, and allusions to celebrations abound. See also Hoskyns, *The Fourth Gospel*, pp. 63-66.

Purifications and washings (Chap. 1-3), sabbath (Chap. 5), Passover (Chap. 6), tabernacles (Chap. 7-8), dedication (or Hanukkah, Chap. 10) are all mentioned and indeed the gospel is structured not in terms of a list of signs but in terms of feasts and institutions of Judaism especially as celebrated at Jerusalem and the temple.

But there is still more. Jesus is the incarnate Word. He is the Word which became flesh and "dwelled" or "tabernacled" among us (1:14). The Greek word underlying "tabernacled" *(eskēnōsen, skēnē)* alludes to the Shekinah or Presence of God in the tent or tabernacle of ancient Israel. The ark of the covenant was the most important piece of furniture in the most mysterious part of the tent.

John the Baptist testified that Jesus is "the Lamb of God" (1:33, 36). That designation calls to mind all the many kinds of sacrifices enacted before the tent and all the cultic devices of the past for dealing with sin.

Jesus forcibly drove money-changers and sacrificial animals from the temple precincts and spoke of the destruction and reconstruction of the temple in three days. The author interprets that word about the house of God to be a declaration about the death and resurrection of the body of Jesus (2:19-22).

The author's interest in the place or focus of worship is vividly expressed in the narrative of the Samaritan woman. Central to the account is the exchange between the woman and Jesus regarding the relative merits of Mount Gerizim near the well of Samaria and Mount Zion at Jerusalem (4:20-22). In the conversation Jesus goes beyond supporting Jewish claims against Samaritan. He speaks of worshiping God "in spirit and in truth" (4:23-24). But what kind of worship is that? "In spirit and in truth" might be understood as characterizing worship as non-geographical, nontemporal, purely inward, and otherworldly. However, the author of the Fourth Gospel anchors salvation in this world and its history so securely that it can be said to be "of the Jews" (4:22). Salvation is locatable at least to that extent, and when Jesus speaks of worshiping not at Gerizim and not in Jerusalem he is hinting broadly that he is himself somehow the place and locale of salvation and worship.

If the position of the angels, one at the head and one at the foot, is intended to correspond to the position of the two men crucified with Jesus, one on either side (19:18), then Golgotha and the empty tomb are once again associated as closely as possible, and the evangelist has found another way of declaring that the glorified Jesus—crucified and resurrected—is the source of salvation.

23. Brown, *Gospel according to John*, 2:1016, with reference to Ruth 1:16 says that Jesus' speaking successively of "my Father and your Father" and of "my God and your God" expresses not distinction between Jesus and the others, he as unique and natural Son and all the others children only by the sufferance of gracious adoption, but connection and identification. Barrett, *Commentary*, p. 566, along with many others, holds that the passage describes Jesus' relation to the Father as unique.

Mark Appold, *The Oneness Motif in the Fourth Gospel* (Tubingen: J.
C. B. Mohr, 1976), speaks of oneness as the central Johannine motif. John
uses the motif of oneness to sum up his christology (Jesus is one with the
Father), his soteriology (gathered into one), and his ecclesiology (one
flock). See also Appold, "Christ Alive, Church Alive: Reflections on the
Prayer of Jesus in John 17," *Currents* 5 (1978): 365-373.

24. However, the initial paragraph of this section (verses 19-23) seems oddly
to echo Matthew 16:16-19 with its bestowal of authority to forgive sins
(cf. Matt. 18:18).

25. *emphysaō* is used eleven times in the LXX. See Schnackenburg,
Commentary, and Bultmann, *Gospel of John*.

26. Hans Freiherr von Campenhausen, *Ecclesiastical Authority and Spiritual Power* (Palo Alto: Stanford, 1969), pp. 139-140, says John emphasizes forgiveness by reversing the Matthean order and then also stresses
that forgiveness is a present and not merely a future reality.

27. Schnackenburg, *Commentary*, points out parallels in structure and motif between this scene about Thomas and the one at the beginning of the
gospel involving Nathanael (1:43-51). Those parallels strengthen the
conviction that the promise to Nathanael about seeing angels descending
and ascending is fulfilled in the Easter story; angels have borne testimony to the crucified Jesus as the place of meeting with God (20:12), and so
Jesus is correctly confessed as "My Lord and my God" (20:28).

28. Lindars, p. 128, speaks of John's presentation of the passion as an "im-
mensely fruitful" act.

29. Excellent bibliography and review of the question in B. A. Mastin, "The
Imperial Cult and the Ascription of the Title *'Theos'* to Jesus (John
20:28)," *Studia Evangelica* 6 (1973): 353-365.

30. The only other beatitude in the gospel is at 13:17.

31. Hoskyns, p. 549, and Brown, *Gospel*, 2:1048, recall the saying of an ancient rabbi that "the proselyte is dearer to God than all the Israelites
who were at Sinai." See also Paul Billerbeck, *Kommentar zum Neuen
Testament aus Talmud und Midrasch* (München: C. H. Beck, 1924),
2:586.

32. Schnackenburg, *Commentary*, 3:409, ponders the proper tag for Chapter
21. It is not a "supplement" (Nachtrag) because it adds nothing new, not
an "appendix" (Anhang) because that word fails to capture the inner
connection and underestimates the weight attached to it by the editor,
not an "epilogue" (Epilog) because that makes it sound too unimportant.
It is an "editorial conclusion" (redaktionelles Schlusskapitel) with a
revelatory function for readers in the church at the time of composition.

33. On style and vocabulary see Bultmann, *Gospel of John*, pp. 700-701, and
Barrett, *Commentary*, pp. 567-568.

34. Not every commentator reads the relationship between the Beloved Disciple and Peter as rivalry. Barrett, *Commentary*, p. 577, thinks the two

are represented as partners. Brown, *Gospel according to John*, 2:1121 (cf. 2:1005 on 20:3-10) says the passage may well be read as an effort to promote the Beloved Disciple by associating him with the great Peter. The report of the ecumenical discussions on *Peter in the New Testament* suggests that Brown's influence was quite potent. See note 15 above.

35. Barrett, *Commentary*, p. 578, calls "appear" *(phaneroō)* a Johannine word and notes occurrences in 1:31; 2:11; 3:21; 7:4; 9:3; 17:6; cf. Mark 16:12, 14.

36. See Wilhelm Wuellner, *The Meaning of "Fishers of Men"* (Philadelphia: Westminster, 1967), and Quentin Quesnell, *The Mind of Mark* (Rome: Pontifical Biblical Institute, 1969), pp. 268-270.

37. Hoskyns, pp. 552-554, prints out the triangle of 153 dots and suggests that the number—so neat, so intriguing, so symmetrical—symbolizes the converts to Christian faith. The disciples have made "the perfect catch of fish, one of every kind," in concrete fulfillment of Ezek. 47:10 and Matt. 13:47-48. For other interpretations see Quesnell, pp. 270-274.

38. See also 1 Clement 5:4; Eusebius *EH* 2.25.5 and 3.1.2-3.

39. Philo, *On the Posterity and Exile of Cain* 144; *Moses* 1.213; cf. 1 Macc. 9:22. Compare and contrast John 21:25 with 20:30-31.

40. Poignantly described in Browning's "A Death in the Desert," quoted by Amos Niven Wilder, "The First, Second and Third Epistles of John," in *The Interpreter's Bible*, ed. George Buttrick (Nashville: Abingdon, 1957), 12:209.

41. Rudolf Bultmann, *Theology of the New Testament* (New York: Scribner's, 1955), 2:3-92; Ernst Kasemann, *The Testament of Jesus;* and to a lesser extent Schnackenburg, *Commentary*, 2:426-437, 532-534, interpret the author of the Fourth Gospel as having rethought the old eschatology of salvation history and as having exchanged the traditional horizontal terms for new vertical, spatial, and perhaps gnostic terms and perspectives.

     Alf Correll, *Consummatum Est* (London: S. P. C. K., 1958); Josef Blank, *Krisis: Untersuchungen zur johanneischen Christologie und Eschatologie* (Freiburg: Lambertus, 1964); and Paola Ricca, *Die Eschatologie des vierten Evangeliums* (Zurich: Gotthelf, 1966), see the evangelist as stressing the connection between eschatology and christology, personalizing eschatology, but tend to affirm the continued presence in John's gospel of a strongly futurist perspective characteristic of salvation history.

42. C. H. Dodd, *Interpretation of the Fourth Gospel*, p. 290, defined an episode as a unit of material "consisting of one or more narratives of significant acts of Jesus accompanied by one or more discourses designed to bring out the significance of the narratives." He found seven episodes in the Book of Signs (Chap. 2-10). The movement from recognition of Jesus as teacher to seeing him as Mosaic prophet-messiah and finally as Son is analyzed by Martyn, *History and Theology*, Chapters 6-7.

43. Culpepper has described the Johannine community as a school and has carefully defined what he means. Kasemann has spoken of the Johannine community as community of the word. The sketch offered here of a backward looking or historically oriented community operating with a low christology is of course not what Culpepper or Kasemann has in mind.

44. Oscar Cullmann, *Early Christian Worship* (Chicago: Regnery, 1953). See Raymond E. Brown, "The Johannine Sacramentary," *New Testament Essays* (Milwaukee: Bruce, 1965), pp. 51-75, and Kysar, *The Fourth Evangelist*, pp. 249-259.

45. On the paraclete in the Fourth Gospel see Brown, *Gospel according to John*, 2:1135-1144; Otto Betz, *Der Paraklet* (Leiden: Brill, 1963); George Johnston, *The Spirit-Paraclete in the Gospel of John* (New York: Cambridge, 1970); A. R. C. Leaney, "The Johannine Paraclete and the Qumran Scrolls," in *John and Qumran*, ed. J. H. Charlesworth (London: Chapman, 1972), pp. 38-61; Martyn, *History and Theology*, pp. 143-151; Kysar, *Fourth Evangelist*, pp. 234-240.

46. Kasemann, p. 73.

47. Dodd, pp. 396-399, offers statistics and comments that metaphysical terms, common in the religious world of Hellenism, recede in favor of personal and ethical terms more at home in the biblical tradition. The teaching of the later chapters does not contradict or even totally supplant that of the earlier but rather deepens it and focuses it, emphasizing that it is in *agapē* that one knows God, shares his life and becomes one with him. Appold, *The Oneness Motif*, disagrees with Dodd's reading of a gradual personalization and ethicization in the unfolding of the narrative. He declares that the oneness between the Father and the Son is the central motif of the gospel, determining the meaning of love, knowledge, glory, witness, work, and all the other important themes of the gospel. Oneness is a mark of preexistent identification of the Father and the Son, transcending time, and when believers are drawn into God's reality, into truth, into glory, into the presence of Christ, then they are bound in a relationship of oneness with Jesus, which is the essence of salvation. See Appold, pp. 18-47, 282-284.

    While Dodd failed to recognize the significance of the theme of oneness in the Fourth Gospel, Appold in his criticism of Dodd seems to overstate that significance and to minimize the deeply personal and ethical dimension in the evangelist's message.

Appendix

1. The short ending is read by Greek uncial mss L (8th c.), W (8th or 9th c.), 099 (7th c.) and 0122 (7th c.), and by minuscule mss 274 (marginal reading, 10th) and 579 (13th c.). It is found also in Codex Bobiensis (Old Latin ms k of the 4th or 5th c.), appears in the margin of the Harclean edition of the Syriac (7th c.), several codices of the Sahidic and Bohairic and some Ethiopic mss. All these except Codex Bobiensis continue with verses 9-20.

See Metzger, Textual Commentary, pp. 122-6; B. F. Westcott and F. J. A. Hort, *The New Testament in the Original Greek*, vol. 2: *Introduction and Appendix* (Cambridge and London: Macmillan, 1896), p. 38; Streeter, *Four Gospels*, pp. 335f.

2. See Rudolf Pesch, *Das Markusevangelium* (Freiburg: Herder, 1977).

3. The longer ending is absent from the Greek Codices Sinaiticus and Vaticanus, the old Latin Codex Bobiensis (it^k), the Sinaitic Syriac, nine out of 10 of the most important Armenian mss, and the oldest Georgian mss. Neither Clement of Alexandria nor Origen (early third c.) knew it, and Eusebius (ca. 325) and Jerome (later fourth c.) state that "they were afraid" is the end of the gospel in the oldest and best mss known to them.

Justin Martyr (ca. 140) may be referring to 16:20 in *Apology* I.45. Tatian (ca. 170) has the longer ending in his *Diatessaron*. Irenaeus (ca. 180) quotes 16:19 as belonging to Mark (*Against Heresies* III.x.6). Many Greek mss include the longer ending (ACDKXW ΔΘΠΨ 099 0112 f ¹³ 28 33 and others). A tenth century (A.D. 989) Armenian ms has the last twelve verses separated from the body of the gospel and with the note "of the Presbyter Ariston," meaning no doubt the elder Aristion mentioned by Papias (Eus. *EH* III.xxxix.15).

For discussion see Metzger, *Textual Commentary*, pp. 122-126, and Kurt Aland, "Bemerkungen zum Schluss des Markusevangeliuss," in *Neotestamentica et Semitica: Studies in Honour of Matthew Black* ed. E. Earle Ellis and Max Wilcox (Edinburgh: T. & T. Clark, 1969), pp. 157-180.

4. The book was republished in 1959. A summary is contained in David O. Fuller, ed. *Counterfeit or Genuine: Mark 16? John 8?* (Grand Rapids: Kregel, 1975).

5. William R. Farmer, *The Last Twelve Verses of Mark* (Cambridge: The University Press, 1974).

6. Eta Linnemann, "Der (wiedergefundene) Markusschluss," *ZThK* 66 (1969): 255-287.

7. Kurt Aland, "Der wiedergefundene Markusschluss?" *ZThK* 67 (1970): 3-13, and James K. Elliott, "The Text and Language of the Endings to Mark's Gospel," *ThZ* 27 (1971): 255-265. Aland focuses on textual history and Elliott on vocabulary and style in their criticisms of Linnemann. Elliott shows that 16:9-20 is a distinct linguistic unit and cannot be cut in two as Linnemann has done, and furthermore he brings evidence to show that the entire passage is non-Markan. In addition he shows that the short ending and the Freer Logion do not belong to the same linguistic unit as 16:9-20.

8. Pesch, *Markusevangelium*, calls the rhetoric of the longer ending "late," and he gives many references to second century literature. The discussion is indebted to him. See also J. C. O'Neill, *The Theology of Acts in its Historical Setting*, 2nd ed. (London: S. P. C. K., 1970), for a study of linguistic and theological parallels between Luke and second century authors.

9. Weston LaBarre, *They Shall Take Up Serpents* (New York: Shocken, 1969). See also Elliott Wigginton, "The People Who Take Up Serpents" in *Foxfire 7*, edited by Paul F. Gillespie (Garden City: Anchor Press, 1982), pp. 370-428.

10. Midrash on Psalm 91, according to W. Foerster, *TDNT* 5:579. See Vergil's Fourth Eclogue.

11. Text in M. R. James, *The Apocryphal New Testament* (Oxford: Clarendon Press, 1924), pp. 262-263. Swete, *Gospel according to St. Mark*, p. 406, refers to a parallel in Theophylact. See the reservations about the contents of the Acts of John in Hennecke-Schneemelcher, 2:206.

12. Roy A. Harrisville, "Speaking in Tongues: A Lexicographical Study," *CBQ* 38 (1976): 35-48, and *The Concept of Newness in the New Testament* (Minneapolis: Augsburg, 1960), pp. 71-73.

13. See John Reumann, *Creation and New Creation* (Minneapolis: Augsburg, 1973), especially Chapters 4 and 5, for a discussion of these and other passages. Reumann finds the focus in a new community of those redeemed in Jesus Christ.

14. Pesch, *Markusevangelium*, p. 549, expresses the opposite opinion. He thinks the motif of doubt, so prominent in the pericope, serves to emphasize the authority of the apostolic gospel. The first witnesses did not come to faith easily. They were not gullible but had to be won. The appearances recited in the pericope have an etiological and legitimizing function in relation to the mission of the church.

15. Fourth century, in his *Against Pelaguis* ii.15.

16. A brief discussion is offered by Joachim Jeremias in Hennecke-Schneemelcher, 1:188-189. See also K. Haacker, "Bemerkungen zum Freer-Logion," *ZNW* 63 (1972): 125-129; E. Helzle, "Der Schluss des Markusevangeliums (Mk 16:9-20) und das Freer-Logion (Mk 16:14W), ihre Tendenzen und ihr gegenseitiges Verhaltnis," *TLZ* 85 (1960): 470-472; and G. Schwarz, "Zum Freer-Logion—ein Nachtrag," *ZNW* 70 (1979): 119.